Current Issues
in Fiscal Policy

Current Issues in Fiscal Policy

edited by *S. T. Cook*
and *P. M. Jackson*

MARTIN ROBERTSON

First published in 1979 by Martin Robertson & Co. Ltd., 108 Cowley Road, Oxford OX4 1JF.

ISBN 0 85520 290 4

Typeset by Santype International Ltd., Salisbury, Wilts.
Printed and bound at The Pitman Press, Bath

Contents

Contributors

J. ALT — Lecturer, Department of Government, University of Essex.

M. ARTIS — Professor of Economics, University of Manchester.

F. T. BLACKABY — Deputy Director, National Institute of Economic and Social Research.

A. BUDD — Williams and Glyn's Research Fellow in Banking at the London Business School.

P. BURROWS — Senior Lecturer, Department of Economics, University of York.

A. CHRYSTAL — Lecturer, Department of Economics, University of Essex.

S. T. COOK — Economic Adviser, Civil Service College, London, on secondment from the Department of Education and Science.

D. A. CURRIE — Lecturer, Department of Economics, Queen Mary College, University of London.

P. M. JACKSON — Professor of Economics and Director, Public Sector Economics Research Centre, University of Leicester. Sometime member of HM Treasury.

G. R. LEWIS — Economic Adviser, HM Treasury, London.

J. C. ODLING-SMEE — Senior Economic Adviser, HM Treasury, London.

P. A. ORMEROD — Senior Research Officer, National Institute of Economic and Social Research.

M. V. POSNER — Pembroke College, Cambridge.

G. K. SHAW — Reader, Department of Economics, University of St Andrews.

C. T. TAYLOR — Economist with Economic Intelligence Department, Bank of England.

Acknowledgements

The papers that compose this volume were originally presented to a Government Economic Service refresher seminar held at the Sunningdale centre of the Civil Service College over the four days 22–25 May 1978. The seminar was attended by members of the departments of Employment, Energy, Environment and Transport, Health and Social Security, the Central Statistical Office, HM Customs and Excise, the Inland Revenue and HM Treasury.

The pace of change in economic science is fast and the division of labour amongst economists deep, so that those in the business of applying their economics to particular areas of government policy are apt to find their professional human capital divided between tolerably up to date vintages within their specialism and out of date vintages, rendered even less productive by disuse, without. The College's refresher seminars are intended to provide compact surveys of areas of economics likely to be of general interest to government economists. As their name suggests, they offer those who do not work in the surveyed area an opportunity to recover old ground and become acquainted with some of the more recent developments in the area. To those who do work in the area, they offer an opportunity to check on the completeness of their understanding, to reflect on their work in a way that is rarely possible during normal working time and to contribute to the seminar from their fund of knowledge and experience.

The organisation of refresher seminars makes considerable demands on the College's course support staff and our thanks are due to Mike Wright, Anne Stimpson and Jean Strange for their patience and perseverance. The papers were prepared for the press with the much valued secretarial assistance of Pat Greatorex at PSERC and of Joan Cross and Marie Walsingham at the College. Our thanks are due to Monica Crooks at the College who assembled the bibliography. We are also heavily indebted to our academic colleagues, particularly Rod Whittaker who kept us well provided with good advice and stepped in at short notice to act as discussant for David Currie's paper.

Finally we must thank all the contributors to the seminar for the speed with which they prepared and revised their papers, for the help and advice they gave so freely and, of course, for providing us with such a stimulating four days.

We would also like to thank our publishers, Martin Robertson, and their staff who have provided us with invaluable assistance at all stages in preparing these papers for press.

In putting this collection of papers before a wider audience than is usual for a refresher seminar we should emphasise that the views expressed therein are those of their authors alone. They should not be taken to represent the views of the Civil Service College, the authors' employers or any government department.

July 1978

Stephen Cook
London Civil Service College

Peter M. Jackson
Public Sector Economics Research Centre
University of Leicester

Note: Billion is used throughout as thousand millions (or milliards) and not million millions, which was the old European usage.

to Aileen, Alison, Laura and Susan

Prologue

S. T. Cook and P. M. Jackson

INTRODUCTION

The issues at stake in the debate about the role and effectiveness of fiscal policy strike at the heart of the theory and practise of macroeconomic management. The enduring bequest of the Keynesian revolution was a belief that governments could exert a close control over the level of aggregate demand, and hence the volume of output and employment, by controlling the balance of its own budget. If demand was insufficient to support some desirable level of economic activity, then governments should spend more than they received in tax and other revenues and run a budget deficit. If demand was excessive, then the balance should be changed so that the budget was in surplus. This belief, and the optimistic gloss it gave to the making of economic policy, has been under seige for more than a decade by the forces of the monetarist counter-revolution armed with the modern quantity theory of money, their resolve strengthened by the unhappy economic experiences of the 1970s. That some believe the besiegers to have been victorious is attested by the proliferation of papers with titles in the vein of 'Does Fiscal Policy Matter?' (Blinder and Solow, 1973) and 'Is Fiscal Policy Dead?' (Peacock and Shaw, 1978); but the conviction of the besieged that they have relinquished, at most, only some relatively unimportant outworks is often to be found eloquently expressed in the text that accompanies these titles.

No one would seriously question the idea that fiscal policy has often failed to produce the results expected of it. The historical record is replete with examples of destabilising fiscal actions (Hansen, 1969). In their evidence to the House of Commons Expenditure Committee, Cripps, Godley and Fetherstone of the Department of Applied Economics at Cambridge argued that '... the record of demand management during the past twenty years has been extremely poor ... fiscal policy has been operated in alternating directions to produce periods of strong demand expansion followed by reversals of policy in crisis conditions' (Cripps, Godley and Fetherstone, 1974). Similarly, Perry has argued from his study of US experience that '... past recessions have often resulted from attempts to slow an expansion by the use of fiscal policy' (Perry, 1976).

1

Much of the debate between the 'fiscal activists' and their opponents hinges upon the interpretation and explanation of this experience. It is a commonplace view that governments can misjudge both the size and timing of their interventions; that they pursue many objectives apart from internal stability by fiscal means; and that the eagerness with which they pursue particular objectives, their preferences for particular instruments of policy and the speed with which they respond to the onset of economic difficulties vary for reasons unconnected with the technical requirements of macroeconomic management. For the opponents of the fiscal activists these explanations are insufficient. They argue that fiscal policy, unaccompanied by an accommodating monetary policy, is impotent; but that an accommodating monetary policy has its effects on the economy after a long but variable and therefore unpredictable lag, which ensures that its effects are almost certain to be destabilising. Hence their preference for a rule-bound approach to economic policy that eschews discretionary actions, whether fiscal or monetary. The reasons that they have advanced for the alleged impotence of fiscal policy form the substance of the debate.

THE PURPOSE AND STRUCTURE OF THE BOOK

The way in which the profession thinks about the theoretical and empirical foundations of macroeconomic policy in general and of fiscal policy in particular has changed very substantially in the last decade and a half. Although there are, in our view, signs of an emerging consensus on the mechanics of fiscal and monetary policy, the ferment of debate shows little sign of abating. The only certain conclusion is that vulgar 'money-does-not-matter' Keynesianism has been firmly knocked on the head and is nowhere to be seen. We incline to the belief that vulgar 'money-alone-matters' monetarism is just as dead; but it still appears in the literature and has powerful popular champions so we are reluctant to press this opinion on the reader.

Our aim in designing the seminar programme, from which this collection of papers emerged, was to provide a review of the debate for economists who felt that they had not managed to keep up with all of its twists and turns. Our intention in publishing this collection of essays is the same: to give students who are new to the subject, or economists who may feel rusty, an overview of a debate that is of great importance to some of the major questions of macroeconomic theory and policy in the late 1970s.

In a compass as small as a four-day seminar we could not, of course, hope to cover all aspects in the detail they merit. In particular readers will notice that we have not pursued at any length the newer pathways of debate through rational expectations to the microeconomic foundations of macroeconomics. We would like to have followed that route but thought it wiser to leave the burgeoning and difficult literature for a future seminar.[1]

As we have set them out here, the essays fall into three distinct groups. Although they constitute an integral whole when taken together, that is not a reason for the reader to feel obliged to read them in sequence or to refrain from dipping into chapters at random. We do suggest, however, that the reader look first at Michael Artis's survey of recent developments in the theory of fiscal policy in chapter 1.

Part I: The Major Theoretical Issues

The essays gathered together to form Part I deal with some of the major theoretical issues in the debate. It begins with Michael Artis's survey which is, as we have indicated already, central to the book's purpose since it provides a context for many of the subsequent essays. Artis indentifies several strands of development and picks out four for closer examination.

The government budget constraint   First among these is the extensive literature associated with the role of the government budget constraint and the significance of the wealth effects that accompany the financing of budget deficits and surpluses. Many undergraduates in economics in the 1950s and 1960s grew up in the habit of thinking of fiscal and monetary policy as the separate concerns of different branches of government. By and large, the monetary authorities managed the supply of reserve assets and of advice to the banks and so controlled either the supply of money or the level of interest rates in pursuit of price level and exchange rate objectives. The budgetary authorities on the other hand controlled the balance of government expenditures and revenues with an eye to maintaining a satisfactory level of aggregate demand and, therefore, employment. Complications were recognised. The operations of the budgetary authorities could affect the balance of payments and so the exchange rate and price level; while monetary actions had some repercussions on the level of aggregate demand, mainly through the effects of interest rates on private investment and inventories. Similarly, if the government financed a budget deficit by issuing eligible liabilities, that could have the effect of increasing the money supply; and so on. However, these complications were often sacrificed to analytical convenience once the full Hicks–Hansen IS/LM analysis came into sight. More often than not, fiscal and monetary policy were left separate once more.

In this section of his survey Artis shows how the government budget constraint can be incorporated into the geometry and algebra of the standard IS/LM model so that it explicitly recognises that government expenditures must equal financing from tax revenues plus or minus new net borrowing or new money creation; in other words, that every fiscal policy has implicitly attached to it a monetary policy. Artis then goes on to demonstrate how the budget constraint and the effects of bond issues and retirements on the level and composition of private wealth modify the standard analysis. He shows, in particular, how the inclusion of interest payments on government debt in the budget constraint can overturn the conventional conclusion that money-financed fiscal initiatives are more powerful than bond-financed initiatives; and how the 'New Cambridge' result, that budget deficits and surpluses are mirrored in the balance of external payments, can be derived from the modified IS/LM framework (a point that reappears in the later essay by David Currie).

Paul Burrows takes up these twin themes of the budget constraint and wealth effects in his essay 'The Government Budget Constraint and the Monetarist–Keynesian Debate'. Of particular interest to students and teachers alike is Burrows' careful synthesis of the evolving debate and his demonstration of how monetarists' views on the substantive disagreements between themselves and the Keynesians have changed as the latter group have modified their models in order to incorporate monetarist insights.

'Crowding out'   The second development dealt with by Artis and taken up in more detail by Christopher Taylor in chapter 4 is the explicit recognition of supply constraints and the possibility that increases in government spending may displace, or 'crowd out', private spending. Such crowding out may be of the direct (or resource) type, in which there is a direct displacement of private output by publicly provided goods and services; or it may be indirect financial crowding out. In this latter case, increases in government expenditure raise income, the demand for transactions balances and, unless there is an accommodating monetary expansion, interest rates rise. The increase in interest rates depresses interest-sensitive private sector expenditures directly; and, because it also depresses the market value of the existing stock of government bonds, which are part of the private sector's net wealth, it will further depress private expenditures, even those that are not sensitive to changes in interest rates. Indeed, these perverse wealth effects may be so strong that an apparently expansionary fiscal policy may end up by reducing the level of national income.[2] Moreover, a shift in the composition of output as between the public and private sectors may adversely affect the productive potential of the private sector and the rate of economic growth.

As Taylor points out, it is difficult to discover whether crowding out has actually occurred. Thus, for example, private investment expenditures that may be crowded out by higher rates of interest may not have been undertaken at lower rates if these lower rates were the consequence of continuing recession. Furthermore, he makes the important point that crowding out '... is equally likely to arise ... if non-adjusting money targets are followed in the face of a spontaneous revival of activity ... [Fiscal policy] simply provides the context in which crowding out happens most usually to be discussed'.

Expectations The anticipations of economic agents have played a central role in macroeconomic theory since the *General Theory*, and the role of rational expectations in the debate about fiscal policy is the third line of development examined by Artis. The most familiar application of expectations to macroeconomic theory is probably the attack on the idea of a negatively sloped long-run Phillips curve. Here it was argued that stabilisation policies would have transitory effects on real output and employment, persisting only for as long as economic agents failed to anticipate fully the effects of the policy on the aggregate price level. In the long run, as expectations of price and wage changes caught up with realised changes, stabilisation policy could be seen to have had a permanent effect only upon the rate of change of the aggregate price level.

Michael Artis shows how an 'expectations-augmented' is/lm model generates long-run fiscal multipliers smaller than the short-run, impact, multipliers.[3]

Ultrarationality The fourth and final development reviewed in chapter 1 is the notion of ultrarationality – the belief that the private sector regards public and private savings as perfect substitutes so that the effects of a government deficit are offset by an increase in private sector saving. This result is christened 'ex ante crowding out' by David and Scadding (1974) since it is not a result of changes in the interest rate, the price level or the exchange rate. There is more than one route to ex ante crowding out. David and Scadding argue that the private sector behaves as if it 'believes' that private and public saving are perfect substitutes; while Barro (1974) argues that outstanding bonds are not part of the private sector's net wealth because the present value of the coupon payments to the private sector are matched by the present value of its liability to the taxes that will finance these coupon payments. In either case, public expenditures are directly substituted for private expenditures so that fiscal policy can have no effect on the level of economic activity. Artis (and, in chapter 7, Paul Ormerod) suggests that the theoretical and empirical foundations of ultrarationality are very flimsy indeed; although there are some goods and services in which private and public provision may be substituted for one another.

The measurement of fiscal stance   Quite apart from the various theoretical objections to the use of fiscal policy it has long been recognised that the actual balance of the government budget is an inadequate index of the authorities' fiscal stance because some items of expenditure and revenue are determined by the prevailing level of income rather than determining it. So in periods of recession, expenditure on unemployment benefits will be increased while tax revenue falls, thus moving the balance of the budget automatically in the direction of a deficit. As the economy recovers these expenditures fall, revenues rise and the budget moves automatically towards a surplus. But these automatic effects may not reflect, and may actually conceal, the true stance of the authorities' discretionary policy.

In chapter 2, Keith Shaw reviews some of the attempts that economists have made to eliminate the effects of built-in stabilisers and so measure the budget balance at some hypothetical constant or full employment level of income. He shows that the full employment budget surplus is a 'better' measure than the actual budget surplus (or deficit) for describing the course of fiscal policy, but that it does not solve all the problems. Thus it does not take account of the different multiplier effects of taxes and expenditures or of different types of expenditures and taxes; it does not allow for the pursuit of other objectives, particularly a balanced external account, by means of budgetary policy; and, of course, it is silent on the financing of budget imbalances. Shaw concludes that it is a mistake to imagine that any single measure could adequately capture the full ramifications of fiscal policy – a point we return to in Part II.

The open economy   In his opening survey Michael Artis shows that the relative efficacy of fiscal and monetary policy in an open economy will depend upon the exchange rate regime within which the economy operates and the strength of the wealth effects associated with bond issues and retirements. These themes are taken up by David Currie in his essay 'Stabilisation Policy in an Open Economy', which looks at the extent to which policy-makers in a small open economy can, acting in isolation, either permanently shift the time path of the economy or stabilise it along some established path. The first part of his essay is concerned with policies designed permanently to shift the time path of the economy. Here, Currie shows that wealth effects and inflationary expectations can reverse the standard Fleming–Mundell results concerning the relative efficacy of fiscal and monetary policy under floating exchange rates (at least for balanced budget fiscal changes). He then shows that if fiscal policy and monetary policy are considered together, there is in principle always some combination of the two that will yield internal and external equilibrium simultaneously. Moreover, Currie suggests that there exists a fair measure of agreement on the modelling of financial effects of budgetary and balance of payments disequilibria and that disagreements about policy prescriptions reflect disagreements on the nature of the supply and balance of payments constraints on policy.

Turning to the design of automatic stabilisation policy, Currie emphasises that in the short run the government's budget constraint compels it to react to unanticipated shocks that disturb the flow of tax and other government revenues. He demonstrates that different types of shock call for different combinations of alternative monetary and exchange rate policies but reminds us that consequential changes in the stock of assets may destabilise the economy in the longer run. Because there is considerable scope for dispute about the relative importance of different types of disturbance, and since the longer run effects of changes in asset stocks are difficult to determine analytically, the prospect of agreement on the design of automatic stabilisation policy is remote.

Endogenous policy-making Standard Keynesian and monetarist formulations of economic stabilisation policies are alike in not analysing political decision-makers' responses to economic events and their changing chances of re-election. Recent attempts to remedy this gap in our knowledge are to be found in Nordhaus (1975), Lindbeck (1976) and Frey (1978). According to Lindbeck:

> ... it seems that the differences between various short term economic forecasts today depend less on divergent views on the functioning of the private sector than on different assumptions about the future of economic policy. An important aspect of such assumptions is various hypotheses as to how governments most likely will react to future economic events. This means that it is useful to treat the government as an *endogenous* rather than an exogenous variable in the macro-economic system.

In the first part of chapter 6 Chrystal and Alt take up a number of technical issues that are raised when stabilisation policy becomes endogenous to the analysis. They criticise the methodology of estimating the reaction functions of the authorities from single equations that make the stance of some instrument the dependent variable and the state of the economy the independent variable. They level against such 'reduced forms' all the objections levelled against the more familiar St Louis type 'reduced form' models of income determination (see p. 126) and turn for guidance to the work of Goldfeld and Blinder (1972) whose concern was to estimate the likely biases in traditional fiscal multipliers that arise from assuming that policy instruments are statistically, as well as economically, exogenous. Their preferred procedure is to specify the structural equations of the model, append the reaction functions of the policy-makers and estimate the whole system simultaneously.

The second part of chapter 6 examines the long-run behaviour of the government expenditure function. For the purpose of this exercise Chrystal and Alt exclude transfer payments from their definition of public expenditure. After reviewing the standard theories of public expenditure growth, the authors proceed to demonstrate empirically that public expenditure does not account for an uncharacteristically high proportion of GNP in the UK; nor has it been growing much faster than in other countries. A stable long-run government expenditure function is then identified and explained in terms of a permanent-income hypothesis of government behaviour.

Chrystal and Alt take care to point out that their work is in its early stages and that much remains to be done in providing a satisfactory theory of the long-run behaviour of public expenditure.

Part II: The Simulation of Fiscal Policy

The two essays in this section, one by Paul Ormerod the other by Ormerod and Geoffrey Lewis, deal with the use of large-scale macroeconomic models for policy simulation and forecasting.

Until recently most of the large structural models favoured by 'fiscalists' in both the USA and the UK had relatively rudimentary financial sectors and paid scant regard to effects of changes in asset stocks on the behaviour of the economy. They were thus open to the criticism that by assumption and construction such models could not detect the financing implications of budget imbalances that so exercised the theorists. The monetarists for their part were usually content with single equation models in the spirit of St Louis, with income appearing as the dependent variable on the left-hand side of the equation and measures of the authorities' fiscal and monetary stance appearing as independent variables on the right-hand side. Generally, these sorts of models threw up coefficients that showed fiscal policy to be weak and monetary policy strong.[4] Unfortunately, it is easy to demonstrate that if either of the instrument variables are managed so as perfectly to offset fluctuations in the level of income then the single equation will register a zero correlation between it and the level of income. The more successful are fiscal, monetary or fiscal-and-monetary policy, the weaker they will appear to be. Furthermore, single equation estimates invariably employ summary measures of fiscal stance that are open to all the objections catalogued by Keith Shaw; and they tend to neglect exogenous variables other than fiscal and monetary policy so that the reduced form is mis-specified.

By and large, structural models avoid the last two pitfalls, but they still tumble into the first, that of treating the economically exogenous instruments of fiscal and monetary policy as if they were statistically exogenous; and, as Chrystal and Alt point out in their discussion of Goldfeld and Blinder, the absence of correctly specified reaction functions for the authorities must bias the behaviour of such models. For this and other reasons, forecasting techniques cannot be applied mechanically in the formation of economic policy.

In chapter 7 Paul Ormerod discusses the role of macro-models in policy formation in a way that students of applied economics and econometrics will find instructive. He lays great emphasis on the part played by forecasters' judgements in modifying or imposing parameter values and structural relationships on the model where free estimation may lead the model to make predictions that are unacceptable on theoretical or experimental grounds. Forecasters know only too well that models are imperfect representations of reality. Important explanatory variables may be missing because their influence was too weak to be detected in the estimation period or because of deficiencies in the data; economic agents, including governments, may learn to modify their behaviour as a result of the experience of past policy interventions; some variables (like the trend growth of output per head) that may reasonably be treated as if they were exogenous in the short run cannot be so treated for longer run forecasts; the properties of the model may be significantly affected by small variations of parameter values within, say, one standard error; and empirical formulations of some relationships may be consistent with a number of theoretical hypotheses. One important function of simulation exercises is thus to reveal the properties of a model so that they may be compared with the properties of other models and the expected behaviour of the real economy.

In chapter 8 Lewis and Ormerod present a set of five such policy simulations, two of which represent balanced budget stimuli. The simulations were carried out on the then current version of the Treasury and the National Institute of Economic and Social Research (NIESR) models. Both models possess comparatively simple monetary sectors, the Treasury's comprehensive monetary model not having been fully integrated with the income–expenditure model at that time. However, the consumption sector of the Treasury model had been completely respecified to incorporate wealth effects on consumers' expenditure; and, in addition, a retentions ratio had been built into the Phillips curve. The retentions ratio measures the ratio of gross to net wages and has the effect of reducing the response of gross wages to price increases when income tax is reduced.

The wealth effects on consumers' expenditure have the effect of reducing the expenditure multiplier in the Treasury model; but, in conjunction with the retentions ratio, they strengthen the tax multiplier. The balanced budget multiplier turns out to be less than unity in both the Treasury and National Institute models, much smaller than is typical for the major US models.

Part III: Making Fiscal Policy

Two two final chapters and the postscript examine the performance of fiscal policy over the recent past and whether fiscal policy has a secure future in the array of techniques for managing the economy. Although the discussion takes place in the context of the British experience, the issues raised have a wider significance.

Frank Blackaby in chapter 9 and Alan Budd in chapter 10 deal with the growing disillusionment with Keynesian-style demand management policies. Blackaby argues strongly that many of the world's current economic difficulties stem from the increasing interdependence of national economies, which makes it harder for national authorities to pursue independent economic policies. In effect, the world needs concerted policy rather than a concatenation of uncoordinated policy actions. He criticises commentators who conclude from recent experience that demand management no longer 'works' and dismisses the idea that the postwar experience of the UK fits either the 'natural rate' or 'crowding out' hypotheses. He thus rejects fashionable notions for restricting governments' freedom to pursue an active fiscal policy and has little sympathy for the recent suggestion of Buchanan, Burton and Wagner (1978) that it should be made constitutionally impossible for governments to run budget deficits. Furthermore, he argues, the recent increase in the savings ratio of the personal sector may require the government to run continual budget deficits to mop up these surplus savings if the corporate sector shows little enthusiasm for investing them.[5]

Alan Budd follows Frank Blackaby in emphasising the variety of criticisms brought to bear on conventional demand management and the assortment of points of view that underpin each of the criticisms. He argues that there is now a general recognition that the constraints that bind would-be demand managers are more severe than was once thought. Thus, he suggests, 'postwar economic history shows that it has become increasingly difficult to use the exchange rate as an effective instrument for changing real wages'; and the balance of payments constraint continues to restrict the scope for domestic reflation despite the experience of floating exchange rates. He then goes on to review the criticisms of conventional demand management and to suggest that the broad choices for the future are between rather more intervention, rather less intervention or the same amount of intervention as at present. He favours less intervention, arguing that there should be more scope for market forces to disseminate information, provide incentives for its proper use and so promote structural change in the UK economy. He accepts that the price of less intervention may be more pronounced fluctuations in employment but suggests that this would be accompanied, possibly, by smaller fluctuations in the rate of inflation.

CONCLUSION

The vigour of the current debate among macroeconomic theorists and policy-makers is eloquent testimony to the continued survival and importance of fiscal policy. The major change in theoretical perspective is the widespread recognition of the implications of the symbiotic relationship of fiscal and monetary policy. That recognition does not, however, solve the problem of policy design. Our understanding of the detailed mechanics of fiscal and monetary policy is still far from complete; and there is little sign of agreement on the operation and severity of the constraints imposed by the economy's aggregate supply responses, the balance of payments and the wage determination process. There can be little chance, therefore, of agreement on the adequacy and efficacy of the instruments of management, be they orthodox or unorthodox in nature.

NOTES AND REFERENCES

1. For a survey of the relevant literature see Poole (1976).
2. The argument is incomplete. The wealth effects on private sector expenditures outlined here reduce the efficacy of fiscal policy while enhancing the efficacy of monetary policy. They may, however, be partially or wholly offset by wealth effects on the demand for money.
3. These multipliers are 'long run' in the familiar, but nevertheless peculiar, context of a fixed stock of real capital.
4. When Benjamin Friedman (1977) re-estimated the St Louis model of Anderson and Jordan for the period up to 1976 he found a significant government expenditure multiplier of 1.5, but the strong impact of monetary actions was still apparent.
5. Evidence to support a belief in a persistently high personal sector savings ratio has been recently supplied by Coghlan and Jackson (1978).

PART I

The Major Issues

CHAPTER 1

Recent Developments in the Theory of Fiscal Policy: A Survey

M. J. Artis*

INTRODUCTION

The purpose of this paper is to give a selective review of recent developments in the theory of fiscal policy, thus providing a context in which the later contributions to this book can be placed. Anyone setting out to provide such a perspective inevitably owes a great debt to the work of David Currie, who in two recent papers (1978a, 1978b) has already surveyed the literature spawned by the controversy over the significance of the mode of financing of fiscal policy. The central focus of attention in this literature is the role of the government budget constraint. The concerns of the present paper are, in fact, a little wider. It will prove useful, therefore, to take advantage of the fact that the essential contribution that recognition of the government budget constraint provides can be illustrated with comparative economy by assuming output to be demand determined. This paves the way for separate consideration of the issues raised by recognition of the supply constraints under which the economy operates. A further set of issues is enjoined by the need to take account of expectational effects in fiscal policy. In principle, these require recognition of the significance of the policies followed by the authorities in other areas: e.g., whether they pursue an incomes policy or not, and whether the exchange rate regime is one of 'fixed' or 'flexible' rates. These issues overlap with those raised by the rational expectations literature.

THE GOVERNMENT BUDGET CONSTRAINT

The government budget constraint is just the financing rule that a government deficit must be 'covered' by issues of government debt, either demand

* The author is grateful to both David Currie and David Vine for helpful comments on earlier drafts.

debt ('money') or deferred obligations ('bonds'). It is one of the gentler paradoxes of the literature that recognition that a deficit must be accompanied by some mode of financing led, initially, to the result that the equilibrium fiscal policy multiplier was independent of the mode of financing and, at that, larger in value than the fiscal multiplier either of traditional *IS/LM* analysis or of ordinary income–expenditure analysis. In the hands of Blinder and Solow (1973) the stronger paradox was arrived at, that bond-financed deficits led to greater expansion of income than money-financed deficits, a result due to their recognition of the deficit-expanding effects of the service costs of bond finance, and the incorporation of these costs in the government budget constraint.

The earlier analyses of this matter (those by Ott and Ott, 1965, and by Silber, 1970, for the closed economy, and those by Oates, 1966, and McKinnon, 1969, for the open economy) had already taken the essential steps, however. The incorporation of the government budget constraint here is motivated by recognising the presence of wealth effects in private sector expenditure and/or money-demand functions and by recognising government debt, like net claims on the rest of the world, as 'outside wealth'. It follows that if a new equilibrium is to be achieved, this will be at a point where wealth is not changing; in the closed economy, this is given by a position of budget balance, in the open economy by the point where the government budget deficit is just offset by a corresponding balance of payments deficit. Christ's motivation was different and applicable only to the money-financed case (Christ, 1968) but with a similar result for that case. The comparable results also claimed by the proponents of the 'New Cambridge' approach seemed at first to be best rationalised as dependent on a strong assumption that the marginal propensity to absorb of the private sector approximated unity; subsequently this, too, has been re-stated in terms that more explicitly indicate that a 'wealth' rationalisation applies.[1]

It may be useful to show how these contributions can be fitted into the traditional *IS/LM* mode of analysis. This can be done by reference to Figures 1.1 and 1.2, the corresponding algebra being given in the Appendix. Certain simplifying assumptions have been made for purposes of this summary exposition; in particular, the economies described are ones in which prices are fixed (though we can consider the effects of parametric changes in the price level) and output is demand determined. Also, the effect of variations in the rate of interest on the valuation of wealth is ignored here, as is, for the most part, the effect of incorporating debt service costs in the budget constraint. The former of these two omissions may be justified for present purposes as affecting neither the equilibrium positions we seek to identify (wherein the rate of interest must be constant) nor, on the assumption of linearity and of interest elasticity in the demand for money, the nature of the stability conditions. The latter omission is less easily justified, but we may

note that insofar as the principal effect of incorporating bond coupon payments is to enlarge the deficit initially created by an increase in government
spending, this can be 'undone' by re-specifying the increase in government
spending as gross of the (net of tax) costs of associated debt service.[2] Finally,
although wealth is defined to include real capital stock, the proper analysis
of adjustments to changes in this item of wealth is evaded here by asserting
that such changes are trivially small.[3]

Figure 1.1, for the closed economy, shows an IS/LM system in the top
quadrant, and government expenditure and taxation schedules in the lower
quandrant. Starting from an initial position of budget balance, with government spending $\bar{G}_1$, income Y_1 and interest rate at r_1, suppose the level of

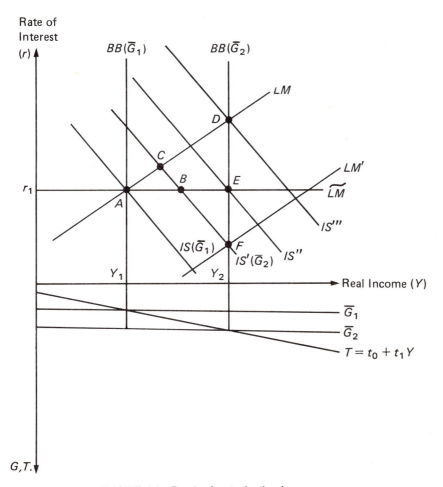

FIGURE 1.1   *Fiscal policy in the closed economy.*

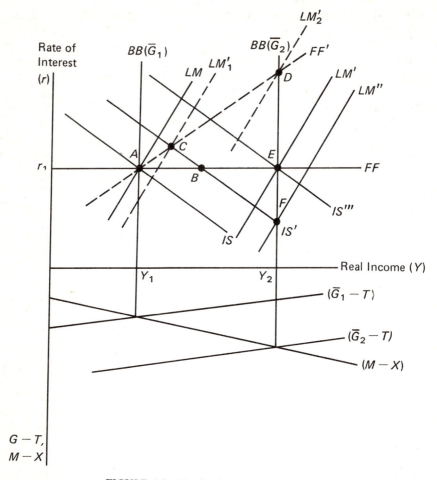

FIGURE 1.2 *Fiscal policy in the open economy.*

government spending to be increased to $\bar{G}_2$. The 'ordinary' income–expenditure multiplier would give the expansion of income as corresponding to the movement from A to B: an accommodating monetary policy (shown as $\widetilde{LM}$) 'puts the rate of interest to sleep'. The traditional IS/LM multiplier puts the expansion of income as that corresponding to the movement from A to C (the money supply being held constant along LM), with the operation of the 'ordinary' multiplier constrained by the dampening of expenditures associated with the increase in the interest rate in the face of rising income and unchanged money supply. The lines $BB(\bar{G}_1)$ and $BB(\bar{G}_2)$ indicate the level of income consistent with a balanced budget before and after the increase in government spending. The movement from A to a point like E

illustrates the income expansion if the marginal propensity to absorb of the private sector is unity ('New Cambridge Mark 1').[4] The movement to a point like F corresponds to the money-financed regime envisaged by Christ (1968); here there are no wealth effects at work, but as long as a deficit persists the money supply will be increasing, so the LM curve will only stabilise if budget balance is achieved. The interest rate associated with this result is the lowest that will be associated with the income expansion process where wealth effects *are* at work since these will, *ceteris paribus*, be associated with an outward movement of the IS schedule and an inward shift of the LM schedule. The point D does not represent a corresponding maximum, but indicates the position that would be reached if the wealth effects in the LM schedule are just neutralised by sufficient money financing whilst positive wealth effects drive the IS schedule to IS'''.

Similar results are shown for the open economy case in Figure 1.2. The lower quadrant of this figure shows the budget and balance of payments deficit schedules. Again, according to the wealth effects literature, equilibrium will be established (if one exists) where outside wealth is not changing, reflected here in the two BB lines. Once again, the 'ordinary' multipliers of income–expenditure and IS/LM analysis are shown by the movement of income corresponding, respectively, to the distances AB and AC, the latter assuming external balance and imperfect capital mobility. The New Cambridge multiplier gives the income expansion corresponding to AE, as is also implied by the presence of wealth effects combined with perfect capital mobility (FF).[5] In the latter case, the current account deficit at E will be covered by sales of bonds to foreign residents just equal to the continuing deficit. If there is less than perfect (but non-zero) substitutability, the FF line should have an upward slope as FF', so that at a point like D, the balance of payments deficit will again be fully covered by bond sales, which are achieved at the cost of an increase in the rate of interest above r_1. With zero capital mobility, an equilibrium along $BB(\bar{G}_2)$ can be achieved, on the condition indicated by Turnovsky (1976), namely that the proportion of the budget deficit financed by money creation should be just equal to the proportion of the balance of payments deficit *not* sterilised by the authorities. This will maintain money, bonds and total financial asset stocks constant. Here of course the reserves are falling by the amount of the budget deficit and there is a query about the 'long-run' nature of such an equilibrium. But equilibria like E or D are, in fact, little better since they presuppose that a balance of payments is continual capital account surplus and current account deficit is a viable proposition. Once again, it seems more reasonable to suggest that these equilibria are rather short run in nature.

These equilibria do not, therefore, appear to be any more robust than those proposed by Mundell (1963) where the same objections apply to the long-run viability of the balance of payments mix, just as they also do to

Mundell's earlier and influential argument (Mundell, 1962) that envisaged the 'assignment' of monetary policy to external balance and of fiscal policy to internal balance. Moreover, both the present analysis and Mundell's assume that capital *flows*, rather than the distribution of capital stocks, is functionally related to the differential between the 'world' rate and the domestic rate of interest.

Whilst influential analyses of the role of fiscal policy under flexible exchange rate regimes exist, the assumption of fixed prices makes an odd bed-fellow for the assumption of flexible exchange rates, so we defer consideration of this point until later.

Instability

Whilst the diagrams and the simple algebra of the Appendix convey the flavour of the results that follow from incorporating the budget constraint, we have assumed so far the existence of a stable equilibrium. A major part of the literature has, however, been motivated by a concern for the possibility of instability. Blinder and Solow pointed out that if the net wealth effects in the *IS* and *LM* schedules are negative then, under bond financing, income will tend to zero; for any reduction in income will only serve to increase the deficit, thus adding to the negative net wealth effects in a cumulative fashion.[6] Where the cost of servicing bond-financed deficits is also taken into account in the government budget constraint, this instability problem is aggravated and a further one is added: it is possible that the net wealth effects, though expansionary, are weak enough to allow both income and the budget deficit to rise. In this case, the (positive) income multiplier is unbounded.[7]

Similar types of instability result have been detected in open economy versions of the model (Turnovsky, 1976) and other variants. Bond coupon payments turn out to be a potent source of instability, or of the added likelihood of instability, in a number of cases, and in this sense the results would often appear to favour money financing.[8] The precise significance to be attached to some of these results is, however, a matter for debate. Appeal to the correspondence principle here carries no resounding conviction, if construed as a test of the 'realism' of the model, in the sense that discretionary action to halt instability can often reasonably be invoked (as, for example, in Sparks, 1976; cf. also Carlson and Spencer, 1975) and it seems equally reasonable, in general, to suppose that governments will be led to conduct 'sensible' financing policies that do not promote instability in the economy.

Setting this problem on one side, the results of incorporating the government budget constraint do seem to have been fruitful. Adjustment to the wealth changes provoked by fiscal actions may very well be an important ingredient in the real world, as would presumably be claimed by, among others, the adherents of the 'New Cambridge' approach. Empirically, we still have much to learn about the nature of the wealth effects in the money-demand and expenditure functions, however. Meanwhile, three important implications for the analysis of fiscal policy may be noted. First, sustained parametric increases in the price level (say, induced by a political wage pressure exogenous to the model) will result in a downward pressure on the level of demand; if the 'long-run' multiplier for fiscal policy is as powerful as the wealth effects literature suggests, so is the depressive influence of inflation. The implied inflation tax might perhaps be properly incorporated in measures of fiscal policy.[9] Second, recognition of wealth effects gives acceptable rationalisation to the policy-relevant views of the New Cambridge Group, which in their initial formulation were rejected as involving over-strong assumptions.[10] Third, an implication of this view is that the balanced budget multiplier is, generally, zero[11] and that the procedure of differentially weighting the components of the budget in fiscal policy measurement is misconceived.[12]

However, it is not being suggested here that these implications should be accepted 'as if proven', if only because, as already indicated, our knowledge of the relevant empirical values is very scanty; in particular, it is clear that speeds of adjustment are of the essence if any of these results are to have relevance for stabilisation policy, and little is known about these.

Bonds as Net Wealth?

The wealth effects assumed turn on the assumption that bonds are (at least to some extent) net wealth;[13] there has been some questioning of this assumption (see Barro, 1974, in particular) on the grounds that since the value of a bond is the present discounted value of the future stream of coupons attached to it, there is a corresponding stream (and PDV) of the associated added taxes required to finance the coupons, which is just equal in value. Objections to this observation may be viewed as denials that the relevant discount rates are in fact equal and in particular that the discount rate that is effectively applied to future added tax liabilities is higher (if not infinite) than the discount rate applied to bond coupons. Such considerations may be motivated, for example, by the observation that in typically imperfect capital markets, the discount rate for those whose wealth is predominantly in human form may very well be much higher than the discount rate applicable to those whose wealth has a large non-human component. It may also be claimed that all taxpayers suffer from 'tax illusion', and suppose that the obligation to pay taxes will fall on someone else, including future generations, whose welfare and actions do not impinge upon themselves. Whilst Tobin long ago (Tobin, 1952) observed that there is something a little odd about the idea that a society can make itself better off by issuing bonds to itself, it can be equally be argued (e.g., Currie, 1978a) that the supposition that bond coupons *must* be tax financed betrays an assumption that the economy is already at 'full employment'; but if it is not and if society does not discount future tax liabilities, the resultant expansionary effects of bond-financed fiscal policy will, in fact, raise current and permanent income, thus indirectly and *ex post facto* 'justifying' the initial differential discounting.

SUPPLY CONSTRAINTS

No one denies that at 'full employment' the potential for fiscal policy must be directed to determining the division of output between public and private sectors, with 100 per cent 'crowding out' of private by public expenditures. The remaining questions are then those concerning the *mechanism* by which this crowding out takes place and the longer run consequences for productive potential of such shifts in the division of output. As regards the former, the mechanisms envisaged involve price level adjustments leading to crowding out through a financial mechanism, inflation involving the collection of an inflation tax (which may also involve a financial disturbance) and exchange rate depreciation (involving inflation). As regards the implication for long-run growth, the literature offers fewer convincing leads, partly because little or no account is taken of the productive nature of (some) government expenditures. Bacon and Eltis (1976) have revived a physiocratic view of the economy involving reductions in capital intensity and increasing inflation as a result of an expanding public sector.

The idea of a definite zone of 'full employment' may be based on the reverse-L shaped aggregate supply curve characteristic of traditional *IS/LM* analysis. In this case, with a fixed money wage and price level prior to the full employment point, the response of the underemployed economy to fiscal policy is as previously described above. At the point of full employment – in the 'classical' zone – it is evident that fiscal deficits must be crowded out. The traditional account of how this occurs involves the argument that the higher demand pressure provoked by a bond-financed expansionary fiscal deficit will lead to a rise in the price level, reducing real money balances and activating a Pigou effect on expenditure, so that equilibrium is eventually attained at the same level of real income and at a higher price level and rate of interest. In this account, bonds are not counted as net wealth, though real money balances are, and there are no wealth effects in the demand for money. Taking account of these items restricts the possibility of a stable full employment equilibrium being achieved by a once-ever price level adjustment to the case of a balanced budget expansion or one where fiscal drag exists but introduces the possibility of an inflationary equilibrium for the more general case. In the first instance, if the new equilibrium is to be stable, it must, as before, require budget balance implying that taxes must rise to match government spending. The existence of fiscal drag suggests that there should be a price level adjustment sufficient to bring this about; in the absence of fiscal drag, the requisite fiscal action can be envisaged as a balanced budget expansion which leads via a price level-induced reduction in real wealth to a net leftward shift of the *LM* schedule (the effect of the fall in the real value of money balances offsetting a rightward wealth effect-induced shift) and a leftward shift of the *IS* schedule reflecting wealth effects, the new equilibrium involving a higher price level and interest rate. In these cases the crowding out mechanism generally provides for a combination of price level and induced interest rate adjustment effects with corresponding impacts on the components of real private expenditure.

In the case of an inflationary equilibrium, what is envisaged is the establishment of an equilibrium in which a continuing budget deficit is just offset by a continuing inflation tax, and in which portfolio balance requires that money and bonds grow in equal proportions (and at a rate equal to the inflation rate). Turnovsky (1978) explores the difficult dynamic properties of a system characterised by such an equilibrium. Analysis of inflationary equilibria of this kind suggests the use of an augmented Phillips curve mechanism, which may be reinterpreted as an aggregate supply schedule relating output positively to unanticipated inflation. This provides scope for output expansion above the long-run equilibrium while inflation remains less than fully anticipated, but does not affect the analysis of the long run, since this is typified by perfectly anticipated inflation. If a variable capital stock is allowed for, there is a possibility of a long-run rise in output since an increase in capital stock (against what would otherwise occur) should shift the supply constraint. This case has been analysed by Buiter (1977), where it depends on a reduction in the real rate of interest; it is argued that this may occur if the lag in the inflation expectations generating mechanism is short enough and the nominal rate, dependent on the mix of financing, fails to rise by as much as the expected rate of inflation. Alternative combinations of these parameters may, however, lead to a rise in the real rate and so to a fall in productive capital stock.

In the open economy case, the existence of supply constraints need not lead directly to inflation (though it may do so indirectly via exchange rate depreciation). However, taking first the case of fixed exchange rates, McKinnon (1976) has recently argued that the income multiplier effect of fiscal policy, with supply constraints, is zero. The argument is very simple. If the economy produces only tradeable goods that are available from and sold to the world markets at a fixed price, and if the aggregate supply schedule, with the money wage fixed, is upward sloping in the price level as indicated by

Keynes, then any attempt via fiscal action to raise demand will merely result in corresponding added imports since the domestic economy is incapable of profitably producing further output. The expansionary potential of fiscal policy is in essence limited to government purchases of non-traded outputs (e.g., the services of civil servants). A comparable result is arrived at by Dixit (1978) using a disequilibrium macroeconomic framework of analysis. Again, the economy is thought of as producing only tradeables; recognition of the foreign trade sector then implies that consumers will not be rationed for goods and firms will not face a sales constraint since the one can buy, and the other sell, any amount overseas. On this basis, it is not surprising that a policy of raising aggregate *domestic* demand with these factors unchanged should have no effect: the added demand simply appears as increased imports.[14] Again, it appears that this result would be modified by recognition of non-traded goods.

The wealth conditions of equilibrium associated with McKinnon's fixed exchange rate result are as analysed earlier. The bond issues financing the budget deficit cover the balance of payments loss on current account. The zero multiplier result also applies to the flexible exchange rate case. In contrast with Mundell's (1963) conclusion that under flexible rates fiscal policy drives out net exports through the appreciation of the exchange rate consequent on the sale of bonds to foreign residents, McKinnon argues that the exchange rate will remain unchanged in the final equilibrium, with wealth effects neutralised by equivalent budget and balance of payments deficits just as in the fixed rate case.[15]

This result is significant in establishing the impotence of fiscal policy (except for the non-tradeables component) in open economies whatever the exchange rate regime, contrary to the received (Mundell–Fleming) wisdom that fiscal policy is potent under fixed rates but impotent under flexible rates.[16] The result depends on specifying a supply constraint, the effect of which is to make imports the residual balancing factor in demand; thus it is no longer possible for the import function to play a role in determining output expansion as under the demand-determined output regimes with wealth adjustments that were analysed earlier. This applies also to the case of non-tradeables where, although expansion of government purchases can have an effect on income (a multiplier of unity in the fixed exchange rate case and rather less in the flexible rate case), tax remissions still have zero impact under either regime.

It seems odd not to incorporate inflation expectations and inflationary processes in models that envisage flexible exchange rates; however, this is not done either in Mundell–Fleming or in McKinnon. In the first case, there is an assumption that wage and price levels are fixed. In the second, the need to incorporate such mechanisms is avoided by the demonstration that sustained changes in the exchange rate are not required to re-establish equilibrium. However, if inflation expectations and exchange rate depreciation are linked, it seems reasonable to suppose that an alternative equilibrium position under flexible rates would be one in which the wealth adjustment criteria for equilibrium are satisfied by a situation where the exchange rate depreciation and associated inflation produce an inflation tax that neutralises the effect of the continued budget deficit. The balance of payments deficit would be zero in such a case, and the level of income unchanged, the nominal exchange rate having undergoing continuous depreciation. Such an equilibrium is the easier to motivate if the Mundell–McKinnon assumption regarding capital mobility is exchanged for the idea of capital stock adjustment.

The point here is that whereas the traditional theoretical assumption was that a continuing capital inflow could be attracted into a country by a given one-for-all interest rate change (infinitesimally small in the case of perfect capital mobility, finite in the case of imperfect capital mobility) empirical work in the area has increasingly stressed the idea that the correct principle is one of stock adjustment, with capital flows occurring in response to a once-over rearrangement of portfolios in favour of the country raising its interest rate. The extent of the capital stock readjustment and (given some costs of adjustments) of the resultant per quarter capital flows would, of course, be related to the degree of substitutability of bonds of various national denomination in portfolios, but would, in principle, be finite. Thus, apart from any effect due to the natural growth of portfolios, a continuing capital flow would require continuing *increases* in interest rates.

If, in fact, the appropriate principle is one of stock adjustment, there are two immediate consequences of significance. First, the relevance of Mundell–Fleming equilibria is very short run indeed; second, the exchange rate could reasonably be thought of as seeking a long-run value determined by current account equilibrium.[17] In this event, an equilibrium can be envisaged in which expansive fiscal action leads to continuous nominal depreciation of the exchange rate equal to the rate of inflation so that fiscal policy will crowd out private expenditure via the inflation tax described above, rather than via a decline in net exports. It is one thing, of course, to envisage such an equilibrium, and another to demonstrate its stability. However, one aspect of the result worth stressing is that the effect of assuming *both* flexible exchange rates *and* capital mobility in the stock adjustment sense is to validate the closed economy result arrived at previously.

In fact, agreed analytical conclusions are hard to find in this area. Apart from the issue of the correct choice of assumption regarding the interpretation of (perfect) capital mobility, there are significant unsettled issues regarding the assumptions to be made with respect to prices and wages, and the determination of the exchange rate. In the latter case, the application of rational expectations requires appeal to a model that, *inter alia*, must settle the previous issues raised. The traditional Keynesian assumption of fixed domestic wages and prices can be easily modified to include the effects of import costs on prices and, via a Phillips (or real wage) mechanism, on wages. The 'law of one price', which motivates global monetarism, is another possible assumption, the one explored by McKinnon to the effect noted above.[18]

FISCAL POLICY AND 'EXPECTATIONS'

This section draws attention to the role credited to expectations in some recent (and not so recent) work on fiscal policy.

Here the most significant contribution was foreshadowed by some comments made by M. Friedman (1957) in his permanent income theory of consumption. At the end of his exposition of this theory, Friedman drew attention to the implication that the income multiplier, in the light of the permanent income theory of consumption, must be reduced in value as compared with that derived from customary 'current income' theories of consumption, with obvious implications for fiscal policy. The subsequent development of dynamic *IS/LM* analysis, however, which entertains permanent income as one among a number of reasons for supposing that both current expenditures and current money demand must be written as lagged functions of income (and other variables) revealed those comments to Friedman's to be partial equilibrium statements. For it turns out that the lags in the response of income to fiscal stimulus may be offset by the introduction of lags in the money demand function.[19] This proposition is illustrated in Figure 1.3. The 'true' income variable in the behavioural equations underlying the *IS* and *LM* curves is assumed to be permanent income, generated as a distributed lag of current and past income. Since, in the long run, the two concepts of income are equal, the schedules labelled *IS*, *IS'* and *LM* may be thought of as 'long-run' schedules. The schedules labelled with a tilde (˜) are the corresponding short-run schedules. The steeper (negative) slope of the short-run *IS* schedule results from the fact that permanent income, the 'true' income variable in the expenditure function, changes by less than current income in the short run; by similar argument, the short-run *LM* schedule is less steeply sloped than the corresponding long-run schedule An expansionary fiscal policy shifts *IS* to *IS'* and *IS* to *IS'*. The corresponding income expansion to the movement from *A* to *C*, the new short-run equilibrium, is clearly less than the long-run income expansion corresponding to the movement from *A* to *B*, which is Friedman's point. If, however, there is also a lag in the demand for money function, the short-run expansion point for the

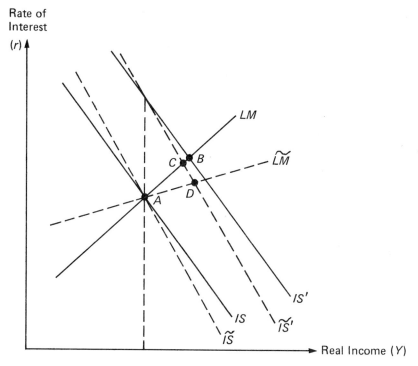

FIGURE 1.3   *Permanent income and fiscal policy.*

same fiscal action is given by the point *D*, which lies to the right of *C*, and may – as drawn – also lie to the right of *B*.

In any event, the widespread adoption of permanent income hypothesis style consumption functions in empirical work did not lead to any major reassessment of fiscal policy, except in cases where the fiscal change in question could be seen as itself a temporary one, expected to be reversed. This application, which may be regarded as a special case of rational expectations, has received particular attention, with inconclusive results, in the analysis of the 1968 income tax surcharge in the United States, which was known to be temporary (see, in particular, Okun, 1971; 1977, and Springer, 1975; 1977). This is a special case of rational expectations to the extent that, even when no particular announcement is made, the public may be expected to second-guess the government's counter-cyclical intentions and hence to anticipate the reversal of tax reductions made in recession and to expect the reduction of taxes increased in the boom. Such anticipations clearly reduce the impact of current fiscal changes on permanent income and thus on consumption. Anticipatory behaviour does at the same time, however, open up to governments the possibility of exerting strong timing effects on expenditures if expenditure taxes or subsidies are changed, with advance notice being given of the changes to be implemented.

The rigorous application of rational expectations hypothesis to problems of fiscal policy analysis has as yet far to go, however. It may be no accident that the principal analytical applications have so far been to problems of monetary policy, where some strong and intuitive 'long-run' conclusions (e.g., as to the neutrality of money) are in some sense reasonably well agreed, though even here problems arise from the fixity of contracts in some markets; more generally the application of the rational expectations hypothesis is inhibited at the very least by the widely differing information structure characterising different markets (see Fischer, 1977, and Schiller, 1978). The principle of rational expectations has, however, been used with some effect by Lucas (1976) as an argument against the usefulness of macroeconometric simulations to reveal the effects of fiscal (or any other) policy change on the grounds that, in general, agents' behaviour reflects knowledge of the policies pursued by governments, but that the conditional nature of this behaviour is not captured by typical macroeconometric simulation exercises. There do seem to be ways in which this criticism can be met, however (see Schiller, 1978).

ULTRARATIONALITY

Recent discussion of fiscal policy, in the context of crowding out, has made some use of the notion that government expenditures are, to some extent, and may be seen as, substitutes for private expenditures. In its full-blown form, whereby the private sector is envisaged as behaving as if the government were an extension of itself, the hypothesis has come to be called 'ultra-rationality'. The notion of government expenditures as a substitute for private expenditures certainly goes back as far as Bailey's classic textbook (Bailey, 1962), if not earlier. The principal direct implication of ultrarationality is that 'crowding out' may take the form of direct substitution not impelled by adjustments in the interest rate, the price level, inflation or the exchange rate. In David and Scadding (1974), the hypothesis is put forward as an extension of Denison's Law, which suggests the integration of the personal and corporate sectors, in much the same way as the New Cambridge approach has suggested, on the grounds that the total private sector savings ratio is more stable than that of either of the two individual sectors taken alone. However, much less evidence has been produced for believing that similar conditions for integrability hold in respect of the government and private sectors. Another implication of the substitution hypothesis is that the private sector may attribute characteristics to government expenditure according to its financing; specifically, David and Scadding suggest bond-financed expenditure may be identified as productive capital expenditures. One consequence of this is that the expectation that bond issues imply future tax increases may not follow rationally even in full employment conditions since the proceeds of the productive investment could be expected to finance the coupon payments. (Accordingly, household investment falls directly.) However, the prefix 'ultra' in 'ultrarationality' surely betrays correctly that what is being said is 'extreme'; the positive byproducts of this line of argument do not seem especially impressive. Even so, it is perhaps worth noting that the physiocratic analysis sponsored by Bacon and Eltis by contrast goes to another extreme; at least beyond some (undetermined) margin, it seems here as though public expenditure is regarded as valueless, with the associated tax increases leading to wage rises, pressure on profits and diminution of investment. Here, fiscal expansion leads to a deterioration in long-run growth potential, both because investment is reduced and because labour is pre-empted by the public sector. All this, however, is rather distincly another story.

CONCLUSIONS

The traditional analysis of fiscal policy assumes that output is demand determined; in such a context aggregate demand, output and employment can be increased by expansive fiscal policy, a result confirmed for the closed economy by the modern disequilibrium macroeconomic interpretation of Keynesian economics (see, for example, Barro and Grossman, 1976; Dixit, 1978, and Malinvand, 1977). The adjustment process embraced by the traditional account envisages the possibility of some crowding out as a result of the choice of the financing mode for the budget deficit.

Recent developments in the theory of fiscal policy are of several distinct kinds and the impression that the field is in a state of ferment is substantially a correct one. In the account above, four distinct developments were singled out for review; of these, the first, which consists of the joint recognition of the government budget constraint and of wealth adjustments, could be regarded, on a formal level, as merely extending the traditional Keynesian 'short run' to a longer horizon. Unfortunately for this fine distinction, it does seem a real possibility that such adjustments do occur substantially within a policy-relevant time horizon, as at any rate seems implicit in the claims made by proponents of 'New Cambridge'. The wealth adjustments literature affords other insights also with regard to inflationary equilibria and the phenomenon of 'inflation taxation'. This has to be associated with the second development reviewed above, the more explicit recognition of supply constraints. The well-worn contrast between 'Keynesian', i.e. underemployment adjustments, and 'classical', i.e. full employment adjustments, is clear evidence that this recognition is not exactly new; nevertheless, what does seem new(er) is the particular application to the small open economy, the analysis of inflationary equilibria and the treatment of the Phillips curve as an aggregate supply schedule. Unfortunately, it seems clear that the choice of stylised assumptions in the open economy, flexible exchange rate case, the one most relevant to current policy analysis for the UK, has not yet stabilised. Another development that is still in train is that associated with rational expectations; the practical policy-maker has long been concerned with the question of 'expectations'. The argument of 'perverse' expectations was used against Keynes to support the 'Treasury view', and against the policy of the New Deal, though these are perhaps examples of irrational expectations. The immediate difficulty raised by rational expectations for the theory of fiscal policy is that it inhibits resort to macroeconometric simulations to 'solve' problems. Finally, we noted the contribution of ultrarationality to the debate over the effectiveness of fiscal policy. All told, the number and complexity of recent developments is large, and it is clear that their implications do not yet command the kind of consensus that could formerly be counted upon in the analysis of fiscal policy.

APPENDIX
THE ANALYSIS OF FISCAL POLICY: A SIMPLE ALGEBRAIC EXPOSITION

Introduction

These notes set out the simple algebra and diagrammatic exposition of the traditional *IS/LM* analysis and show how the addition of a government budget financing constraint and of wealth effects leads to rather radical modifications in the analysis. The analysis assumes a fixed price level and a fixed physical capital stock; there are no supply constraints so output is demand determined. Until the last section, where the assumption is relaxed, a closed economy is maintained.

The analysis is intended to track the results, previously arrived at, of Laidler (1971), Teigen (1974), Christ (1968), Ott and Ott (1965), Silber (1970), Blinder and Solow (1973), McKinnon (1969) and Turnovsky (1976), to which reference is made at various points.

Traditional IS/LM Analysis

A model describing the traditional *IS/LM* analysis is set out below. Starting with the real sector, equations for the *IS* schedule are derived; from the equations for the monetary sector the *LM* schedule is derived next. Full equilibrium is established at the intersection of the *IS* and *LM* schedules. The algebraic reduced form for *Y* at the point of full equilibrium leads to the identification of multipliers discussed in the last part of this section.

The real sector The real sector comprises behavioural equations (1)–(4), and the goods market equilibrium condition is given by (5), or (5a). Substitution from (1)–(4) into (5) gives equations for the *IS* schedule with *Y* as the left-hand-side variable (7) and with *r* as the left-hand-side variable (8).

$$C = c_0 + c_1(Y - T) \qquad \text{Consumption function} \qquad (1)$$

$$T = t_0 + t_1 Y \qquad \text{Tax function} \qquad (2)$$

$$G = \bar{G} \qquad \text{Government spending function} \qquad (3)$$

$$I = a - br \qquad \text{Investment function} \qquad (4)$$

Y is national income, *r* 'the' rate of interest

$$Y = C + I + G \qquad \text{Goods market} \qquad (5)$$
$$S + T = I + G \qquad \text{equilibrium} \qquad (5a)$$

Substituting from (1)–(4) into (5):

$$Y = c_0 + c_1(Y - t_0 - t_1 Y) + a - br + \bar{G} \qquad (6)$$

which gives an equation for the *IS* schedule with *Y* as the left-hand-side variable as

$$Y = \frac{w - br}{z} \qquad \text{IS schedule } (Y) \qquad (7)$$

where *z* is the reciprocal of the unconstrained multiplier; i.e.

$$z = 1 - c_1(1 - t_1)$$

and *w* is an expression in the autonomous factors of the expenditure functions,

$$w = c_0 - c_1 t_0 + a + \bar{G}.$$

Alternatively, the *IS* schedule with *r* as the left-hand-side variable is given by:

$$r = \frac{w - Yz}{b} \qquad \text{IS schedule } (r) \qquad (8)$$

The monetary sector   The monetary sector consists of two behavioural equations, (9) and (10), and the condition of money market equilibrium (11). Substitution from (9) and (10) into (11) yields equations for the *LM* curve with Y as the left-hand-side variable (12) and with r as the left-hand-side variable (13).

$$M_d = h + dY - er \qquad \text{Money demand function} \qquad (9)$$

$$M_s = \bar{M} \qquad \text{Money supply function} \qquad (10)$$

$$M_s = M_d \qquad \text{Money market equilibrium} \qquad (11)$$

M, the money stock, is treated as the government's demand debt here.
  Substituting from (9) and (10) into (11) gives

$$Y = \frac{\bar{M} - h + er}{d} \qquad \text{LM schedule } (Y) \qquad (12)$$

$$r = \frac{h + dY - \bar{M}}{e} \qquad \text{LM schedule } (r) \qquad (13)$$

Full equilibrium   Full equilibrium of the system requires the simultaneous satisfaction of (7) and 12) and, equivalently, of (8) and (13). (Diagrammatically, this involves solving for the point of intersection of the *IS* and *LM* schedules.)
  Solving for Y, we obtain, by equating (8) and (13), the equation:

$$Y = \frac{w}{db/e + z} + \frac{(\bar{M} - h)}{d + ze/b} = wk_f + (\bar{M} - h)k_m \qquad (14)$$

Implications of the traditional IS/LM *analysis*   (1) The greater the ratio b/e – the ratio of the interest sensitivity of investment to the interest sensitivity of demand for money – the greater the value of the monetary multiplier (k_m) and the less the value of the 'fiscal' multiplier (k_f).
  (2) In extreme cases, involving 'extreme' values for b and e, one or other multiplier converges to zero. When k_f converges to zero, k_m goes to $1/d$, when k_m converges to zero, k_f goes to $1/z$, the simple unconstrained multiplier.
  These implications are noted in Laidler (1971), and in Teigen (1974), who additionally notes the effect of allowing for a positive interest elasticity of supply of money on the monetary multiplier (irrelevant here, because of the assumption that all money is high-powered money). *Ceteris paribus*, someone who 'believes in' a 'high' value for the ratio b/e believes in a 'high'

degree of crowding out of fiscal policy; complete crowding out follows in the traditional *IS/LM* model, however, only from 'extreme' assumptions about the parameters b or e (viz $b \to \infty$ or $e \to 0$).

IS/LM *analysis with a government budget constraint*

Christ (1968) explored the effects on traditional *IS/LM* analysis of recognising the government budget financing constraint. Formally, this involves adding the condition that a deficit adds to the net total of money plus bonds, as in equation (15). The full system is now represented by four real sector behavioural equations (1)–(4), two monetary sector behavioural equations (9) and (10), two equilibrium condition equations (5) and (11) and the financing constraint equation:

$$G - T = \partial(B + M), \tag{15}$$

or, starting from initial balance:

$$\partial G - \partial T = \partial(B + M). \tag{15a}$$

Bonds do not appear elsewhere in the model, so there is no reason why (15) should be binding for the case of bond financing. Money financing is a different matter. A deficit covered by additions to the money supply will involve shifts in the *LM* schedule, an effect comprehended in the model. Ruling out net open market operations so that if

$$\partial G - \partial T > 0, \text{ then } \left.\begin{array}{l} \partial B \geq 0 \\ \partial M \geq 0 \end{array}\right|$$

and writing ρ for the proportion of the deficit covered by addition to the money stock, we have

$$\partial M = \rho(\partial G - \partial T). \tag{16}$$

The impact multiplier Writing (14) in suitable differential form, the impact multiplier for a change in government spending financed as to 100ρ per cent by addition to the money stock can be written as

$$\partial Y = k_f \, \partial G + k_m \, \partial M_g \tag{17}$$

where ∂M_g is the deficit-associated increase in money supply. (It is assumed that the budget is balanced in the initial position.) Substituting for ∂M_g from (16), we obtain

$$\partial Y = k_f \, \partial G + k_m \rho(\partial G - t_1 \, \partial Y) \tag{18}$$

rearranging and dividing the right-hand side top and bottom by k_f gives

$$\frac{\partial Y}{\partial G} = \frac{1 + \frac{k_m}{k_f}\rho}{\frac{1}{k_f} + \frac{k_m}{k_f}\rho t_1}$$

$$= \frac{1 + \frac{b}{e}\rho}{z + \frac{b}{e}(d + \rho t_1)}, \tag{19}$$

which, with the restriction $\rho = 1$ is identical to the result obtained by Christ for the impact effect of a money-financed increase in government spending. If $\rho = 0$ (the bond financing case) then (19) reduces to the expression

$$\frac{1}{z + \frac{bd}{e}},$$

i.e., to k_f, the fiscal multiplier of the traditional *IS/LM* analysis already derived in equation (14). It is clear that the money-financed impact multiplier exceeds in value the traditional *IS/LM* multiplier for

$$\frac{1 + \frac{b}{e}}{\frac{b}{e}d + z + t_1\frac{b}{e}} > \frac{1}{\frac{b}{e}d + z}.$$

However, the money-financed impact multiplier may or may not exceed the unconstrained multiplier $1/z$, since whether

$$\frac{1 + \frac{b}{e}}{\frac{b}{e}d + z + t_1\frac{b}{e}} \gtrless \frac{1}{z}$$

depends on

$$\frac{1}{d + t_1} \gtrless \frac{1}{1 - c_1(1 - t_1)}$$

or

$$d \lessgtr (1 - c_1)(1 - t_1).$$

The impact effect is more likely to be bigger than the unconstrained multiplier the smaller the income 'elasticity' of demand for money (d), the smaller the marginal propensity to consume and the smaller the marginal tax rate. The first condition follows from the fact that the extent of the shift in the *LM* curve for a given increase in money supply depends inversely on the income elasticity of demand for money, and the second from the fact that the extent of the shift of the *IS* curve depends positively upon the marginal propensity to consume. The third effect emerges as a counterbalancing of two factors: first, the smaller the tax rate, the greater the extent of the shift in the *IS* schedule; second, the smaller the tax rate, the greater the incremental deficit associated with a given rise in income and hence the greater the associated increase in the money supply.

The long-run effect   Christ's principal point, however, was that long-run equilibrium in the money financing case requires a balanced budget. This holds, no matter what proportion of the deficits is covered by the issue of new money, so long as this is positive since the money supply will be increasing while a deficit remains and the *LM* curve will be shifting outwards. Hence, income will not reach a new long-run equilibrium until

$$\partial M = \rho(\partial G - t_1 \, \partial Y) = 0 \tag{20}$$

or

$$\partial G/\partial Y = \frac{1}{t_1}. \tag{21}$$

This long-run multiplier is unambiguously larger than either the impact multiplier or the unconstrained multiplier.

Wealth Effects

The recognition of the government budget constraint creates, or highlights, an apparent asymmetry in *IS/LM* analysis between the role given to the stock of bonds and the role given to the stock of money. Whereas changes in the latter are explicitly accounted for through the *LM* curve, changes in the stock of bonds (except as the counterpart of an opposite change in the money supply) are not accounted for.

Ott and Ott (1965) and Silber (1970) attempt to remove the asymmetry by incorporating in the demand for money function a term in wealth. Thus changes in the stock of bonds not offset by an opposite change in the stock of money appear as a change in wealth, and so affect the demand for money and the *LM* schedule. A wealth term in the demand for money function seems to invite a wealth term in the consumption function.

We can therefore replace our original consumption and money demand functions by the equations:

$$C = c_0 + c_1(Y - T) + jW \qquad (1)'$$

$$M_d = h + dY - er + gW, \qquad (9)'$$

where W, wealth, is defined as

$$W = B + M. \qquad (22)$$

Stocks of physical capital, which are to be kept fixed in the equilibrium solutions to the model may accordingly be omitted. The system, with behavioural equations augmented by wealth effects, and retaining the budget financing constraint (15) may now be solved for the impact multiplier.

The differential equation for income may be written as

$$\partial Y = k_f \, \partial G + k_m \, \partial M_g - k_m g \, \partial W_g + k_f j \, \partial W_g \qquad (23)$$

where ∂M_g and ∂W_g are the changes in money stock and in wealth associated with the policy of increasing government spending, from a position of initial balance, by ∂G. Since the change in wealth is identical with the deficit $(\partial G - t_1 \, \partial Y)$ and the deficit is financed as to 100ρ per cent by money creation, (23) can be rewritten as

$$\frac{\partial Y}{\partial G} = \frac{k_f + k_m \rho - k_m g + k_f j}{1 + k_m \rho t_1 - k_m g t_1 + k_f j t_1} \qquad (24)$$

Dividing by k_f and noting that $k_m / k_f = b/e$, this reduces to

$$\frac{\partial Y}{\partial G} = \frac{1 + \dfrac{b}{e}(\rho - g) + j}{\dfrac{b}{e}d + z + t_1 \left[\dfrac{b}{e}(\rho - g) + j \right]} \qquad (25)$$

With $t_1 = 0$, this expression is directly comparable with one of the results quoted by Silber (1970).

If the system is stable, the long-run multiplier is again $1/t_1$; adjustment towards this is now assisted by an outward movement of the *IS* schedule as long as a deficit persists, but hampered by an inward movement of the *LM* schedule due to wealth effects.

There are now four elements concerned in the adjustment and in the impact multiplier, viz:

(a) the direct (expansionary) effect of the increase in government spending on the *IS* schedule;

(b) the indirect (expansionary) effect (if $\rho > 0$) on the money supply through the financing of the deficit;

(c) the indirect (contractionary) effect on the demand for money due to the impact of the deficit in increasing wealth and the demand for money;

(d) the indirect (expansionary) effect on the *IS* schedule of the wealth effect in the consumption function.

In view of the opposing effects on the *LM* schedule (b) and (c), it is possible to imagine, as a special case, a policy of expansionary money financing just sufficient to offset the contractionary wealth-induced effects on the demand for money. As can be shown from equation (25) money financing provides a larger impact multiplier and, given the long-run multiplier, a faster rate of adjustment.

Instability   The impact multiplier (25) need not be positive, and even if it is positive the system need not be stable. The system will not be stable if the balance of the deficit-related effects is negative, i.e., if the sum of the terms (b), (c), (d) mentioned above is negative. If they are negative, any deficit remaining after the initial 'impact' period must tend to reduce income, and any further reduction in income will *increase* the deficit so adding a further net negative (wealth-cum-financing) effect. Income tends to fall to zero, hence the system will be unstable; *a fortiori*, if the impact multiplier as a whole is negative (i.e., the negative net sum of the terms (b), (c), (d) outweighs the positive term (a)) the system will be unstable.

So instability arises if

$$k_m \, \partial M_g - k_m g \, \partial W_g + k_f j \, \partial W_g < 0.$$

Recalling that $\partial M_g = \rho \partial W_g = \rho(\partial G - t_1 \, \partial Y)$ this reduces to

$$k_m \rho - k_m g + k_f j < 0$$

or, dividing by k_f and simplifying:

$$\frac{g}{\rho} > 1 + \frac{e}{b} j \frac{1}{\rho}.$$

In the absence of a wealth effect on consumption ($j = 0$) this reduces to saying that instability ensues if the increase in demand for money associated with a deficit exceeds the increase in the supply of money associated with it.

Silber notes the equality of their effects (on the special assumption that $j = 0$) as leading to a fixed *LM* schedule, and to the validation of the traditional *IS/LM* multiplier, for in this case the system loses the mechanism by which the long-run equilibrium, given by the multiplier of $1/t_1$, can be reached, and the deficit persists indefinitely.

Bond Coupons

Blinder and Solow (1973) additionally argue that, once account is taken of the need to service bond debt, the bond-financed fiscal multiplier will exceed the value of $1/t_1$.

If the system is stable, long-run equilibrium can be found from the government budget financing constraint, rewritten to account for the net (after tax) coupon payments on the bonds issued as a result of the rise in government spending. For the sake of convenience bonds are measured in units just such that the coupon is equal to unity. Accordingly, the budget financing constraint becomes

$$\partial G + (1 - t_1)\frac{\partial B}{\partial G} - t_1\,\partial Y = 0 \tag{26}$$

so that

$$\frac{\partial Y}{\partial G} = \frac{1 + (1 - t_1)\,\partial B_g}{t_1} > 0 \tag{27}$$

Since under money financing $\partial B/\partial G$ (and $\partial B_g) = 0$, bond-financed government spending appears to have more expansionary effects than money-financed government spending, the reverse of the implications of both the traditional *IS/LM* analysis and of the ordering of the impact effects of traditional analysis modified to allow for wealth effects and the government budget financing constraint.

The conventional result, can, however, be retained by rewriting the fiscal spending parameter as

$$\partial G' = \partial G + (1 - t_1)\,\partial B/\partial G \tag{28}$$

so that by substitution in (26)

$$\partial Y/\partial G' = 1/t_1 \tag{29}$$

In this case (cf. Tobin and Buiter, 1976) the definition of government spending is taken as exhaustive expenditures (∂G) *plus* associated net service costs $((1 - t_1)\,\partial B/\partial G)$.

Blinder and Solow (1973), as do others, additionally consider that the inclusion of bond service payments in the financing constraint should be balanced by a corresponding change in the tax function so that disposable income, and hence consumption, will be increased. This would affect the *IS* schedule and the impact multiplier. It is not clear, however, that such an effect should be added on top of the wealth effect associated with the issue of bonds, since to do so is to indulge in a kind of double-counting of bonds, first as a stock and then as a flow: cf. Sparks (1976) and Miller (1976).

The Open Economy

The extension of the same kind of model to the case of the open economy crucially involves the further adjustment of the wealth constraint. Since the current account is equal with opposite sign to the net capital account, and still assuming a given stock of fixed capital equipment, the wealth constraint is rewritten as

$$\partial W = \partial X - \partial M' + \partial G - \partial T = 0 \tag{30}$$

where X is exports, and M' imports of goods and services.

This constraint can be satisfied by the equality of the balance of the payments deficit, $\partial M' - \partial X$ and the government budget deficit.

Assuming, as before, that output is demand determined and also that the exchange rate is fixed, then recalling the tax function (2), (30) can be rewritten as

$$\partial Y / \partial G = \frac{1}{m_1 + t_1} \tag{31}$$

or alternatively as

$$\partial Y / \partial G = \frac{1 - m_1}{m_1 + t_1(1 - m_1)} \tag{31a}$$

according to whether the important propensity is described as $M' = m_0 + m_1 Y$ (for 31) or $M' = m_0 + m_1(Y + M')$ (for 31a).

The expression (31a) and the conclusion that full equilibrium requires only the equality of the government budget deficit and the balance of payments deficit are to be found in McKinnon (1969), Oates (1966) and McKinnon and Oates (1966).

This may not, in fact, be a sufficient condition for full equilibrium, as argued by Turnovsky (1976). For the closed economy, the condition of budget balance rules out any change in the stock of money (or the supply of bonds) since the financing questions at issue pertain to the finance of deficits and do not embrace open market operations. Clearly, this condition does not follow from the requirement, simply, that the government budget deficit and balance of payments deficits be equal. The money supply (and therefore the stock of bonds) could be changing while this were true. One or two further requirements must be added to ensure that the money stock is stationary in full equilibrium.

The requirement that the change in the stock of money should be zero in equilibrium requires that

$$\partial M = \partial M_D + \partial M_F = 0 \tag{32}$$

or

$$\partial M_D = -\partial M_F$$

i.e., that the increase in the stock of money of 'domestic' origin should be just offset by the decrease in the stock of money of 'external' origin. Denoting by s the proportion of a balance of payments deficit that is sterilised, this requires

$$\partial M_D = \rho(\partial G - t_1 \, \partial Y) = -\partial M_F = -(1 - s)(\partial X - m_1 \, \partial Y)$$

or $\qquad \rho = (1 - s)$ if $G - T = X - M'$.

Or, in precisely similar fashion, the change in the stock of domestic bonds (∂B_D) must equal with opposite sign the change in the stock of foreign bonds (∂B_F), i.e.,

$$\partial B_D = (1 - \rho)(\partial G - t_1 \, \partial Y) = \partial B_F = -s(\partial X - m_1 \, \partial Y)$$

so if the proportion of monetary financing of the deficit (ρ) is equal to the proportion of the balance of payments deficit not sterilised $(1 - s)$, wealth and the stock of money (hence the stock of bonds) will be stationary.

As an alternative, perfect substitutability of foreign and domestic bonds will produce the same result. Suppose that we start from a position like (31) with no change in net wealth or its constituents. Then suppose the government (say) reduces ρ, financing more of the deficit by bond issue. Then, since the added domestic bonds are perfect substitutes for foreign bonds, there will be an offsetting decline in the stock of foreign bonds held. As a result of this assumption, the rate of interest must be assumed given at the exogenously determined 'world' level. The fixity of 'the' interest rate at the world level, given the perfect substitutability of domestic and foreign bonds, has as an implication that the instability possibility referred to earlier in the closed economy case is no longer a difficulty. The reason may be seen from Figure 1.2 (p. 18). In that diagram the external balance line FF (and under present assumptions conterminously an LM schedule for infinitely elastic money supplies) is drawn as a horizontal line, at the 'world' interest rate r_1. This means that the troublesome wealth effect in the demand for money schedule is no longer capable of causing a rise in the rate of interest that would crowd out private investment; instead, excess bond holdings can be liquidated at the fixed rate of interest (sold for money overseas). The IS schedule will continue to drift to the right, however, until the wealth effect operative on consumption is neutralised at the point where private sector wealth ceases to grow.

'*New Cambridge*'

A characteristic 'New Cambridge' result is that the government budget deficit is mirrored (eventually) in the balance of payments. In this sense the New Cambridge result is similar to the Oates–McKinnon result, although presented and derived in a different fashion.

A key assumption of the New Cambridge doctrine, at least as initially interpreted, is that the private sector's marginal propensity to absorb out of disposable income is unity. The marginal propensity to absorb of the economy as a whole may be regarded as a weighted average of the private sector's and the government sector's marginal propensities.

Letting A stand for absorption

$$A = a_0 + a_1 Y; \partial A = a_1 \partial Y \tag{33}$$

$$a_1 = w_1 \alpha_1 + (1 - w_1)\alpha_2 \tag{34}$$

where α_1 is the private sector's marginal propensity to absorb (MPA) and α_2 is the government sector's MPA; w_1 and w_2 are weights that give the proportionate marginal distribution of ∂Y between the two sectors as

$$w_1 = \frac{\partial(Y - T)}{\partial Y} = 1 - t_1$$

$$w_2 = \frac{\partial T}{\partial Y} = t_1.$$

Consequently, the balance of payments, which according to the absorption principle improves according to

$$\partial \beta = \partial Y - \partial A, \tag{35}$$

can be written as

$$\partial \beta = \partial Y - (1 - t_1)\alpha_1 \partial Y - \alpha_2 t_1 \partial Y \tag{36}$$

or, taking the 'New Cambridge' assumption of $\alpha_1 = 1$,

$$\partial \beta = \partial T - \partial G \tag{37}$$

The 'New Cambridge' income multiplier, accordingly, appears to be given by (31a) above.

This representation of the private sector's MPA is 'too strong' as a property holding both *in and out* of equilibrium and in fact the earlier Cambridge empirical estimates suggested that what was envisaged was, to begin with, some involuntary 'hoarding' followed (within two years) by dishoarding of a roughly equivalent amount. In subsequent accounts it has been clarified that the process is one of (wealth) stock adjustments; in this case, the 'strong' MPA assumption holds at points of equilibrium, and as between them, subject only to a modification arising from the idea that desired wealth is a function of income.

NOTES AND REFERENCES

1. See CEPG *Economic Policy Review*, March 1978, No. 4, Ch. 6. In the Appendix we indicate a formal derivation of the earlier 'New Cambridge' statements, utilising the assumption of a unity private sector marginal absorption propensity.
2. Cf. Tobin and Buiter (1976). Although it is often convenient to appeal to this redefinition, it should be recognised that certain of the consequences of doing so are uncomfortable: as, for example, Currie (1978a) points out, open market operations should, by this same token, be accompanied by counterbalancing changes in exhaustive government spending to offset the effects on debt service costs.
3. This otherwise inconsistent assumption may be regarded as a concealed, but plausible, appeal to the idea that wealth adjustments with respect to financial claims are faster than those associated with real capital; in any event, to grapple with the latter properly requires a much longer time horizon and a different mode of analysis (see McKinnon, 1976, for a nice account of all this).
4. This is just the 'ordinary multiplier', $1/[1 - c_1(1 - t_1)]$, but with c_1 construed as a marginal propensity to absorb of unity, and an accommodating monetary policy. Although not shown in the diagram, it is clearly implied that the *IS* schedule applicable here is flatter than for the traditional case.
5. In the Appendix to this paper, the 'Mark I' version of New Cambridge is briefly stated. The comparability of these results with those of the wealth approach was commented upon by McKinnon (1976) who noted that the unity marginal propensity to absorb was only an *equilibrium* feature of the wealth approach, but seemed to have to hold *in and out of* equilibrium for New Cambridge. Subsequently, the expenditure functions of the New Cambridge approach have been given a more explicit wealth adjustment basis (see note 1).
6. Money-financed deficits will be stable, however, since the negative net wealth effect in the demand for money could not exceed the increase in wealth represented by the deficit and financed by equivalent monetary creation. Instability may still be a problem for 'mixed' financing regimes, therefore.
7. Silber (1970) specified 'lump sum' tax functions, which clearly must also give rise to a multiplier of $+\infty$ if wealth effects are net expansionary.
8. Williamson (1971) remarked on the instability induced by recognition of debt service costs in his critique of the influential Mundell (1962) model, well before the example of Blinder and Solow (1973) set the fashion for explicit recognition of bond coupon payments. Williamson noted that Mundell's recommendation for a rise in interest rates (and expansion of the budget deficit) following an exogenous deterioration in the external equilibrium schedule would imply in following periods a further deterioration of the same type, as the bond coupons fall due to be paid.
9. See, e.g., Siegel (1976); Miller and Temple (1977) have computed such effects for the United Kingdom in recent years and have concluded that they broadly match the value of the (unadjusted) budget deficit.
10. The rationalisation thus also justifies the assignment rules proposed by the New Cambridge approach, though it may be objected that assignment exercises themselves are somewhat unrealistic, in that they ignore the possibilities for the appropriate simultaneous decision-making by the relevant governmental authorities.
11. Strictly, this is so only on the assumption that asset demands are unaffected by changes in fiscal parameters, which is perhaps not a very general condition.

12. In the case of the open economy, this conclusion goes through only on the assumption that the import function applies to total income.
13. For most purposes, the results indicated above follow even if bonds are 'only a little' net wealth since, if they are so, the equilibrium requirement that wealth be not changing still requires budget balance and so does not change the 'multiplier' results.
14. This was of looking at the problem does seem to raise an aggregation problem, though. For each small economy in a world of such economies, taken individually, it might seem reasonable to argue that its own recession was due to its inability to reduce real wages and its unemployment is, hence, classical. But it would not seem correct to deny the possibility of Keynesian unemployment arising at the world level and, if so, we would expect the constituent economies to share in this unemployment.
15. McKinnon motivates his arguments by showing how a Mundellian exchange rate appreciation would lead to inconsistencies in his own model, which would have to be resolved by a corresponding depreciation. It would appear that the added import demand, and deficit on the current account, would be met in the new equilibrium by equivalent sales of bonds overseas so requiring no change in wealth. The 'effective' (comparative static) value of the 'marginal propensity to import' (related to expenditure) is unity, so the formula $\partial Y/\partial G = (1 - m)/(m + t + mt)$ reduces to zero.
16. As indicated, in the case of flexible rates, crowding out was achieved in Mundell–Flemming by an appreciation leading to a fall in net exports. In the fixed exchange rate case, the constraining effect of the rising LM schedule is avoided as bonds can be sold overseas at unchanged interest rates, an assumption that simultaneously renders monetary policy impotent, in this case, and fiscal policy as fully potent as the 'ordinary' income–expenditure multiplier has it, or more potent if wealth effects are allowed, cf. Figure 1.2.
17. Argy and Porter (1972) have previously argued that the short-run Mundell result is vulnerable to a different exchange rate assumption. They suggest a regressive expectations model so that the exchange rate, having appreciated, would be expected again to depreciate. This requires the domestic interest rate to increase so as to offset the expected depreciation, which yields the possibility of an increase in income. Of course, if the exchange rate actually does not depreciate, the expectation that it will must be assumed to be revised. In the case reviewed in the text there is by assumption no scope for an expansion of output in the long run.
18. Gordon (1977) confronts the domestic Phillips curve approach with that of global monetarism and suggests a hybrid model that 'corresponds more closely to the real world than either extreme view from which it is derived'.
19. There are a number of papers in the dynamic IS/LM literature; that by Meyer (1974) provides a comprehensive account and comments explicitly on the matter referred to here.

CHAPTER 2

The Measurement of Fiscal Influence

G. K. Shaw*

Evaluation of fiscal policy and of the ultimate effects of the Budget may differ, depending on whether the monetary authorities accommodate the liquidity implications of the budget [Chand, 1977].

1. THE RATIONALE FOR THE FULL EMPLOYMENT BUDGET SURPLUS

Before one can begin to evaluate the effectiveness of fiscal policy or compare its impact with alternative policy measures, it is necessary to decide how fiscal intervention should be assessed and quantified. That is to say, we require some means of deciding whether a given fiscal change is exerting an expansionary or contractionary influence and whether such influence can be categorised as strong or weak. Ideally, we would want to be able to rank alternative fiscal measures in terms of their comparative weight. For our purposes, we define fiscal policy[1] to encompass any *discretionary* change in the level, composition or timing of central government outlays,[2] whether upon goods and services or in the form of transfer payments;[3] and equally any *discretionary* alteration in the burden, structure or frequency of the tax payment. Insistence upon the discretionary element permits us to distinguish deliberate acts by the fiscal authorities from fluctuations in outlays and revenues that arise as an automatic consequence of variations in the level of economic activity.

The concern with the measurement of fiscal influence sprang in large measure from the inadequacy of the actual budget surplus or deficit as an indicator of the ease or stringency of fiscal policy. In the United States in the 1930s for example, the depression had been accompanied by large budget deficits that apparently exercised little expansionary impact upon the econ-

* I am indebted to my colleague R. B. Cross for constructive comments upon an earlier draft.

omy. This experience led many to the view that Keynesian-type fiscal policy measures would be ineffectual in aiding the recovery from depression or recession, and possibly reinforced the traditional 'Treasury view' that increased public expenditure would necessarily be at the expense of private outlays. In a pioneering article in the 1950s, E. Cary Brown re-examined this experience (Brown, 1956) and demonstrated that, on balance, fiscal policy had been relatively restrictive; the substantial budget deficits merely reflected the shortfall in government revenues stemming from the depressed level of economic activity. The alternative proposed by Brown was to evaluate the change in the budget surplus (deficit) resulting from a fiscal measure that would have occurred had the income level remained constant. The change in the budget surplus (deficit) occurring at an income level corresponding to full employment would indicate the *direction* of fiscal policy in the sense of indicating the intentions of the fiscal authorities in their attempt to stimulate or constrain the economy. The subsequent history of the measurement of fiscal influence has reflected the attempt to refine and improve upon the concept of the full employment budget surplus as an adequate indicator of the direction of policy.

Brown's critique of the actual budget surplus (deficit) as an indicator of policy and his advocacy of the full employment surplus measure can be illustrated by reference to Figure 2.1. Part (b) of the figure depicts the budget surplus as a positive function of money national income, the positive slope being a consequence of the greater responsiveness of tax revenues vis-à-vis outlays to income fluctuation.[4] Point A depicts a balanced budget. Let us assume the economy is at point B with an initial surplus of $0X$ when the decision is taken to raise taxes. The tax hike will be reflected in an upward shift of the budget function and in the tax curve (indicated by the dotted lines). However, if increased taxes so depress the economy that the income level falls, let us say to point C, a budget deficit will be generated equal to $0Y$. Focusing upon the actual surplus (deficit) at C suggests expansionary policy whereas had the surplus been calculated for the constant income level B, the raising of the surplus of $0Z$ would more correctly depict the restrictive intentions of the fiscal authorities.

2. Limitations of the Full Employment Surplus Measure

Clearly, the full employment budget surplus measure represents a conceptual advance upon the actual budget surplus (deficit) as an indicator of policy.[5] However, it is not entirely free of defects, that may generate misleading impressions about the stance and strength of fiscal policy.

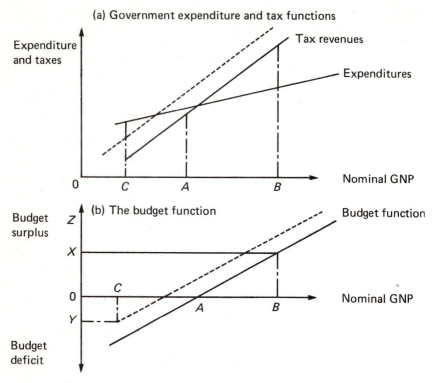

FIGURE 2.1   *The full employment surplus*

(a) *Absence of Weighting*

The full employment budget surplus as described above does not distinguish between changes in taxes and changes in expenditures, or between changes in expenditure upon goods and services and changes in transfer payments. A £1 increase in the full employment budget surplus is assumed to exert the same restrictive impact upon the macro-economy regardless of its origin. However, this result, as has long been recognised, is contrary to the doctrine of the balanced budget multiplier, which *ceteris paribus* imparts a greater weight to increased spending upon goods and services as compared to an equivalent reduction in taxation or alternatively to an equivalent increase in transfer payments. To overcome this difficulty the concept of the weighted full employment budget surplus has been proposed that attaches different weights to expenditure and taxes – with transfer payments being treated as negative taxes.[6] The weighted full employment budget surplus thus indicates a less contradictory fiscal attitude upon the part of the authorities when contraction is achieved by taxation, as compared to the unweighted surplus;

and equally indicates a less expansionary policy when expansion is achieved by decreased taxation, than indicated by the unweighted surplus (assuming a marginal propensity to consume of less than unity).

(b) The Composition of the Tax Mix

The weighted full employment budget surplus was an attempt to take account of the greater macroeconomic impact of government outlays vis-à-vis comparable adjustments in taxation as suggested by the famous Haavelmo–Gelting balanced budget multiplier theorem. However, no attempt is made to allow for the alleged greater macroeconomic impact of indirect vis-à-vis direct taxes. It is simply assumed that an increase in the budget surplus occasioned by an indirect tax change will exert the identical macroeconomic impact as an equal yielding direct tax change.

The belief that indirect taxes exert a greater deflationary impact than equal yielding income taxes is firmly established in the public finance literature although it is only comparatively recently that a formal demonstration was provided within the context of a multi-tax setting (Peston, 1971). The argument is implicit in Keynes' formulation of the consumption function, which is non-linear and exhibits a declining marginal propensity to consume with rising income. It only requires indirect taxes to be more regressive than direct taxes for the former to merit greater weight in the definition of the weighted full employment surplus.

To this rather intuitive foundation was added the important formal contribution of Cary Brown (Brown, 1950) who demonstrated that a sales tax would exert a greater macroeconomic impact than an equal yielding income tax even assuming a uniform marginal propensity to consume.[7] Brown's analysis depended upon a comparison of two single tax states: one possessing income taxes and no sales taxes, the other possessing sales taxes but no income taxes. It is for this reason that the statement put forward by Peston (1971) takes on renewed significance. Peston showed that in a multi-tax world with sales taxes and direct taxes existing side by side, a change in the tax mix in favour of direct taxes, with total tax proceeds held constant, would exert an expansionary impact upon the level of economic activity.

Moreover, to this formal analysis would need to be added possible differential impacts upon interest rates and investment. Since indirect taxes add to prices then, with a fixed money stock, interest rates will rise and presumably there will be some impact upon investment spending. In addition, the indirect tax-induced price rise should adversely impinge upon consumption outlays operating via reverse Pigou effects. In short, therefore, there are firm grounds for believing that indirect taxes exert greater impacts than equal yielding direct taxes. It follows that if we are going to invoke a weighted full employment budget surplus concept to evaluate fiscal policy, then differential weights would have to be attached according to the nature of the various tax components. Theoretically, without such an adjustment, there is no reason why an increase in the full employment budget surplus achieved by increasing taxes, accompanied by a major switch from indirect to direct taxation, could not be expansionary *in toto*.

(c) Differential Balance of Payments Impact

The foregoing has suggested the need to amend the simple full employment budget surplus by a set of weights, first to discriminate between government expenditures and taxes and transfers, and second to distinguish between the different impact effects of indirect and direct taxes. Equally, however, it is necessary to distinguish between the differing balance of payments consequences of like changes in the full employment budget. If the marginal propensity to import of the public sector significantly differs from that of the private sector, then any changes in the full employment surplus occasioned by expenditure changes will imply differing consequences from those occasioned by tax changes.[8] In like manner, changes in corporate taxation will exert different import repercussions from those arising from changes in personal taxation. In principle, such influences can always be taken into account in determining the weighting procedure to be attached to any fiscal policy change, but estimation problems and time constraints delineate the resultant trade-off.[9]

(d) Biased Estimates of Actual Impact

The full employment budget surplus, whether weighted or not, indicates the strength of any fiscal policy change evaluated at the full employment income level. Nonetheless, its purpose is to indicate the direction and comparative strength of fiscal intervention at actual income levels – the full employment estimate being merely a device to overcome the difficulties occasioned by built-in flexibility. Is there any reason to assume that the full employment estimate may give a distorted impression of the actual fiscal influence? Unfortunately, there is. Consider, for example, the decision to increase unemployment benefits. Presumably, this will have little or no impact upon the estimate of the full employment budget surplus (depending upon how full employment is actually determined). Yet the expansionary impact of such a measure upon current income levels could be considerable in times of heavy unemployment. The full employment surplus would, in this case, seriously understate the strength of the fiscal change: this situation is illustrated by reference to Figure 2.2.[10]

It will be appreciated that what is involved here is a change in the slope of the function. Strictly speaking, the full employment budget surplus will only

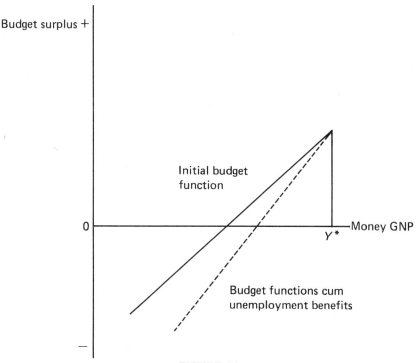

FIGURE 2.2

give an accurate estimate of the actual fiscal impact if the fiscal policy change
promotes a *parametric* shift of the budget function. Where the policy change
promotes a change in slope, as for example by the adoption of more progressive tax schedules, then the true size of the discretionary fiscal action will
vary according to the income level currently prevailing. Furthermore, once it
is conceded that discretionary fiscal policy may change the slope of the
budget function, then further problems are created, for now the full employment budget surplus will no longer be an unambiguous indicator of policy.
In Figure 2.3, for example, the budget function I implies a far more restrictive discretionary policy than budget function II, evaluated at the full employment income level, Y^*. But if the economy were actually at the income
level Y_1, could we reasonably maintain this to be so?[11]

In addition, most advanced economies discriminate with regard to the
taxation of labour and capital incomes, in terms of progressivity, actual
effective rates, allowances and so forth. This consideration becomes of importance if the pattern of income distribution varies over the course of the
trade cycle, for then the change in the budget surplus evaluated at full
employment, arising from any given fiscal measure, need no longer correspond to the actual change at other stages in the cycle.

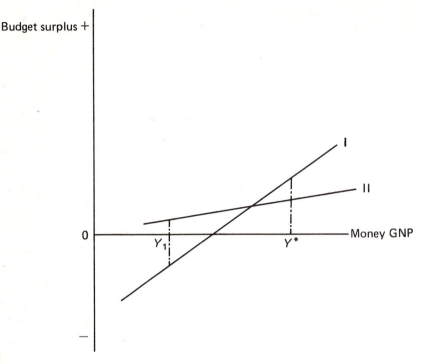

FIGURE 2.3

Considerations such as these have led to attempts to construct a budget surplus measure to evaluate fiscal influence at a constant income level near that currently prevailing. In the United Kingdom, for example, where the gap between actual and full employment income has been substantial and long-lasting, an attempt has been made to construct a standardised budget balance at 3 per cent and 5 per cent unemployment levels respectively. The differences, when expressed as a percentage of GNP, are not insubstantial, as indicated in Table 2.1.

TABLE 2.1   *Estimates of standardised budget balances as a proportion of* GDP*

	1974	1975	1976	1977
Standardised at 5% unemployment	−9.8%	−10.8%	−8.1%	−4.6%
Standardised at 3% unemployment	−5.8%	−7.1%	−4.4%	−1.1%

* Calendar years
Source: Hartley and Bean (1978)

(*e*) *The Problem of Fiscal Drag*

One of the great virtues claimed for the original full employment budget surplus measure was that it distinguished between discretionary and automatic fiscal changes. In the simplest terms, a movement along a given budget function illustrated the degree of built-in flexibility of the fiscal system – the automatic adjustment of yields and outlays to income change[12] – whereas a parametric shift of the budget function denoted discretionary policy. Such a distinction is important in the evaluation of the efficacy of fiscal policy; in particular the automatic fiscal stabilisers serve to weaken the impact of discretionary fiscal change. However, this alleged virtue holds good only in the case of a stationary economy experiencing zero rates of inflation. If full employment income is growing, either because of an increase in the labour force or because of improved productivity,[13] then, since revenues reveal greater responsiveness to income change than do outlays, the full employment budget surplus will progressively increase. This tendency is reinforced by the effects of inflation on the yield of a progressive tax system and the real value of government outlays denominated in nominal terms. Unless these influences are adjusted for, the full employment budget surplus will lead to the understanding of expansionary fiscal intervention, when evaluated in a dynamic context.[14] The entire concept of the full employment surplus becomes bedevilled once inflation is introduced into the analysis – unless the economy happens to be operating at full employment income – because an estimate of full capacity output is needed before the implications of government policies for revenues and outlays can be assessed. But if we are not at full employment what price index are we to use to evaluate the money value of full employment GNP? In practice, the current price index is invoked, which may be far from that experienced at full employment; with a progressive tax structure this may have a significant effect on the resulting estimate of the full employment surplus.[15] In a growing economy, characterised by inflation, the full employment budget surplus encounters precisely the same objections as does the actual budget surplus – namely the inability to distinguish automatic from discretionary components without invoking procedures that at best might appear arbitrary.

(*f*) *Other Considerations*

Three further points may be noted. First, the full employment budget surplus is essentially static in its application and no provision is made for lags in effect. This is clearly unsatisfactory. For example, if at time t_1 the economy is experiencing under-utilised resources, this does not necessarily imply that the correct response should be a decrease in the full employment surplus, for the economy may still be responding to budgetary measures undertaken at time t_0. It cannot be assumed *a priori* that the existence of a budget surplus (deficit) when the margin of spare capacity is high (low) is evidence of establising policy. Second, little information can be culled from inter-country comparisons of the full employment surplus when expressed as a percentage of GNP (see Neild and Ward, 1976) and similar percentage changes need not imply identical or similar fiscal intervention – partly because the potency of the automatic stabilisers that discretionary policy has to overcome will in all probability differ between countries. Finally, it will be appreciated that the domestic impact of any fiscal change will depend in part upon the prevailing policy with respect to exchange rates. The leakage into imports and the accompanying monetary changes will differ under a regime of fixed as opposed to fully floating exchange rates.

3. Evaluation of the Full Employment Budget Surplus

The full employment budget surplus represents an attempt to sum up in one value both the direction and strength of a given discretionary fiscal change. Its proponents consider it superior to the actual budget surplus figure. In this respect they attempt to summarise for fiscal policy what those single valued variables, M_1 and M_3, purport to do for monetary policy. Approached in this manner, it becomes easier to place the full employment surplus in perspective. No one should seriously expect that a unique measure of this kind would always prove an infallible indicator of fiscal policy or would always operate in a truly precise manner, any more than the monetarist would focus solely upon M_1 or M_3 and ignore entirely the corresponding movement in interest rates. The great virtue of the unweighted full employment budget surplus, as with the monetary aggregates, lies in its being a measure of policy change devised without regard to any specific model of the economy: it does not make any particular claim to Keynesian or monetarist interpretations and equally it is neutral in the controversy over the relative merits of fiscal versus monetary intervention.

Nonetheless, its relevance to policy formation may be called into question, especially then the economy may depart from full employment income for long periods of time – and indeed when the authorities may be pursuing objectives other than full employment. Particularly in the United Kingdom, where balance of payments and inflation objectives have frequently taken precedence, attention has focused more upon the *actual* budget surplus as opposed to its full employment counterpart. It is the actual surplus (deficit) that is important in determining the public sector borrowing requirement, which in turn carries relevance to the pursuit of a money supply target. Likewise, the New Cambridge School has identified the current budget deficit with the prospective balance of payments deficit in its assault upon the conventional Keynesian wisdom and in its advocacy of the imposition of import controls.[16] Criticism along these lines has led to the attempt to evaluate the strength of policy changes upon *actual* income levels as opposed to some hypothetical full capacity utilisation level. Such attempts have moved away from the neutrality of the budget measure in that being attempts to evaluate fiscal *impact* they implicitly assume a formal model analysis. Moreover, being concerned with the actual fiscal impact of a budget change upon current income levels they become interlinked not just with the measurement of fiscal influence but also with the attempt to assess the efficacy of the fiscal instrument. Once we move away from the limited aim of attaching a value upon a budgetary measure to the idea of estimating fiscal impact and assessing the efficacy of fiscal policy we encounter two difficulties. First, we need to invoke, if only implicitly, some formal model with respect to how the economy actually behaves. Second, and more importantly, it is impossible to assess the effectiveness of any policy measure without first delineating the policy objectives. In this respect, the majority of studies have been sadly disappointing.[17] For the most part, they have adopted a unidimensional objective function and have concentrated upon measuring the impact of fiscal policy solely upon the level of domestic aggregate demand.[18] Scant attention is paid to other macroeconomic objectives, particularly economic growth, balance of payments and the price level. It is clearly inadequate to assess the efficacy of fiscal policy by reference to its demand and employment impacts if the authorities in question are in fact manipulating it to secure other goals of policy (not least electoral advantage). This qualification should constantly be borne in mind when examining alternative measures of fiscal influence.

4. OTHER MEASURES OF FISCAL INFLUENCES

(a) *Fiscal Leverage*

Probably the best-known alternative measure to the full employment budget surplus is that of fiscal leverage proposed by Musgrave (1964). As opposed to a pure budgetary measure, the concept put forward by Musgrave is concerned to measure actual fiscal impact and assess the cyclical role of fiscal intervention. Stated simply, fiscal leverage, L, is given by

$$L = 6(1G + 1R_s + 1R_b + .9R_p + .3R_i - .5T_c - .9T_o) \qquad (1)$$

where G = expenditure upon goods and services
$\quad\quad R_s$ = transfers to state governments
$\quad\quad R_b$ = transfers to business
$\quad\quad R_p$ = transfers to persons
$\quad\quad R_i$ = interest payments on government debt
$\quad\quad T_o$ = the yield of all other taxes[19]

and where the coefficients specify the assumptions made about the differential rates of responding out of various income flows. The multiplier of 6 relates to the propensity to consume out of income after tax and corresponds to a multiplier with tax leakage of 2.5. A number of comments appear pertinent. First, fiscal leverage is concerned solely with the estimate of the fiscal policy change upon the level of demand (and implicitly employment) and ignores alternative objectives. Second, its validity in assessing the effectiveness of policy measures to narrow the gap between actual and potential output depends upon the econometric model and the estimation procedure adopted in determining the values of the coefficients used. Third, this formulation of fiscal leverage does not distinguish between discretionary and automatic changes in the budget balance.[20] We can think of fiscal leverage as:

$$L = (\Delta G - \Delta T)k \qquad (2)$$

where ΔG and ΔT are now taken to be the aggregated weighted change in the budget deficit[21] and where k is the conventional multiplier. The bracketed term thus indicates the weighted actual budget surplus (deficit)[22] and provides an index of the first-round impact of the budgetary change on aggregate demand, which when multiplied by the multiplier gives the total impact. The great virtue of the fiscal leverage concept is that it deals with the actual budget and attempts to evaluate its impact. Its weakness lies in the demands it makes upon formal econometric estimates of the relevant weights involved – which is precisely the difficulty encountered in the full employment budget surplus concept when attempts are made to give it greater precision. Moreover, problems arise in the estimation of the multiplier. If we dispense with the multiplier then we are left with a weighted first-round impact of the actual budget that differs from the weighted full employment budget surplus only to the extent that the latter is evaluated at a constant income level and this abstracts from built-in flexibility.

(b) *Fiscal performance measures*

Numerous studies have attempted to obtain a direct appraisal of fiscal policy performances in terms of its contribution to stabilising the level of income upon the one hand and to promoting a desirable income level upon the other.[23] By far the most ambitious approach along these lines was that made by Hansen (1969), which surveyed fiscal policy experience in seven countries over the period 1955–1965. His starting point is to estimate, using the fiscal leverage concept, the total impact of the budget upon the volume of GNP. Subtracting this estimate from actually observed GNP data provides an estimate of the so-called 'pure cycle', the hypothetical progress of the economy in the absence of budgetary measures.[24] When the actual GNP data fall closer to the trend growth rate of GNP than the pure cycle data, then the budget may be considered stabilising and *vice versa*. The coincidence of actual GNP data with the trend growth rate of GNP would imply perfectly stabilising fiscal policy. Figure 2.4 illustrates the case of stabilising budgetary policy.

As previously mentioned, there is no particular merit in stabilising income around a trend growth rate in itself; what is required is stabilisation around the desirable or potential full employment growth path of GNP. To deal with the latter problem Snyder has proposed a modification to the Hansen index, which seeks to measure the fiscally induced reduction in the GNP gap that otherwise would have prevailed in the absence of policy (Snyder, 1970). In a similar manner, Auld (1967, 1969) has proposed a measure of the 'output saved' by fiscal policy intervention when compared to the estimated output level that would have prevailed in the absence of policy measures. In simplistic terms what this reduces to is making an estimate at time t of what the income level would be at time t_1 in the absence of positive fiscal intervention and comparing it with what occurred in fact. Assuming initially the economy is at a cyclical peak with income Y_t at time t, Y_f the observed income level

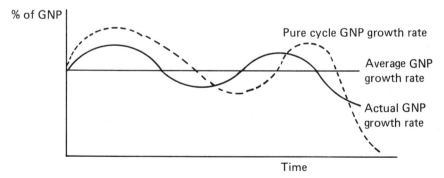

FIGURE 2.4

occurring at time t_1 with fiscal intervention, and Y_a the estimated income level that would have prevailed in the absence of policy, then the ratio

$$\frac{Y_f - Y_a}{Y_t - Y_a} \qquad (3)$$

provides an estimate of the success of fiscal policy. A ratio equal to 1 implies fiscal policy is perfectly successful; a zero value would imply the policy was completely non-successful. Moreover, a negative value would imply the policy operated in a decidedly perverse manner and intensified the recessionary down-turn. There are all sorts of objections to simple measures of this kind (Smyth, 1968), but the principal one lies in the uni-valued objective function. Whether approached in terms of stabilisation *per se* or of closing the gap between actual and potential GNP, the policy is always to be evaluated in terms of output volume – presumably a proxy for employment objectives. Other objectives, particularly economic growth, inflation and balance of payment goals, are not related to the assessment of policy performance, a procedure only justified if it can be assumed that policy objectives are complementary to each other and do not in fact conflict. Hansen, it should be noted, in his important OECD study (Hansen, 1969) does recognise this difficulty and qualified his major empirical finding, namely that fiscal policy in the United Kingdom has been destabilising, by recognising that the authorities may have given primary attention to balance of payments objectives at the expense of output and employment. Unless assessments of policy performance studies are able to deal with a multiplicity of macroeconomic objectives, there would appear to be a strong case for relying upon simple budgetary measures that can be applied to whatever aspect of stabilisation policy the occasion demands.

5. FISCAL INFLUENCE AND THE BUDGET CONSTRAINT

The various measures we have discussed thus far possess one common feature, namely that they ignore the financial implications of fiscal intervention and thus exclude consideration of any wealth effects.[25] However, as the recent monetarist revival has made clear, the financial implications may be of crucial importance in determining the fiscal impact. This revival has been closely linked with the concept of the budget constraint,[26] and the associated controversy surrounding the 'crowding out' of fiscal policy measures.[27] The position adopted in the present paper, as indicated in the quotation that precedes it, is that any measure of fiscal influence that ignores the financing implications can at best be but a first approximation. For example, it will make a considerable difference to the overall impact whether a fiscally induced surplus is used to retire domestically held national debt, to cut back upon the rate of growth of the money supply or to repay external debt.

Equally, it will make a considerable difference whether a deficit is financed by increasing the money supply or by issuing new bonds, and in the case of the latter it will make a difference whether the bonds are acquired by the banking sector, by the non-bank private sector or by institutions and individuals abroad. In principle, it is not really permissible to separate the financing of the fiscal change from the change itself in the measurement of fiscal influence.[28] To consider this point more formally, let us write the budget constraint as

$$G + TP + IP - T = \Delta M + \Delta D_n + \Delta D_b + \Delta D_f \qquad (4)$$

where G represents government expenditure upon goods and services, TP represents transfer payments such as unemployment benefits and so forth, IP interest payments upon government debt,[29] T total tax receipts, ΔM the change in the high-powered money supply, and the terms ΔD_n, ΔD_b and ΔD_f signify the change in debt held by the non-bank private sector, the banking sector and foreigners respectively.[30]

The left-hand side of (4) is thus total outlays minus total tax receipts and this is what is commonly understood by the term budget surplus when positive, or deficit when negative. Given the force of the budget constraint, which must be satisfied at all points in time, any change in the left-hand side of (4) must imply some correspondence change in ΔM, ΔD_n, ΔD_b or ΔD_f or alternatively some combination of these.[31] Now the fallacy implied in concepts such as the full employment budget surplus, or equally fiscal leverage, is that it is permissible to disregard where these accommodating financing arrangements occur in determining the direction and comparative strength of the fiscal policy change. Clearly, one need not endorse the monetarist position to challenge this underlying assumption. One would imagine, for example, that a far greater degree of 'crowding out' would occur if a budget deficit is financed by the sale of bonds to the non-bank private sector than if they are sold to the banking sector when the latter hold substantial excess reserves.[32] Moreover, comparing two identical fiscal policies, differential total impacts may occur even when the same accommodating agent is used. On one occasion, for example, it may be relatively easy to finance a given deficit by sales to the non-bank sector; on another occasion, considerable inducement may have to be offered in the form of low bond prices and high yields depending upon the mood and expectations of the non-bank private sector.[33]

Similar fiscal measures, therefore, may carry vastly differing implications, for interest rate changes reflected in differing wealth effects and investment outlays.

6. Conclusion

Whatever measure we adopt, the attempt to summarise the stance and
strength of fiscal policy by reference to one elementary value must be logi-
cally suspect; a useful starting point but little more, to be used with considerable qualification and caution. It is, perhaps, well to remind ourselves of
Marshall's famous dictum: 'every short statement in economics is false –
with the possible exception of my present one'.

NOTES AND REFERENCES

1. It is remarkable how many studies of fiscal influence omit to define precisely the meaning of
   'fiscal'. The importance of this point is ably demonstrated by F. Forte and H. M. Hockman
   (1969) and M. Friedman and W. H. Heller (1969).
2. We explicitly exclude local government outlays and taxes although in a federal revenue
   structure one could possibly make out a case for their inclusion.
3. Transfer payments are thus considered a part of government outlays in keeping with our
   subsequent discussion of the budget constraint, but equally they could be considered as
   negative taxes – the procedure normally followed in model building.
4. Conceptually the opposite situation, a negatively sloped budget function, is a distinct
   possibility. Particularly in periods of rapid inflation, specific unit taxes decline in real terms
   while certain government outlays are effectively index linked. Thus increases in nominal
   income may generate increases in the public sector borrowing requirement – a phenomenon referred to as 'fiscal starvation'.
5. Moreover, it exercised a profound and fairly immediate impact upon fiscal policy-making.
   Considerable use of the concept was made by the largely Keynesian-oriented Council of
   Economic Advisers in their *The Economic Report of the President* in 1962, which laid the
   foundation for the hitherto unprecedented cut of $12 billion in taxes effected in 1964. See
   CEA (1962). In the United Kingdom the preferred terminology has become 'the full employment financial balance'; cf. Neild and Ward (1976).
6. For expositional purposes we have treated the weighted full employment surplus as a
   logical sequential development stemming from the unweighted full employment surplus. It
   should perhaps be noted, therefore, that both concepts were expounded in Brown's original
   article (Brown, 1956).
7. The formal demonstration rested upon the assumption that sales taxes are shifted forward
   in their entirety as well as the belief that saving would be positive for the aggregate
   economy.
8. In the UK (and most other industrial countries) the marginal propensity to import of the
   private sector usually exceeds that of the public sector in its outlays upon goods and
   services, thus reinforcing the conventional wisdom that expenditure changes are more high
   powered upon the domestic economy than equivalent reductions in taxation.
9. For a discussion of some of these issues see, especially, Morss and Peacock (1969) and
   Borpujari and Ter-Minassian (1973).
10. Indeed, it is quite possible for the full employment measure to indicate the wrong sign of the
    actual impact. Blinder and Solow (1974) offers this illustrative example. A decrease in
    personal income taxation combined with an increase in corporate taxation might decrease
    the budget surplus in times of recession, when corporate profits are depressed, but could
    actually increase the surplus as evaluated at full employment when corporate profits are
    buoyant.

11. See Oakland (1969) and Dixon (1973) on the implications of differences in slope of the respective budget function.
12. It is sometimes assumed that built-in flexibility, indicated by the slope of the budget function, indicates the degree of automatic stabilisation incorporated into the fiscal structure. The view, however, is erroneous since automatic stabilisation requires a multiplier impact and as previously indicated, the multiplier can be completely independent of the slope of the budget function.
13. It is not always made clear that the full employment budget surplus is evaluated in terms of the percentage of the labour force actually employed.
14. It will be appreciated that the way these issues are resolved will be of crucial importance to those studies that resort to the reduced form approach to judge fiscal potency. cf. Anderson and Jordan (1968), Artis and Nobay (1969), Keran (1969) and B. Friedman (1977). In the UK, the autonomous growth of North Sea oil revenues is an additional factor that will progressively exaggerate the restrictive stance of the fiscal authorities unless specifically allowed for.
15. The procedure described here is that practised in the United States where the full employment budget surplus has received the greatest endorsement and has certainly exercised the greatest policy influence. Alternative measures with similar objectives include the Cyclically Neutral Balance (CNB) practised in the Federal Republic of West Germany, and the Structural Budget Margin (SBM) and Budget Impulse (BI) adopted in Holland. For a comparison of these measures and applicability to the UK see especially Chand (1977).
16. Cf. Cripps and Godley (1976). The importance of the actual budget surplus in the Cambridge model relies heavily upon the stability of the private sector financial surplus – a stability that has been called into question.
17. For an extended critique of existing studies see especially Stringer (1977).
18. Presumably, employment is assumed a function of output; i.e., aggregate demand serves as a proxy for the real objective, employment. Needless to add, neoclassical theory would not posit a linear relationship, creating difficulties for assessment of policy changes.
19. Regardless of whether they are direct or indirect. Cf. section 2(b) above.
20. A purer fiscal measure is obtainable by calculating fiscal leverage at a constant level of income.
21. With the weights corresponding to the coefficients in equation (1) above.
22. Cf. Oakland (1969).
23. Needless to say, the two do not necessarily coincide. There is no intrinsic value attached to the actual trend of GNP in itself; 'stabilisation around the trend during these periods [of prolonged unemployment] should not necessarily be considered a positive feature' (Hansen, 1969).
24. Considerable conceptual difficulties emerge with respect to the concept of the 'pure cycle'. It incorporates, for example, other stabilisation policies apart from fiscal policy yet these alternative policies were presumably designed in the anticipation of positive fiscal intervention. Moreover, the pure cycle will also incorporate fiscal policy changes emanating from the previous time period. This latter point derives from Stringer (1977) in a penetrating critique of the concept of neutrality.
25. Implicit in the changed volume of outside money and bonds held by the private sector.
26. Amongst the more important contributions are, Blinder and Solow (1973), Christ (1968, 1969), Currie (1976), Hansen (1973), Infante and Stein (1976), McGrath (1977), Meyer (1975), Meyer and Hart (1975), Ott and Ott (1965), Scarth (1975), Silber (1970) and Steindl (1974). For an elementary exposition of the concept see Shaw (1977) chapter 8 or Peacock and Shaw (1978). A full analysis of the budget constraint will be found in the chapter by Burrows in this volume.
27. See especially Carlson and Spencer (1975) and chapters 4 and 5 by Taylor and Currie in this volume. It may be noted that in many respects the crowding out controversy reflects a return to the 'Treasury view' already substantially analysed as early as 1929. See Keynes and Henderson (1929) especially chapter IX.
28. In essence, this is to argue that measures of fiscal influence are irrelevant and should be replaced by the more comprehensive measure of budgetary influence, which would specifically allow for the financing implications. Alternatively, and recently advocated, fiscal policy

might be defined as changes in government outlays financed by tax changes or bond issue (retirement) and sharply distinguished from changes financed by changes in the money stock – the latter being classified as monetary policy.

29. Interest payments on government debt are, of course, a form of transfer payment. However, considering the budget constraint, there are good reasons to distinguish them from alternative transfer payments since their volume varies directly with the issuance or retirement of the debt – that is, with the operation of the constraint *per se*.

30. ΔD_n, ΔD_b and ΔD_f are, of course, to be understood as indicating the proceeds actually realised by the government on the sale of additional debt.

31. Except in the special case of a balanced budget change, where alternations in outlays and tax receipts are precisely offsetting.

32. In addition, the degree of crowing out may well depend upon the phase of the trade cycle, being greater at full employment income levels when loanable funds are comparatively in short supply.

33. In a similar vein, the ease with which one can finance deficits externally will be conditioned by expectations about exchange rates, which recently have exhibited extreme volatility.

CHAPTER 3

The Government Budget Constraint and the Monetarist–Keynesian Debate

*P. Burrows**

1. AIMS

The first aim of this paper is to survey some important contributions to the literature that has explored the implications of incorporating a government budget constraint into macroeconomic theory. The second aim is to outline the development of the controversy between monetarists and Keynesians over the relative effectiveness of fiscal and monetary stabilisation policies, and to see at which points the analysis of budget constrained stabilisation policy relates to this development. The main significance of recognising the existence of a government budget constraint is that it brings to the fore the monetary aspects of fiscal policy, and edges us out of the simple world in which fiscal and monetary policies are thought to be separate and independent. An attempt to relate the more complicated view of interdependent instruments to the monetarists–Keynesian controversy runs into the problem of identifying the central areas of disagreement. Unfortunately, the points of disagreement between the two camps have been like mirages in the desert: running in the soft sand of combative debate has done little to bring them nearer for a closer examination. On the contrary, the very effort of running seems to replace one mirage with another yet more elusive. The most we can do here is to sketch the four mirages that have appeared so far.

The paper will be organised as follows. In section 2 a summary of the conventional analysis of the impact of fiscal and monetary instruments will be presented, to provide a starting point for the discussion of the government budget constraint and interdependent instruments in section 3. Links with the monetarist–Keynesian debate will be identified in both of these sections. Finally, some conclusions are drawn from this discussion in section 4.

* *I should like to thank Keith Shaw for his comments on this paper.*

61

2. THE CONVENTIONAL ANALYSIS OF FISCAL AND MONETARY POLICY IMPACT

While in certain respects an oversimplification, it is true to say that the bulk of the theory of fiscal and monetary impact in the postwar period has consisted of comparative-static exercises using relatively simple aggregative models of the economic system.[1] Considerable research effort has been put into developing particular components of these policy models, such as the formulation of an external sector to represent the balance of payments consequences of stabilisation policy.[2] It will suffice for the purposes of section 3 to outline the central propositions of the conventional comparative-static theory of fiscal and monetary policy in a closed economy.

The policy analysis uses a two-sector, static model in which one sector identifies the condition for equilibrium in the goods market and the other the condition for monetary equilibrium. The details of the formulation of this *IS/LM* model can be found in many texts;[3] three characteristics we need to note are:

(1) households and firms in their roles as consumers, investors and demanders of money respond only to the flow of aggregate income, Y, and to the cost of using money for spending or as an asset to hold (the cost being the rate of interest, r). Consequently, their behaviour is independent of their net wealth (assets minus liabilities) position.[4]

(2) the government's stabilisation problem is seen as the need to reduce the changes in aggregate income inherent in the uncontrolled economy. It is not possible in the simple model to break down changes in (nominal) income into changes in output and in the price level. For this a third sector must be added to explain price, output and employment decisions. But for the particular questions at issue in this paper, the analysis will not be adversely affected by the simplifying assumption that changes in income reflect only changes in output at a given price level.

(3) the instruments of stabilisation policy are:

changes in exogenous government
   expenditure (G) ⎫
changes in exogenous tax revenue (T_0) ⎬ fiscal instruments
changes in the size of a balanced
   budget (*BB*) ⎭

changes in the money supply through ⎱ monetary
open market operations ⎰ instrument

It is assumed that each instrument can be altered with the others remaining constant so that the impact of any instrument change can be identified *ceteris paribus*. Fiscal policy that involves a fiscal deficit implicitly requires extra bonds to be floated to finance the government expenditure in excess of revenue, when the money supply is fixed.

The impact of each of the policy instruments on aggregate income is found by solving the two-sector model to find the equilibrium values of income and the rate of interest, and asking how these values will change if any instrument is varied. The emphasis here is on the *flow* equilibrium at which the demand for goods and money that is generated by the flow of income equals the supplies.[5] Budget deficits and surpluses give rise to changes in the stock of assets in private hands. Yet with the concentration on flows no consideration is given to the willingness of households or firms to hold more or less assets or to the implications of changes in asset stocks for the demand flows. This gives rise to problems of interpretation as we shall see. Consider first the policy impacts resulting from changes in fiscal instruments.

Fiscal Instruments

Characterising the initial full equilibrium as the values of the rate of interest and income that correspond to the intersection of the initial IS and LM curves, a permanent increase in G or in BB, or cut in T, raises income and the rate of interest by shifting the IS curve to the right with the position of LM unchanged.[6] The IS shift is the result of the public spending injection in the first case, the injection of private spending in the third, and the net effect of a public spending injection and a private spending cut in the second. The leverage of the tax revenue cut is less than that of an equivalent injection of government spending on goods and services as long as the 'recipients' of the tax cut (consumers) have a marginal propensity to consume less than unity. Consequently, an increase in G and T of the same magnitude, that is an expansion of a balanced budget, is expansionary on balance. These results assume that the government is *able* to inject net expenditure, which is true as long as the recipients of the government services do not regard them as a substitute for private spending and consequently cut back their own spending in response. With such a response there is said to be 'direct crowding out' of private spending by government expenditure (Buiter, 1977, pp. 311–12), but this possibility is not the subject of this paper, so private and public spending will be regarded as non-substitutes.[7] However, the fiscal instruments do have another effect that constitutes a type of monetary crowding out.[8] Even though a change in a fiscal instrument does not necessitate a change in the monetary *instrument*, the resulting expansion of income does induce an increase in the transactions demand for money, leading to a rise in the rate of interest, which reduces expenditure and the income impact of the fiscal policy. If the rate of interest did *not* increase then the income change associated with the shift from IS_1 to IS_2 in Figure 3.1 would be $(Y_3 - Y_1)$

but, as the money supply is fixed, monetary equilibrium requires a movement from E_1 to E_2 along LM with the interest rate rise offsetting the income effect on the demand for money (the demand and supply of money being equal at all points on LM). The outcome is the smaller income impact $(Y_2 - Y_1)$, the difference $(Y_3 - Y_2)$ being the restraining influence of the negative feedback provided by indirect crowding out.[9] The size of this restraining influence is greater the more responsive is the demand for money to an income change (L_Y) and the less responsive it is to the rate of interest (L_r), and the more responsive is expenditure to the rate of interest $(C_r + I_r)$. In particular we should note that this implies that the steeper is the LM curve, the more the fiscal leverage is reduced by the monetary effect, as can be seen by drawing a steeper LM through E_1 in Figure 3.1.[10]

This description of the impact of fiscal policy, including bond-financed deficits, involves a logical inconsistency that can be resolved only by adopting an unreasonably extreme assumption.[11] The problem lies in ignoring the effect of a deficit on the total stock of assets. If £1 of deficit is financed by £1 of bonds then the net wealth of the private sector is increased by £1.[12] But will people be prepared to hold the extra £1 of wealth in the form of a bond without the inducement of a higher rate of interest? Assume for a moment that they are. Then as the deficit shifts the IS curve to IS_2 in Figure 3.1 the

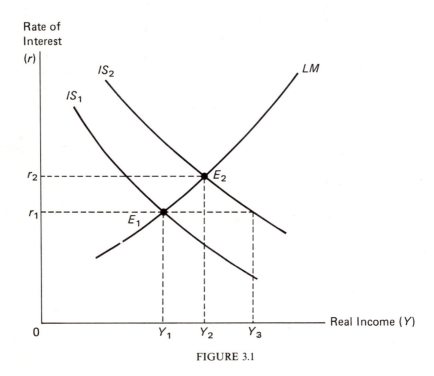

FIGURE 3.1

rate of interest increases from r_1 to r_2, which results *only* from the rise in the transactions demand for money as *incomes* increase. The bond float does not necessitate any further increase in the rate of interest due to the *wealth* increase. If the deficit continues at E_2 for another budget period, the *IS* curve does not shift to the left again and the required extra bonds are floated at the constant rate of interest r_2. All of the extra wealth is held as bonds; liquidity preference does not increase, so the *LM* curve stays put. However, if people prefer to hold part of any extra wealth in the form of money and part in the form of bonds (quite apart from the desire to spend part on goods!) then this analysis simply will not do. Once E_2 has been reached, for example, and the deficit is repeated to *keep* the system at E_2, an increase in the rate of interest above r_2 is required to induce people to hold the extra bonds. Now the extra wealth does increase liquidity preference, moving the *LM* curve to the left, and the independence of the *IS* and *LM* curves, which the conventional analysis assumes, has been violated. Therefore, unless we are prepared to accept the implausible assumption that the coefficient of the wealth variable in the demand for bonds function is unity (£1 of extra wealth is used to demand £1 of extra bonds), the inconsistency can be resolved only by turning to a model in which asset-stock changes and wealth effects are incorporated, which is the subject matter of section 3.

Monetary Instruments

A once-for-all open market operation to expand the money supply through government purchases of bonds at the initial full equilibrium E_1 in Figure 3.2 creates an excess supply of money, and an excess demand for bonds, at r_1. The *LM* curve shifts to the right and the fall in the rate of interest from r_1 to r_2 stimulates aggregate expenditure from Y_1 to Y_2.[13] The fact that the position of the *IS* curve is presumed unaffected by open market operations reflects the assumed absence of wealth effects on demand for goods.[14] The only mechanism by which changes in the money supply are transmitted to expenditure (and therefore to output, employment, etc) in this model is through the money and bonds markets and through changes in 'the' rate of interest. Keynesians have usually interpreted 'the' rate of interest as a representative rate on financial assets and have identified certain parameter values as unfavourable to the leverage of the monetary instrument, namely the limiting cases of interest-insensitive expenditure (steep *IS* curve) and highly interest-sensitive demand for money (liquidity trap: flat *LM* curve).[15] The same circumstances would also be characterised by potent fiscal policy to the extent that indirect crowding out would be weak or ineffective in reducing the fiscal multiplier.[16]

It was in this connection that the first mirage of the monetarist–Keynesian debate came into view. At the end of the 1960s many Keynesians felt that the

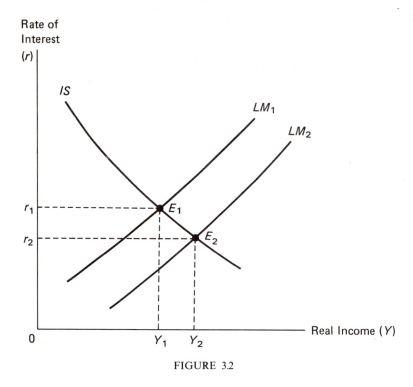

FIGURE 3.2

dispute was about the magnitudes of the important parameters in the multi-plier, in particular the interest sensitivity of the demand for money L_r.[17] They would have been inclined to the empirical judgement that L_r is large enough to suggest a weak transmission of monetary impulses (i.e., minor indirect crowding out) and to the view that the monetarists' case for strong monetary effects (large monetary and small fiscal leverage) rested on the *LM* curve being steep.[18] Monetarists for their part denied the empirical basis for expecting the *LM* curve to be flat and anyway argued that monetary effects are transmitted to expenditure through the rates of return on a wide range of financial *and* real assets. Even if the financial rate of interest did not fall as the money supply increased (liquidity trap), implying that people are happy to raise the ratio of money to bonds in their portfolios, as more money is held the ratio of money to equities, property, physical assets such as houses, etc. would rise thereby increasing the relative attractiveness at the margin of the non-money assets. By implication the open market operations lead to excess money holdings, which are used to buy non-money assets (other than bonds), which raises their prices and lowers their rates of return until they are equal to the (implicit) return on money. For changes in the money supply to have these effects on the demand for other assets, money and other assets would have to be non-perfect substitutes. In principle, therefore, this first version of the point of disagreement should be resolvable through the study of the degree of substitutability between money and other assets. However, hardly had the shimmering of mirage one begun to wane, and the picture came into focus, than the monetarists claimed that the point of disagreement concerned not the character and force of the rate of return transmission mechanism but the theory used to explain the division of changes in money aggregate income into output and price level changes. But before digressing a little from the analysis of fiscal and monetary policy to describe this second mirage, let us conclude the conventional analysis of the monetary instrument by pointing out that the impact of monetary policy is dependent on the fiscal structure just as the fiscal multiplier may be affected by monetary negative feedback. The selection of the rate of tax, t, determines the degree of fiscal built-in stability (negative feedback) and the higher is t, the lower is the money multiplier. The conclusion is, then, that even where the fiscal and monetary *instruments* can be varied independently there are interdependences between fiscal *impact* and the characteristics of the money market and between monetary *impact* and the structure of the budget.

In two papers in the *Journal of Political Economy* in 1970 and 1971, Friedman set out to identify the areas of agreement and disagreement between the monetarists and Keynesians (M. Friedman, 1970; 1971). The details of his argument are beyond the scope of this paper but his main propositions can be reviewed.[19] The 1970 paper claims that the main components of the *IS/LM* model, namely the consumption and investment functions, the demand for money function and the expenditure and monetary sector equilibrium conditions,[20] are *common ground* between the two camps. Two observations on this statement are pertinent to the theme of this paper. First, the demand for money function with the rate of interest as an explanatory variable ($L_r \neq 0$) is inconsistent with the monetarist limiting case of a vertical *LM* curve and proportionate relationship between real expenditure and the nominal money supply. It is therefore being denied that the slope of the *LM* curve represents the crux of the issue. Second, for simplicity Friedman omits wealth variables from the behavioural equations, so apparently they are not crucial to the discrepancy between the views of monetarists and Keynesians on stabilisation policy (which will prove to be significant for section 3).

The question that clearly arises is, if these matters are agreed upon where lies the source of the dispute? Friedman's 1970 paper provides us with the second mirage, namely the suggestion that *the* difference between the two approaches is the method used to solve the basic model when the price level is included as a variable. The problem that he identifies is that when the money supply is endogenous, i.e., a function of the rate of interest, the system contains six equations (the consumption, investment, demand for money and supply of money functions and the expenditure sector and monetary sector equilibrium conditions; the tax function is omitted) but seven variables that are unknown (C, I, L, M, P, r, Y). An extra equation is needed to make the system solvable (determinate). One might wonder why this problem could not be solved by reducing the number of unknowns to six by making the nominal money supply exogenous. The reason is that Friedman has incorrectly identified the problem as the lack of equality between equations and unknowns in the basic equations. The problem really lies in the lack of independence of the equations. Even if the money supply is exogenous, and the number of equations and variables are both six, by substituting for C, I and L into the two equilibrium conditions the system is reduced to two equations in three unknowns, Y, r and P, and still cannot be solved.[21] In Figure 3.3 the real LM curve's position varies with the price level $P_2 > P_1$ (which determines the real supply of money given M). Equilibrium solutions for any two of the three variables can be found *given* the third, for example the solution r_1, Y_1 if the price level is known to be P_1. In economic terms the basic problem with the model is that it is only a theory of aggregate demand (expenditure), and unless the nature of the aggregate supply curve is known, nothing can be said about the extent to which

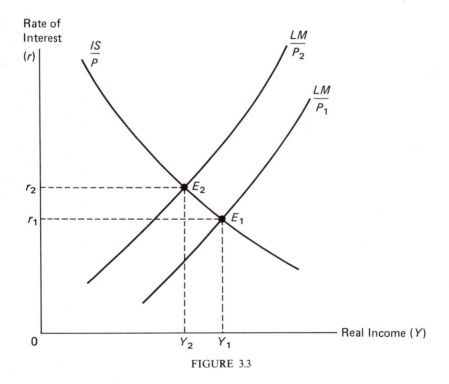

FIGURE 3.3

changes in nominal income, $d(PY)$, are reflected in output, dY, or in the price level, dP.[22]

The most general means of overcoming the problem, and one used by economists of many persuasions, is to add an equation to the system that represents the relationship between P and Y on the supply side, that is an aggregate supply curve, thereby making the price level endogenous to the model.[23] The general case is for an expansionary policy that raises aggregate demand to have price level and output effects that depend on the slope of the aggregate supply curve, which may be expected to steepen as full employment is approached so that the inflationary effect will then tend to dominate. It is curious, therefore, to find Friedman claiming that *the* difference between the monetarists and Keynesians is that the Keynesians solve the system by assuming a fixed price level (horizontal aggregate supply curve) and the monetarists by assuming aggregate real income to be fixed (vertical aggregate supply curve).[24] This may be true of caricature monetarists and Keynesians, but is not true of most members of either group. The second mirage begins to fade as well.

3. THE GOVERNMENT BUDGET CONSTRAINT AND THE WEALTH EFFECTS OF STABILISATION POLICIES

We have seen that the conventional theory of stabilisation policies runs into a problem of internal inconsistency because it takes no account of the changes in asset stocks when the budget is unbalanced and the possible effects on spending and money-holding behaviour when net private wealth is affected. The problem can be overcome by introducing into the conventional model a government budget constraint and wealth variables in the behavioural equations.

Government Budget Constraint

In its essentials the concept of a government budget constraint is extremely simple. It merely says that the government can only spend funds that it has raised from taxation, the printing of money or the floating of bonds. The form of the constraint first used in the literature[25] was

$$G - T(Y) = \Delta M + \frac{\Delta B}{r}$$

where G and T are government expenditure and tax revenue in money terms,[26] ΔM is the change in the nominal supply of money, and $\Delta B/r$ is the change in the bond stock (ΔB) valued at market price. The bonds are assumed to be perpetuals whose price is $1/r$.[27] Five points of elucidation can be made:

(1) The constraint must *always* hold regardless of time period and regardless of the prevailing conditions of the economy, for example whether it is in equilibrium or disequilibrium.

(2) Any of the instrument variables G, T, ΔM and $\Delta B/r$ can be altered if and only if at least one of the other three is changed as well. Combinations of changes in the variables give us a set of stabilisation policies:

Variables changed	*Variables constant*		
(i) $\Delta G = \Delta T$	$\dfrac{\Delta B}{r} = \Delta M = 0$	tax-financed government expenditure (balanced budget change[28])	pure fiscal policy
(ii) $G - T = \dfrac{\Delta B}{r}$	$\Delta M = 0$	bond-financed deficit or surplus (deficit/ surplus plus open market operations)	
(iii) $G - T = \Delta M$	$\dfrac{\Delta B}{r} = 0$	money-financed deficit or surplus (deficit/ surplus plus printing or withdrawing money)	monetary fiscal policy
(iv) $\Delta M = \dfrac{\Delta B}{r}$	$G - T = 0$	open market operations	pure monetary policy

The analysis of (ii) and (iii) will use the deficit case to illustrate.

(3) It is apparent that any deficit (or surplus) will alter the size of the stock of bonds plus money, as we have noted previously. If the stabilisation instrument is a money-financed deficit, the addition to the asset stock is in the form of outside money, which definitely constitutes an increment to *net* private wealth. But if bond financing is used, whether perceived net private wealth is raised depends on people's attitude to bonds. The question 'Are bonds net wealth?' is disarmingly simple at first appearance, yet for twenty years or more has generated much controversy.[29] The point is that when a bond is created the government also incurs the liability to pay a return each year and the par value at the date of maturity (if there is one). The net present value of these commitments to pay is equal to the price of the bond.[30] In theory, therefore, creating a bond also creates an equivalent government liability. Since this liability is likely to imply a liability of the private sector to pay higher taxes in the future, it has been argued that the future tax liability should be netted out to find the *net* private wealth

value of a bond. This ultrarational view has been associated with monetarists, while Keynesians on the whole have taken the view that in practice the future tax liability is *not* capitalised and balanced against the bond asset. We cannot go into the details of this empirically by observing the behaviour of wealth holders when asset stocks vary. Our analysis of stabilisation policies will hedge on the issue by looking at the implications of adopting the extreme assumptions that bonds are 100 per cent net wealth and zero net wealth.

(4) The government budget constraint introduces into an otherwise static model the dynamic response of asset-stock levels to the net injection (or withdrawal) of a flow of demand for goods resulting from an unbalanced budget.[31] In Figure 3.1, for example, once an increase in government expenditure (deficit) has shifted the *IS* curve to IS_2, maintaining the higher level of government expenditure will mean that E_2 represents the new flow equilibrium where the demand for goods is just equal to real income (output) Y_2. However, the dynamic response of asset stocks means that *if* net private wealth changes as well *and* this affects spending behaviour the flow equilibrium E_2 will be disturbed by a change in the demand for goods by the private sector. We shall trace these effects through shortly. The point to be made here is that the flow equilibrium will, in these circumstances, be only a temporary equilibrium. Permanent equilibrium, defined as the constancy of all flows and stocks (i.e., a steady state), can only be achieved where the flow equilibrium is associated with a balanced budget that allows stock levels to remain the same. The short-run multipliers previously derived can, therefore, be misleading as regards the total effect of a stabilisation policy in that they identify the move to a new temporary equilibrium but fail to incorporate the subsequent responses of aggregate income to asset changes and the attendant feedbacks to demand flows. It will be convenient to distinguish three time periods for the subsequent analysis.

(a) *the very short run:* this is defined as a period in which the policy instrument change occurs (say a deficit) and the flow of demand responds, but before the transmission of impact through wealth changes takes effect.[32] At the end of the very short run the system is in its initial temporary flow disequilibrium with the unbalanced budget requiring changes in asset stocks.

(b) *the short run:* this is the period in which wealth changes are taking effect as a result of a budget deficit (asset stocks are still changing) and interest is paid on bonds. A succession of new temporary flow equilibria characterises the short run.

(c) *the long run:* this is a period long enough to allow wealth effects to work themselves out. For the long run to be characterised by full flow and stock equilibrium (i.e., a steady state), the government's budget must be in balance.[33]

(5) The first formulation of the government budget constraint takes no account of the government's expenditure on interest payments on bonds. In reality, the flow of interest payments, £B per period, enters the budget constraint twice, once as an expenditure item and once as an addition to taxable income (which becomes $Y + B$). Note that the symbol B is being used for the number of bonds each of which requires an interest payment of £1 per period. The revised form of the constraint is (Blinder and Solow, 1973, 1974);

$$G + B - T(Y + B) = \Delta M + \frac{\Delta B}{r}.$$

Clearly, even if the government balanced its tax revenue and its goods and services expenditure, G, the flow of interest payments on bonds would require financing through money printing or the floating of further bonds.

Stabilisation Policies with Wealth Effects

To begin with, we must reformulate the basic functions to allow for the effect of changes in net private wealth on the behaviour in the private sector. This is done by hypothesising that both the total private expenditure on goods and services, $(C + I)$, and the demand for money, L, are positive functions of the level of wealth, W.[34] In contrast to the conventional *IS/LM* model, it is no longer necessary to adopt an extreme assumption about the coefficients of the wealth variable in the demand equations for goods, money and bonds.

(a) Consider to begin with the effects of policies when bonds are regarded as net private wealth:

Very short run: in this period the budget constraint must be satisfied but no wealth effects occur. The importance of the constraint here is that the method of financing deficits must be incorporated. In the case of the bond financing of a deficit created by a permanent increase in government spending, the very short-run multiplier is the same as for a change in government expenditure in the conventional model (equation (a) in note 6) and the *IS* curve shifts as in Figure 3.1 but the *LM* temporarily remains unaffected. The consequent change in asset stocks will have its effect when the very short run is over. If money financing is used instead, the deficit proves to be more expansionary in this time period. The very short-run multiplier is the sum of the conventional model's multipliers for a change in G and a change in M.[35] The reason why money financing increases the deficit multiplier here is that the expansion of the money supply mitigates the restraining influence of indirect crowding out. The combination of instruments shifts the *LM* curve to the right in addition to shifting the *IS* curve from IS_1 to IS_2 in Figure 3.1, and the demand-dampening rise in the interest rate is reduced and the income expansion is increased.

With pure monetary policy in the form of a government bond purchase that shifts the *LM* curve to the right, the government budget constraint would be violated, as tax revenues rise with income, unless the surplus is used to withdraw money or bonds. The financial implications of the surplus therefore have subsequent counteracting effects (see below). Until this happens the impact multiplier will be similar to that of a change in M in the conventional model because the *initial* open market operation is compatible with the balanced budget. Similarly an increase in the size of a balanced budget induces extra tax revenue and subsequent counteracting effects result from the use of the surplus to retire bonds or withdraw money.

Short run: we shall concentrate on the effects of deficits under money and bond financing, but first open market operations and balanced budget changes can be dealt with. In the case of a once-for-all open market purchase of bonds, which expanded income in the very short run, two effects occur in the short run when interest payments are due and wealth changes take effect. First, the government's purchase of bonds has reduced the flow of interest payments that is income to the private sector. This is clearly contractionary. Second, the budget surplus due to the income expansion created by the open market operation requires a reduction of the net wealth of the private sector as money or bonds are withdrawn to use the surplus.[36] The reduction in wealth will lower the demand for both goods and money. The effect on the demand for money shifts the *LM* curve from LM_2 to LM_3 in Figure 3.4 (where the move from E_1 on LM_1 to E_2 on LM_2 is the initial impact of the bond purchase), which is expansionary as the interest rate tends to fall. The direct effect on the demand for goods on the other hand, the shift from IS_1 to IS_2, is contractionary. The net effect on the demand for goods of the decline in wealth *may* therefore, be expansionary or contractionary, but generally would be expected to be contractionary (E_2 to E_3 in Figure 3.4). In other words, the demand for goods is expected, on balance, to move in the same direction as net private wealth.[37] This means that the subsequent contractionary effect of the government's bond purchase *may* convert an initially expansionary monetary policy into a contractionary one, E_1 to E_3 in Figure 3.4.[38] Whether such an eventual reversal of impact would be serious for stabilisation policy depends on the frequency with which instrument reversals are required and the time it would take for the impact reversal to occur.

In the case of an expansion in the size of a balanced budget the subsequent surplus proves to be contractionary, but the extent of the contraction, and therefore the direction of the *total* impact of the balanced budget change, in the long run, depends on whether bonds are retired or money is withdrawn.

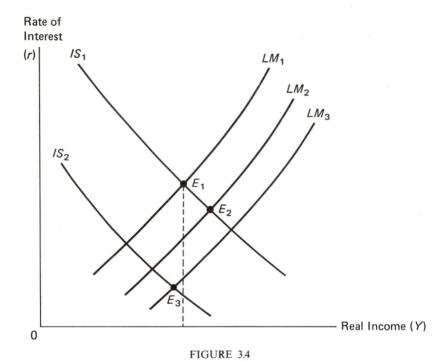

FIGURE 3.4

Turning to the monetary-fiscal policies of bond- or money-financed deficits, the introduction of the government budget constraint and of wealth effects proves to be particularly interesting for bond financing and brings us back again to the monetarist–Keynesian dispute. Since we have seen that it is *possible* for the wealth effects following from a budget imbalance to be perverse in the sense of the change in wealth and the change in the demand for goods being in opposite directions, it should come as no surprise that it is possible for an ostensibly expansionary deficit to generate an increase in wealth that is contractionary and possibly strong enough to offset the initial expansionary effect of the deficit. The third mirage of the monetarist–Keynesian debate is the monetarists' view that it is the impact of the wealth effects of bond-financed deficits, rather than the slope of the *LM* curve or the method used to solve the conventional model, that is the main source of disagreement.[39] They believe that a bond-financed deficit is likely to be *contractionary* in practice. Since they tend to refer to bond-financed deficits as 'fiscal policy' (and money-financed deficits as 'monetary policy'), they therefore draw the conclusion that 'fiscal policy' is ineffective. The definition of fiscal and monetary policy is not important, except to avoid confusion, and we shall retain the pure-fiscal and pure-monetary taxonomy of instruments. But the possible consequences of wealth effects *are* important.[40] The very short-run effect of a deficit is the shift from IS_1 to IS_2 in Figure 3.5, with aggregate demand rising from Y_1 to Y_2. The associated increase in wealth has two consequences. One is that the demand for goods (at any level of income and the rate of interest) increases; the IS curve shifts further to the right, from IS_2 to IS_3. The other is that the LM curve shifts to the left from LM_1 to LM_2 due to the extra demand for money. As regards the demand for goods, the wealth-induced IS and LM shifts are in contention. As they are drawn in Figure 3.5, the wealth effect on the demand for money is stronger than that on the demand for goods, so that aggregate demand is reduced by the wealth effects from Y_2 to Y_3. Will this perverse wealth effect outweigh the initial expansion in demand due to the deficit, $Y_2 - Y_1$? The answer is yes, eventually. The shift from IS_1 to IS_2 is the result of a permanent increase in government expenditure (if the increase were temporary the IS curve would return to IS_1). However, in each budget period the stock of wealth is increased again. Consequently the move from E_2 to E_3 is part of a continuing contractionary process, shown by the arrow in Figure 3.5, as the wealth-induced decline in income reduces tax revenue, generating deficits of increasing size and further contractionary wealth effects.

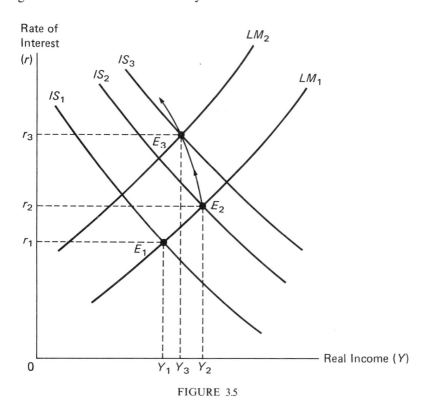

FIGURE 3.5

If they occur, perverse wealth effects prevent bond-financed deficits from expanding aggregate demand. But Blinder and Solow have demonstrated that perverse wealth effects would imply that the economic system is inherently unstable.[41] Ultimately, however, the perversity or non-perversity of real world wealth effects must be resolved by empirical studies.[42] *If* wealth effects are non-perverse, bond-financed deficits would be expansionary (E_3 lies to the right of E_2 and *a fortiori* to the right of E_1 in Figure 3.5), but pure monetary policy in the form of government purchases of bonds may not. There is no ambiguity, on the other hand, in the impact of money-financed deficits. Here the deficit financing increases wealth, but because the new wealth is in the form of money there is no leftward shift of the *LM* curve.[43] The wealth effect accentuates the expansionary effect of the deficit spending, so there is no disputing that money-financed deficits expand aggregate demand.

Long run: a substantial amount of research effort has been put into analysing the long-run, steady state consequences of various policies *in a sgable system*.[44] The results are less interesting from the point of view of short-run stabilisation policy, but they serve as a useful reminder that policies used for short-run objectives can have lingering effects unless they are deliberately neutralised by new policies.

Because full flow and stock equilibrium ($\Delta M = \Delta B = 0$) requires budgetary balance, the long-run analysis centres on the equilibrium condition[45]

$$G + B - T(Y + B) = 0.$$

One of the best-known propositions concerning the long-run effect of stabilisation policy is that budget deficits have multiplier effects that do *not* depend on the method of financing (Christ, 1968, pp. 56 and 65). Omitting interest payments from the equilibrium condition, in the long run

$$G - T_Y Y = 0, \qquad T_Y = \text{tax rate}$$

so

$$\frac{dY}{dG} = \frac{1}{T_Y}.$$

If G increases and the budget must balance, then income must increase by just enough (dG/T_Y) to generate an equivalent amount of extra revenue. The fiscal structure in this case is the *sole* determinant of policy impact in the long run. Unfortunately, for those who appreciate simple results, the neatness of this conclusion is lost when interest payments on bonds are included in the equilibrium condition, for then the long-run multiplier does depend on the method of financing.[46] If money is used to finance the deficit then the situation is as before: the increase in tax revenue must equal dG and the multiplier is $1/T_Y$. But if bonds are used, government spending increases by *dG and* the extra interest payments. As compared with money financing more revenue must be raised to balance the budget, and equilibrium will not be reached until income has risen by a greater amount.[47] Paradoxically, in the long run bond financing is more expansionary (if the system is stable!) than money financing in a closed economy.[48]

Turning finally to open market operations and balanced budget changes, in the long run government purchases of bonds have a contractionary effect on income, not because of perverse wealth effects but because the decline in the stock of bonds reduces government expenditure on interest payments, and the lower tax revenue required to balance the budget necessitates an eventual fall in aggregate income. This is created by the decline in the income flow to the private sector in the form of interest payments. (Steindl, 1974, p. 1144). With an increase in the size of a balanced budget, the induced tax revenue subsequently creates a surplus. If money is retired as a consequence of the surplus, the balanced budget change will have no long-run effect on income: the same income that initially balanced the budget at the new higher tax rates and government spending level will balance it in the long run. Money will have to be retired sufficiently to eliminate the income expansion. If, instead, bonds are retired, the decline in interest payments means that the initial income expansion will have to be more than offset so tax revenue is eventually reduced. The long-run balanced budget multiplier in this case is *negative*.

(b) The analysis of stabilisation policies when wealth effects are present has assumed so far that bonds are regarded as net private wealth. The survey can be concluded by considering the changes that would have to be made to the analysis if bonds were not net wealth. This brings us to the final mirage of the monetarist–Keynesian debate because monetarists take the view that bonds are not net wealth, in contrast to the Keynesian assumption that they are 100 per cent net wealth. (Friedman, 1972; Bruce, 1977). If the monetarists' view were correct, then the wealth effects of policies that involve exchanges of assets or alterations in total asset stocks would be different from those that we have previously described. We must, therefore, take another look at the *short-run* impact of the various *instruments*; but the very short-run and long-run effects of the instruments will remain as before since these are not contingent upon the wealth effects.

In the case of government bond purchases there is a change in the wealth effects for two reasons. Firstly, the original bond purchase, which we previously treated simply as the exchange of one form of wealth for another as far as the private sector is concerned, now places in people's hands extra money, which is wealth, in place of bonds, which aren't. There is, therefore, a second source of expansion from the operation: the increase in wealth does not prevent the *LM* curve shifting to the right as it did before as *M* rose because the extra wealth is in the form of money, but now the *IS* curve also shifts to the right as the increase in wealth raises the demand for goods.[49] As in the previous analysis, the increase in income induces extra tax revenue and the reduced flow of interest payments curtails government expenditure. If the consequent surplus is used to retire money, the subsequent contractionary effect is as previously analysed: wealth declines and if the wealth effects are non-perverse, a contractionary effect occurs that eventually offsets the now larger expansion of income. If, on the other hand, bonds are retired, there is no decline in wealth, but the cut in the flow of interest payments is greater and the subsequent contractionary effect remains. Again, in the long run, the bond purchase is contractionary. In general, therefore, the fact that bonds are not net wealth does not alter the conclusion that an apparently expansionary bond purchase will eventually prove contractionary, although the time taken for the contractionary effect to win out will be longer than if bonds are net wealth. This conclusion contrasts with the monetarist view expressed by Bruce who implies that the effectiveness of open market operations is enhanced when bonds are not net wealth (Bruce, 1977, pp. 1058–9). However, Bruce's conclusion relates only to the expansionary part of the instrument's impact, and ignores the counteracting contraction due to the induced surplus because his model omits the government budget constraint.

With an expansion of a balanced budget the subsequent surplus remains contractionary, for the same reasons as the surplus created by a bond purchase proves contractionary, and the long run impact is unchanged.

In reconsidering bond-financed deficits we shall consider in particular the monetarist view that when bonds are not net wealth the instrument is severely weakened.[50] The source of this prediction is the fact that a bond-financed deficit now has no wealth effect. To interpret this as *weakening* fiscal leverage is apparently to reject another monetarist view, namely that the wealth effects are perverse anyway. In other words, to criticise 'fiscal policy' on the grounds that it has *no* wealth effect (mirage number four) contradicts the indictment of fiscal policy on the grounds that it has *perverse* wealth effects (mirage number three). One cannot have one's monetarist cake *and* eat it! Be that as it may, let us briefly explore the implications of bond-financed deficits when the initial deficit causes no change in wealth (i.e., rejecting mirage number three and accepting mirage four). As before, the response to a bond-financed deficit in the very short run is the shift from IS_1 to IS_2 in Figure 3.6, with aggregate demand rising from Y_1 to Y_2. The deficit creates no new wealth, but the sale of bonds has expanded the bond stock, and the increased government spending on interest payments to the private sector shifts the *IS* curve further to the right, say to IS_3, while the *LM* curve remains stationary at LM_1. Fiscal drag reduces the multiplier effect of both the initial expenditure injection and the short-run injection of

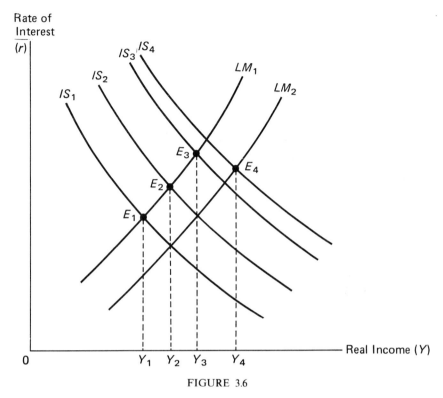

FIGURE 3.6

interest payments, but the net impact of the bond-financed deficit is expansionary to Y_3. Is it more or less expansionary than a money-financed deficit of equal size? A money-financed deficit adds to the initial shift from IS_1 to IS_2 with a further shift in the IS curve (say, IS_2 to IS_4) and a rightward shift in LM (LM_1 to LM_2) as wealth increases. Depending on the strength of the two wealth effects, the point E_4 under money financing may well lie at a higher income level than the E_3 under bond financing for a time. But the higher interest payments flow under bond financing, continually shifting the IS curve to the right, will eventually raise income to a higher level than the long-run equilibrium under money financing. In other words, deficits financed by printing money may well be more effective than bond-financed deficits in the short run, the period of greatest concern to stabilisation policy, but the greater effectiveness does not last indefinitely.

4. CONCLUSIONS

(1) The first lesson taught by the inclusion of the government budget constraint in macroeconomic theory is that the partial analysis of changes in

individual instruments is potentially misleading. The consequences that follow from the financing requirement can, in particular, alter the conventional view of open market operations and bond-financed deficits.

(2) The second related lesson is that, in an analysis that incorporates the wealth effects of changes in asset stocks, the initial (very short-run) impact of an instrument-combination can be offset by a subsequent impact in the opposite direction. Consequently, the ranking of stabilisation policies in terms of their effectiveness as means of altering aggregate income must be time period specific; the very short-run, short-run and long-run rankings are likely to differ.

(3) The controversy between monetarists and Keynesians over the effectiveness of fiscal and monetary instruments for stabilisation has suffered from a failure to agree on even the *definition* of fiscal and monetary policies, and from a tendency for the alleged point of theoretical disagreement to shift through time. The macroeconomic model with a government budget constraint throws light on the implications, for various instrument combinations, of the monetarist cases of perverse wealth effects and of bonds not being counted as net wealth. Analyses of this kind can reveal the determinants of instrument effectiveness that require empirical quantification. An empirical resolution of the differences between the two groups will be achieved, however, if such a resolution is genuinely sought by them. For such is the ingenuity of economists that, if the mood so takes them, they can always conjure up yet another mirage of dispute when the old ones are beginning to fade.

NOTES AND REFERENCES

1. Nevertheless, attempts *have* been made to explore the dynamic properties of stabilisation policies in stochastic models or in models with lagged responses; see for example Holt (1962), Laidler (1973) and Poole (1970). We shall not be concerned in this paper with policy analysis in such explicitly dynamic models.
2. A useful survey of the literature to 1970 is Von Neumann Whitman (1970). A more up to date bibliography can be found in Turnovsky (1977).
3. See for example Burrows and Hitiris (1974), Chapters 2 and 3.
4. The behavioural equations (with C, I, T, L and Y being real values) are

$$C = C_0 + C(Y - T, r) \quad (1), \quad \frac{\partial C}{\partial Y} > 0, \quad \frac{\partial C}{\partial r} < 0 \qquad \text{consumption } (C) \text{ function}$$

$$I = I_0 + I(Y, r) \quad (2), \quad \frac{\partial I}{\partial Y} > 0, \quad \frac{\partial I}{\partial r} < 0 \qquad \text{investment } (I) \text{ function}$$

$$L = L_0 + L(Y, r) \quad (3), \quad \frac{\partial L}{\partial Y} > 0, \quad \frac{\partial L}{\partial r} < 0 \qquad \text{demand for money } (L) \text{ function}$$

We shall abbreviate the partial derivatives to

$$\frac{\partial C}{\partial Y} = C_Y, \qquad \frac{\partial I}{\partial r} = I_r, \text{ etc.}$$

With taxes endogenous we add the tax revenue (T) function $T = T_0 + T(Y)$, $T_Y = \partial T/\partial Y > 0$, the fixed tax rate.
5. The conditions for flow equilibrium in the two sectors are

expenditure sector
(the *IS* curve)
$$Y = C_0 + C(Y - T, r) + I_0 + I(y, r) + \bar{G}$$

monetary sector
(the *LM* curve)
$$L_0 + L(Y, r) = \frac{\bar{M}}{P}, \qquad \bar{M} = \text{nominal money supply}$$

With the price level variable all other variables except $\bar{M}$ are in real terms. For the simultaneous solution of the model for full equilibrium (*IS-LM* intersection) see Burrows and Hitiris (1974), Chapter 3, section 6.
6. The analysis of policy impacts can be reversed for changes in the instruments in the opposite direction. The fiscal impact multipliers are:

$$\frac{\partial Y}{\partial G} = \frac{L_r}{[1 - C_Y(1 - T_Y) - L_Y]L_r + (C_r + I_r)L_Y} > 0 \tag{1a}$$

$$\frac{\partial Y}{\partial T_0} = \frac{-C_Y L_r}{[1 - C_Y(1 - T_Y) - I_Y]L_r + (C_r + I_r)L_Y} < 0 \tag{1b}$$

$$\frac{\partial Y}{\partial B} = \frac{\partial Y}{\partial G} + \frac{\partial Y}{\partial T_0} = \frac{(1 - C_Y)L_r}{[1 - C_Y(1 - T_Y) - L_Y]L_r + (C_r + I_r)L_Y} > 0 \tag{1c}$$

7. See chapter 4 of this book for a discussion of crowding out.
8. Buiter refers to this as 'indirect crowding out' (1977, p. 313).
9. The multiplier with r fixed

$$\frac{1}{1 - C_Y(1 - T_Y) - L_Y}$$

exceeds the multiplier with monetary feedback, equation (a) in note 6, which can be rewritten as

$$\frac{1}{[1 - C_Y(1 - T_Y) - L_Y] + (C_r + I_r)\dfrac{L_Y}{L_r}},$$

where the second term in the denominator is positive and reduces the multiplier just as a fall in C_Y would.
10. This follows from the previous sentence because the slope of the *LM* curve is

$$\frac{\partial r}{\partial Y} = \frac{-L_Y}{L_r} > 0, \; L_Y > 0, \; L_r < 0.$$

11. Silber (1970) pp. 462–3, noted the inconsistency but not the means of resolving it.
12. This assumes that bonds are thought of as net wealth. The question of whether bonds *are* net wealth will arise later in this chapter.
13. The monetary policy impact multiplier is

$$\frac{\partial Y}{\partial M} = \frac{1}{[1 - C_Y(1 - T_Y) - I_Y]L_r + (C_r + I_r)L_Y} > 0$$

14. But see below. In addition, of course, the model does not assume all wealth changes to have any effects anyway.
15. Respectively setting $(C_r + I_r) \to 0$ and $L_r \to -\infty$ in the money multiplier in note 13 produces

$$\frac{\partial Y}{\partial M} \to 0.$$

16. Setting $(C_r + I_r) \to 0$ or $L_r \to -\infty$ in the government expenditure multiplier

$$\frac{\partial Y}{\partial G} = \frac{1}{[1 - C_Y(1 - T_Y) - I_Y] + (C_r + I_r)\dfrac{L_Y}{L_r}}$$

    raises it to

$$\frac{\partial Y}{\partial G} \to \frac{1}{1 - C_Y(1 - T_Y) - I_Y}$$

17. This view is expressed by Tobin (1972) as an interpretation of the state of play prior to Friedman's 1970–71 papers offering a framework for monetary analysis (1970, 1971). Friedman's papers are reprinted in part in Surrey (1976). It will not be possible in this paper to review the attempts to test the effectiveness of fiscal and monetary policies by estimating reduced forms of simple macro-models. See Blinder and Solow (1974), pp. 63–71, Burrows and Hitiris (1974), pp. 165–70 and the references therein.
18. The monetarist limiting case can be viewed as a zero interest sensitivity of the demand for money, $L_r = 0$ (although this misses the point mentioned below concerning the relevant spectrum of rates of return). This implies that the *LM* slope tends to infinity, the curve becomes vertical, and that aggregate income will be proportional to the money supply as the strict Quantity Theory suggests. Thus, inserting $L_r = 0$ in the money multiplier in note 13 we have

$$\frac{\partial Y}{\partial M} = \frac{1}{L_Y},$$

    where L_Y is constant so that the relationship is proportional. On the other hand, the fiscal multiplier, equation (4) in note 6, tends to zero as $L_r \to 0$.
19. For an exposition of the detailed arguments see Chick (1973). There is a danger of oversimplification in taking Friedman's views as representative of monetarists' views but we shall take the risk! However, see Brunner and Meltzer (1972) for a critique of Friedman's 1970 and 1971 papers from a different monetarist standpoint.
20. See notes 4 and 5 above.
21. See note 5 for the equations, omitting the tax variable.
22. The aggregate demand curve is derived by plotting the combinations $Y_1 P_1$, $Y_2 P_2$, etc. from Figure 3.3 in the $P - Y$ plane.
23. See Burrows and Hitiris (1974) Chapter 5, Turnovsky (1977) Chapters 5 and 6.
24. Clearly these two methods represent the adoption of limiting cases of the model of aggregate supply. Friedman offers also a third, 'superior', means of solving the model by setting the rate of interest constant at its long-run expected level. However, he does not, in the final analysis, use this method because he doesn't think we can reasonably assume the real interest rate to be constant when analysing savings and investment decisions! For a critical appraisal of the fixed interest rate model, see Tobin (1972).
25. See Christ (1968), Ott and Ott (1965), Oates (1966), Silber (1970), Steindl (1974). Hansen (1973) postulates a second type of government budget constraint that recognises the separation of powers between the US Treasury and the Federal Reserve System, and restricts deficit financing to the sale of bonds. As regards discretionary stabilisation policy in the form of bond-financed deficits, as distinct from automatic responses of the system, the results are equivalent to those described below (see Meyer and Hart, 1975, section IV).

26. If the price level is fixed, as we shall assume, G and T are in real terms also. In a variable price model the constraint would be written as

$$P(G - T) = M + \frac{\Delta B}{r},$$

where G and T are in real terms. Note that the variables in the budget constraint have not been given time subscripts for simplicity. This will not prevent us from interpreting policy impacts in terms of short- and long-run effects. For a more rigorous development of the dynamic implications of the government budget constraint see Turnovsky (1977) Chapters 3 and 4.

27. For a bond that yields £R each period for t periods and is worth £V at maturity, the price of the bond today (P_B) is the sum of the R's and the V discounted to present value, i.e.,

$$P_B = \frac{R}{(1 + r)} + \frac{R}{(1 + r)^2} \cdots + \frac{R}{(1 + r)^t} + \frac{V}{(1 + r)^t}.$$

This geometric progression reduces to

$$P_B = \frac{R}{r}\left(1 - \frac{1}{(1 + r)^t}\right) + \frac{V}{(1 + r)^t}$$

which for a perpetual bond (consol) with no maturity date $(t \to \infty)$ is $P_B = R/r$.
If the perpetual bond is assumed to yield £1 each period, the price is $P_B = 1/r$ and servicing cost of the bond stock of B bonds is £B.

28. The budget is balanced for the initial change; any subsequently induced deficit or surplus will require a change in the stock of money plus bonds.

29. See, for example, Gurley and Shaw (1960), Pesek and Saving (1967), W. Smith (1970), Barro (1974, 1976), Buchanan (1976) and Feldstein (1976).

30. See note 27.

31. Turnovsky refers to this as the 'intrinsic dynamics of the system' (1977, p. 68).

32. In postulating a delay in the operation of wealth effects we are informally following Turnovsky's insistence that a lag is required because decisions are constrained by wealth owned at the end of the period *prior* to the decision period (Turnovsky, 1977, pp. 39–40). It is purely for convenience in exposition that we assume the flow responses resulting directly from the instrument change to be worked out (in the very short run) before the wealth effects occur (in the short run).

33. This long-run equilibrium condition, that $G - T = \Delta M = \Delta B/r = 0$, says nothing about the conditions under which the system will be stable and converge on the steady state.

34. For the purposes of the analysis to follow it does not matter whether consumption or investment or both are a function of wealth. The following are commonly used versions of the equations (see, for example, Christ, 1968; Oates, 1966; Silber, 1970; Blinder and Solow, 1973):

$$C = C_0 + C(Y - T, r, W), \qquad C_W = \frac{\partial C}{\partial W} > 0 \qquad \text{consumption function}$$

$$I = I_0 + (Y, r) \qquad\qquad\qquad\qquad\qquad\qquad\qquad \text{investment function}$$

$$L = L_0 + L(Y, r, W), \qquad L_W = \frac{\partial L}{\partial W} > 0 \qquad \text{demand for money function}$$

35.
$$\frac{\partial Y}{\partial G}dG + \frac{\partial Y}{\partial M}dM = \frac{(1 + C_r + I_r)/L_r}{[1 - C_Y(1 - T_Y) - L_Y] + L_Y(C_r + I_r)/L_r}$$

which is the sum of the multiplier for dG, equation (4) in note 6, and for dM (see note 13). For a more formally derived, but perhaps less easily understood, presentation of this argument see Turnovsky (1977) Chapter 4, section 3. The injection of money over the very short run will be less than dG by the amount of induced tax revenue as Y rises.

36. Note that we attribute the wealth effect to the utilisation of the surplus *not* to the original open market purchase. The purchase simply exchanges one asset (money) for another (bonds). The increase in the wealth of those who hold outstanding bonds as bond prices rise is tied to the rate of interest change (Keynes Effect) and leads to a movement along the demand for money curve and not a shift in the curve of the kind that results from an increase in wealth at a given rate of interest. Turnovsky (1977) p. 78 by contrast appears to attribute the wealth effect at a given rate of interest to the original open market operation, but the source of this effect is not clear.
37. As Blinder and Solow (1973, 1974) demonstrate, the perverse case of wealth increases that curtail the demand for goods would lead to an unstable system. See note 41 below for the formal stability condition.
38. Whether it does so in the long run will be considered shortly. If the surplus generated is used to retire more bonds instead of withdrawing money, the interest payment flow would be even more contractionary, but the contractionary wealth effect would be absent since money is injected from the surplus in order to buy the bonds.
39. See M. Friedman (1972), Blinder and Solow (1973) pp. 322–33.
40. The following is a summary of the argument presented by Blinder and Solow (1973) section 2, and (1974) pp. 52–5, but see also Silber (1970) and Turnovsky (1977) Chapter 4, sections 6 to 8.
41. The multiplier for bonds

$$\frac{\partial Y}{\partial B} = \frac{1}{[1 - C_Y(1 - T_Y) - I_Y] + (C_r + I_r)\frac{L_Y}{L_r}} \cdot \frac{[C_W - L_W(C_r + I_r)]}{L_r}$$

will be positive if

$$C_W > L_W \frac{(C_r + I_r)}{L_r},$$

where the left-hand term is the wealth effect on consumption and the right-hand term the wealth effect on the demand for money. The extreme case of zero wealth effects on consumption ($C_W = 0$), which was adopted by Scarth (1975), clearly does not meet this requirement. The sufficient condition for the stability of the system is that the budget deficit declines as aggregate income increases (otherwise increasing deficits and income interact without limit in the model of aggregate demand), which requires that induced tax increases exceed induced government spending on interest payments as the bond stock rises. Formally, the stability condition is

$$\frac{\partial Y}{\partial B} > \left(\frac{1 - (\partial T/\partial Y)}{\partial T/\partial Y}\right)$$

which clearly requires the multiplier to be positive.
42. Blinder and Solow (1974) p. 54, present some evidence for the United States and conclude that 'we may feel relatively safe in ruling out the possibility that additional bonds will be contractionary, other things equal'. However, this view cannot be said to be empirically established yet.
43. Assuming £1 of extra wealth does not raise the demand for money by more than £1!
44. Examples of papers that have concentrated almost entirely on long-run analysis are Ott and Ott (1965), Steindl (1971, 1974), Oates (1966) and McGrath (1977). In addition, long-run analysis is added to the short-run analysis in Christ (1968), Turnovsky (1977) Chapter 4, Blinder and Solow (1973, 1974).
45. Oates (1966) p. 493, argues that in an open economy long-run equilibrium requires not budgetary balance but that the budget deficit equals the balance of trade deficit. However, this was subsequently refuted by Turnovsky (1977) Chapter 11, who demonstrated that both the budget *and* the balance of trade must be in equilibrium for a steady state.

46. Christ (1968) recognises that the simple result is a special case. See also Blinder and Solow (1973) section 2.
47. The multiplier with bond financing is

$$dY = \frac{1 + (1 - T_Y)\dfrac{dB}{dG}}{T_Y}$$

which follows from the differential of the long-run equilibrium condition

$$dG + dB - T_Y \, dY - T_Y \, dB = 0.$$

48. But Turnovsky (1977) p. 255, argues that in an open economy Christ's original neat result once again holds sway.
49. See Bruce (1977) p. 1058. If this were the end of the story the wealth-induced shift in the *IS* curve could be seen as overcoming the limitation of the effectiveness of open market operations by the Keynesian limiting cases.
50. Bruce (1977) p. 1058; he refers to bond-financed deficits as 'fiscal policy'.

CHAPTER 4

Crowding Out: Its Meaning and Significance

*C. T. Taylor**

1. INTRODUCTION

In general the term 'crowding out' means expansion by the public (or administratively oriented) sector of the economy at the expense of the private (or market oriented) sector.

Crowding out must inevitably happen in due course when the public sector expands faster than the productive capacity of the economy in a situation of full or near-full employment. This is the kind of development depicted by Bacon and Eltis (1976) and to which they have ascribed a good deal of the recent ills of the British economy. Note, however, that the *ex post* fact in the UK of a trend increase in the share of public expenditure in GDP since the war is not in itself evidence of crowding out; the latter also requires that the share of the private sector would otherwise have been larger, i.e., the public sector was not merely filling a gap left by the private sector. That would be a rather less easy matter to establish.

It is not intended to dwell further here on 'resource' crowding out, except to say that it is an issue that relates principally to the size of public expenditure, and only secondarily to its financing. The subject of this paper is the kind of crowding out that is alleged to occur if public expenditure is financed in certain specific ways, and that might be termed 'financial crowding out'. This version of crowding out may arise, at least in principle, even if the economy is running well below capacity and there is no binding constraint from real resources. As such, it is relevant to the situation of recession that has existed in the UK since late 1974, or so many would argue.[1]

The issue at stake here is how far fiscal policy is likely to be effective in

* *This paper draws heavily on work done by others in the Bank of England and on discussions with colleagues. Nevertheless the broader views expressed are those of the author and should not be interpreted as a reflection of Bank views.*

correcting a deficiency of demand in an underemployed economy. Fiscal policy is taken to refer to the deliberate manipulation of tax rates and/or public expenditure so as to influence total demand for currently produced goods and services. In practice, this means changing the size of the government's budget deficit at a given level of activity.[2] It is also held that fiscal policy, most sensibly defined, involves *no significant change in the proportions of government obligations outstanding* (including high-powered money that is the counterpart to government borrowing from the banking system). This is felt to be the best, if not a perfect, dividing line between fiscal and monetary policy.[3] Monetary policy is then concerned with changing, through open market operations, the proportions of money and government debt held outside the public sector. More accurately, fiscal policy on its own implies no changes in rates of interest on government debt from what they would otherwise be.[4,5]

Those who see financial crowding out as a problem, argue that the emergence of enlarged public sector deficits following a tax cut (and/or expenditure increase) intended to stimulate demand will lead to financial consequences that will sooner or later counteract, wholly or in part, the expansionary effects of the stimulus on economic activity. The principal lines of argument are that sooner or later interest rates and/or prices of goods and services will rise and that by one route or another this will depress real expenditure. Since interest rates in our approach are supposed to be unaffected by fiscal policy *per se*, this entails arguing, *inter alia*, that the authorities will be obliged to tighten monetary policy sooner or later in the wake of a fiscal stimulus. It also involves saying that wages and prices either cannot be or are not for very long effectively limited by prices or incomes policies.

The theoretical arguments about financial crowding out are not new; they have grown up over the ten years or so in which academic economists have turned their attention to the analysis of the consequences of the financing flows resulting from the existence of persistent deficit or surplus sectors.[6] However, circumstances have developed in the UK as in other countries in the past few years that have given the debate a much greater head of steam. Among these, and in addition to the emergence of the deepest recession since the 1930s, are above all the outbreak of very high inflation and coupled with this the onset of unprecedentedly large public sector deficits; the abandonment of the system of relatively fixed exchange rate parities based on Bretton Woods in favour of flexible rates; and, particularly pertinent to this discussion, the adoption by the authorities of tacit, and more recently overt, money supply targets as the mark of a new approach to monetary policy. In the remainder of this paper we look first and fairly briefly at the detailed issues affecting financial crowding out as they appeared in the circumstances of the 1950s and 1960s – termed for short the era of 'Keynesian optimism'; we then examine the new emphases that have developed more recently, in the period of 'practical monetarism' (to borrow a phrase from the Mais Lecture by the Governor of the Bank of England; Richardson, 1978); later we look at the results of some published simulations using large econometric models of the UK economy before finally drawing a few tentative conclusions.

2. KEYNESIAN OPTIMISM

The notion behind Keynesian demand management has always been that the private sector of the economy is prone to generate swings of activity that at times may be only weakly self-correcting, or even in some circumstances hardly self-correcting at all. Fiscal policy has been thought of as a means of stabilising the economy in the face of such cycles, in particular injecting demand into the economy to compensate for excessive private savings at the prevailing level of income by cutting taxes or raising public expenditure. Almost no one would dispute that the immediate effect of an expansionary fiscal 'gesture' is to raise private monetary expenditure through its effect on the income of the recipients (in addition to any increase in the public sector's own expenditure), and that if there are ample unemployed resources, as assumed, this will bring about an equivalent increase in output (expenditure at constant prices); i.e., there will be little immediate reason for prices to rise much. Given a once-for-all fiscal stimulus that is not reversed, output will rise to a new level (compared with what it would otherwise be), the rise depending on the size of the stimulus and the relevant 'multiplier' (really a composite of multiplier and accelerator effects that depend on the size of the leakages into savings, imports and taxation, and on the strength of additional physical investment demand associated with additional income). What could happen to interfere with this corrective process? The popular objection was always that the increase in the budget deficit implied a perpetual increase in the flow of public sector obligations that the rest of the economy would be unwilling to take up at prevailing interest rates; higher interest rates would be needed to induce the public to hold the additional government paper. This argument failed to appreciate that through the multiplier process depicted by Keynes, income will expand to the point at which the rest of the economy (whether the private sector or overseas) is *content* to save at exactly the rate needed to finance the higher rate of public sector borrowing. Moreover, the smaller the economy's willingness to acquire public sector obligations at prevailing levels of income and rates of interest, the larger, paradoxically, will be the leverage on activity exerted by a given fiscal gesture.

The important proviso in the above is that the authorities at all times accommodate private portfolio preferences by issuing and maintaining the mix of obligations that the economy desires to hold, given prevailing interest rates. There are likely to be lags in this process that cause interest rates to fluctuate, but these need not be such as to cause revisions to expenditure plans. In particular, provided the authorities are content to allow the money stock to adjust to whatever is required, nothing in the financial nexus need counteract the fiscal stimulus.

(a) Composition of Gross Saving

A number of qualifications are required to this picture of fiscal stimulus under 'Keynesian optimism'. In concentrating on (net) saving by the private sector in its entirety, i.e., the accumulation of 'outside' – necessarily *financial* – assets by the private sector, it ignores what is happening to private *gross* financial saving, which includes the private sector's acquisition of its own liabilities. Could it happen that a fiscal stimulus, which raises gross as well as net saving, might lead to the private sector holding an excessive proportion of financial assets in public sector debt, and if so should not this tend to raise yields on government bonds in a way that could not easily be countered by open market operations? Since a recession is typically a time in which the marginal propensity to save is high whereas the propensity to invest, and thence for companies to borrow, is low, this possibility seems not implausible. However, these developments are unlikely in themselves to lead to crowding out of private investment but rather to a reduction in the required yield on equities relative to that on bonds as private investors bid to maintain their stake in private industry; the cost of capital in these circumstances is more likely to fall than to rise as a result of fiscal stimulus, since the supply of savings to industry is likely to be greater than otherwise, while profits are likely to gain from higher activity.

(b) Inflation

With spare capacity, the 'demand–pull' pressure on prices could be largely ignored under 'Keynesian optimism' (subject to the stimulus not being such as to produce a rapid and sustained *change* in overall utilisation) and if anything influences on the cost side were expected to be a help rather than a hindrance, for unit costs normally fall when activity rises and few manufacturing industries exhibit diminishing returns for output variations of the scale typically envisaged. With mark-up of prices on *normal* unit costs, profitability should improve without putting pressure on prices, and this should reinforce the stimulus.

An optimistic Keynesian would not of course ignore that, in a relatively open economy operating not too far from full employment, a stimulus that was miscalculated by even a modest margin might lead uncomfortably quickly to overheating, with the attendant inflationary pressures, including of course the possibility of a devaluation if the stimulus were much over-done. But in the era before the large inflations and devaluations of recent years he could reasonably count on a helpful degree of inertia or money illusion on the part of price setters and wage bargainers. This confidence in a relatively 'fixed-price' environment contributed greatly to the efficacy of demand management; in an atmosphere of docile price expectations, inflation itself was inclined to be relatively stable.

(c) The Balance of Payments

Where a fiscal stimulus is given independently of policy in other countries, some deterioration in the balance of payments must almost inevitably result as imports respond to increased home demand. The optimistic Keynesian would see this as a perfectly normal consequence of fiscal stimulus, which would limit the size of the multiplier while hardly in itself representing crowding out of UK activity. However, with fixed exchange rates a current account deficit (or smaller surplus than otherwise) will sooner or later lead to a (comparative) loss of reserves, possibily exacerbated at some stage by a capital outflow. The standard response by the authorities would be to raise interest rates on sterling-denominated securities with the object of reversing the capital flow; this would be accompanied by a domestic credit squeeze (hire purchase controls, calls for special deposits, etc.) if the situation war-ranted it, as for example in the balance of payments crises in the UK of 1955–1956, 1961 and 1964. Such measures would have some depressing effect on interest-sensitive kinds of domestic expenditure, mainly stockbuild-ing – where the cost of financing stocks is an important consideration – and housebuilding, where activity is especially sensitive to the flow of mortgage finance. The mechanism was held to be essentially through the cost and availability of borrowing rather than through the wealth effects, which now-adays tend to be more emphasised. (See below for a fuller discussion of wealth and interest rate effects.) Mitigating factors would be that the import response could be expected to be relatively moderate in a recession and that longer term interest rates would be relatively less affected, since it is normally short rates that are relevant to international capital flows, the volatile element of which tends to be composed of relatively liquid assets.

The exercise of monetary policy to mitigate the adverse consequences of a fiscal stimulus on the balance of payments under fixed exchange rates was the only potentially serious form of crowding out generally recognised in the era of Keynesian optimism. The emergence of balance of payments deficits in the wake of bouts of fiscal expansion was a problem that dogged attempts at demand management in the UK through the 1950s and 1960s, when the economy was operating at a pressure of demand taking one year with another that nowadays would be thought over-ambitiously high. Yet few would see it as a reflection of any impotence of fiscal policy – indeed the phases of 'stop' that followed phases of 'go' represented reversals of fiscal policy rather than periodic frustration of fiscal by monetary policy; it betokened more fundamental weaknesses in the economy, which fiscal policy was neither designed nor expected to overcome.

3. PRACTICAL MONETARISM

Out of the economic upheavals of the early 1970s has emerged a perhaps uneasy coalition of ideas about, and approaches to, demand management that incorporates at least two major new features entirely outside orthodox Keynesian policies: flexible exchange rates and monetary targets. The era of flexible exchange rates began for the UK in June 1972 when the government announced its intention to let sterling float for a time to find its own value in the market. Since then there have been periods of managed floating interspersed with periods, such as that after October 1977, when the authorities refrained for a time from significant intervention in the exchange market. The beginning of the era of monetary targets is less easy to date, for the authorities had been paying attention internally to the growth of monetary aggregates well before the first announcement of an explicit guideline for M3 by the Chancellor of the Exchequer in March 1977 (foreshadowed by ceilings for domestic credit expansion (DCE) and the public sector borrowing requirement (PSBR) in the Letter of Intent to the International Monetary Fund in December 1976). Both of these innovations have had important consequences for the operation of fiscal policy.

(a) Flexible Exchange Rates

A key consequence of the operation of flexible exchange rates in the present context has been that the link between domestic monetary demand (and/or monetary conditions) and the general price level has been much strengthened and speeded up. A fiscal stimulus (accompanied by accommodative money policy) tends to worsen the trade balance, as depicted earlier, and this, *ceteris paribus*, tends to bring about an exchange depreciation.[7] The immediate effect of the depreciation is to improve trade competitiveness and this improvement, if it persists, will magnify the expansionary impact of the fiscal stimulus in comparison with that of the fixed exchange rate case discussed above.

But simultaneously depreciation will raise import prices and these will feed into domestic costs, setting in motion an inflationary spiral that will leave domestic prices significantly higher than otherwise. The extent and speed of the transmission of import price inflation into domestic prices is the subject of considerable debate and research at the moment. The answer will naturally depend on a number of factors, including the way in which price expectations are formed, the degree to which such expectations enter into wage determination, the size of offsetting factors like productivity gains, the extent to which tax reductions mitigate pressure for money wage increases and, of course, the degree of formal or informal restraint on wage settlements. Many researchers seem now to be coming to believe that most if not all of an initial import price increase will be passed through to higher domestic prices in the long run, i.e., domestic prices will eventually rise in the same proportion as import prices, but there is much disagreement about the speed of the process. If wage bargainers take exchange depreciation as a signal that inflation is in store and try to anticipate it, the speed of transmission will be faster than if they simply try to catch up with the inflation that has already happened. If through increasing sophistication wages are bargained for in terms of take-home pay, tax cuts will help to retard the process.

The adjustment of domestic costs following a depreciation will naturally operate to reduce the initial gain in competitiveness, but unless forward-looking price expectations are a very powerful element – which seems questionable given the uncertainties that normally surround wage negotiations – it is likely to take a long time (perhaps five years according to Odling-Smee and Hartley, 1978) before competitiveness gains are substantially wiped out. In the meantime, improvements in the trade balance caused by competitiveness are likely in themselves to be a substantial bonus to fiscal stimulus.

They may, however, be countered by other influences from faster inflation. For any given path of nominal domestic incomes, faster inflation will reduce real incomes compared with otherwise, so that in a period of pay restraint some domestic expenditure is likely to be crowded out compared with the fixed rate case. This obviously happened in the UK in 1976/77 when the combination of sharp depreciation and pay restraint led to an unprecedented cut in real personal disposable income. (But on the other hand, the improvement in trade competitiveness in those circumstances was unusually large, so that the net effect on activity compared with the fixed rate circumstances could still have been expansionary – as well as clearly preferable from the point of view of improving the trade balance at the expense of domestic consumption.)

Wealth effects   A second way in which faster inflation may influence expenditure is through wealth effects. This line of reasoning has come into greater prominence in the last few years as it has become necessary to explain the depressed behaviour of consumer expenditure in the face of high inflation. The theory, simply put, is that (real) wealth is a determinant of private expenditure – particularly personal expenditure – independently of income, and that the real value of assets denominated in money terms (cash, deposits, nominally capital certain securities of all kinds) falls with inflation. When this is perceived to happen, individuals attempt to restore the real value of their holdings by spending less of their incomes; hence the abnormally high saving ratios seen in the UK from about 1974 onwards.

How important are wealth effects likely to be? This is the subject of much research at the present time and only tentative answers can be attempted. For example, some research has been done in the Bank of England to investigate the role of various measures of real wealth as arguments in the consumption function. Its findings so far are that a significant improvement in the explanatory power of conventional equations for non-durables expenditure can be obtained by including real liquid assets as a separate independent variable (Townend, 1970). (Since the parameters on gross liquid assets and on liabilities do not appear to be significantly different, net liquid assets is the preferred measure.) The influence of net liquid assets turns out to be very small when compared with that of income, as can be seen from a simplified long-run version of the equation now in the Bank short-term forecasting model:

$$CND_t = 1360 + 0.45\left(\frac{YD^*}{PCND}\right)_t + 0.06\left(\frac{NLAJ}{PCND_t}t - 1\right) = \text{error term}$$

Where CND is expenditure on non-durable goods (£ million at 1970 prices), YD is nominal personal disposable income (£ million), PCND the implicit price deflator for non-durables expenditure and NLAJ the nominal stock of net liquid assets held by persons (£ million). (Both CND and YD are net of government grants.) The asterisk on YD indicates that YD is smoothed to give an approximate estimate of permanent income. The equation was estimated quarterly, 1965 IV–1975 III. With net liquid assets of persons now standing at some £25 billion in 1970 prices, a 1 per cent reduction in their total (reflecting for example a rise in PCND of 1 per cent), *ceteris paribus*, leads to a reduction in expenditure of £15 million (at 1970 prices) per quarter, the effect tending gradually to diminish through time as additional saving (with given income) steadily restores net liquid assets to their original level. This may seem a small amount, but of course the effect on expenditure continues to build up if prices continue to rise, so that the persistence of a higher rate of inflation over a period of years leads to a significant change in the saving ratio.

The interpretation of such results is not without its problems. So far the inclusion of broader measures of wealth as alternatives to liquid assets has not proved equally successful, while bank advances separately appear a much more powerful determinant of durables expenditure. Moreover the interpretation of the results for liquid assets is not unambiguous. It is uncertain, for example, whether they are acting as a proxy for aggregate personal sector wealth or merely as a measure of liquid resources. If the latter, then the consequences of a rise may not be symmetrical with those of a fall: when liquid resources are reduced, they may be expected to constrain expenditure on goods and services, but when they rise they may simply be channelled into other kinds of financial assets.

At all events, the evidence suggests that inflation is likely to have significant effects on consumer spending through its impact on personal asset holdings, and this provides a useful and in itself quite persuasive argument for those who support the notion of crowding out in circumstances where a fiscal stimulus is prone to provoke depreciation of the exchange rate and thence faster inflation. However, it must also be borne in mind that the enlargement of saving that was earlier seen to accompany the higher incomes resulting from a fiscal stimulus itself represents a faster rate of accumulation of wealth which, if the preceding arguments are correct, will in due course provide a separate boost to expenditure,[8] thereby countering to some extent, and perhaps ultimately more than offsetting, the depressing effect of faster inflation. The net outcome of these opposing influences on expenditure is obviously an empirical question that cannot be solved by *a priori* reasoning.

(b) Monetary Targets

Alongside these issues arising under the new regime of flexible exchange rates are those stemming from the pursuit of money supply targets that do not adjust, or do so (it is supposed here for sake of the argument) only minimally when fiscal policy shifts. Does this pursuit compound the likelihood of crowding out or does it diminish it? In one important respect, that of inflation, it should diminish it, for if inflationary expectations are indeed much influenced by prospective monetary growth and provided it is widely believed that the authorities will adhere to their target despite a fiscal expansion (possibly a significant proviso) monetary stability should help to quell domestic reactions to enlarged public deficits and exchange depreciation. But in most other respects pursuit of monetary targets seems likely to accentuate crowding out.

A pure monetarist would see the matter largely in terms of the relative reduction in the real money supply that would accompany a fiscal stimulus in these circumstances. This would tend to negate any increase in domestic expenditure and any outflow of capital across the exchanges (thereby forestalling sterling depreciation). Others would see the problem largely in terms of consequences for interest rates when the money supply is held down in the face of higher incomes and rising net financial asset holdings in the private sector. How big do the increases in interest rates have to be to reconcile people to hold the (relatively) lower money stock? The answer naturally depends on the nature of the demand for money in the private economy.

The demand for money If money is needed purely and solely as a means of financing transactions, and assuming as before that a fiscal stimulus produces in due course a once-for-all increase in income, there will be a once-for-all increase in interest rates (although lags in the adjustment in the demand for money may produce a sharp initial increase after which rates fall back somewhat to new equilibrium levels) as the velocity of money circulation adjusts to a new, higher, rate. The size of the increase will depend on the size of the increase in income and the elasticity of demand for money with respect to income and to competing rates of interest (with a representative rate of interest on short-term public sector bonds usually taken as the relevant opportunity cost of holding money). Orders of magnitude suggested by the Bank of England's published demand for money (M3) equations suggest the following:

$$M_t^* = \text{constant} + 1.0Y_t + 1.0P_t - 0.25r^s + 0.5r'$$

where M^* is the private sector's desired stock of 'broad' money (M3), Y is real national income, P is the general price level, r^s is a representative competing rate of interest (here the rate on three-month deposits with local authorities) and r' the 'own rate' on money (i.e., the return on money time deposits – here the rate on three-month sterling certificates of deposit); all variables are in logs and the coefficients denote long-run elasticities (Hacche, 1974). The equation was fitted quarterly over the period 1963 IV–1972 IV, with the long-run price elasticity constrained to unity and the 'own rate' put at zero before the introduction of the new arrangements for competition and credit control during 1971. That is to say, a *ceteris paribus* change from 10 per cent to 11 per cent in the rate on local authority deposites (with r' constant) ultimately causes a decrease of $2\frac{1}{2}$ per cent in the demand for M3. Consequently a fiscal stimulus that raises income by 1 per cent will require an increase of 4 per cent (or 0.4 percentage points in this case) if the public are to be induced to hold an unchanged money stock.

This is not a negligible effect, but neither is it a very alarming one. But that is not the end of the story. Under the new arrangements for competition and credit control that have operated since 1971, banks are left much freeer than they used to be to bid for deposits in the money markets, and competition between them is likely to drive up the 'own rate' on money when competing rates rise. Accordingly, to obtain a given change in interest rate differentials, a larger increase in competing rates is needed than would be the case in the days before the 'new approach'. How much larger? The answer is unsure, but a change of several percentage points in the above example might be plausible.

Second, the variety of demand for money equation referred to includes no allowance for the possibility that money may be required not merely as a means of financing transactions (related to Y and P) but also as a stock of wealth, or a source of liquidity the demand for which varies with wealth. If so, a policy that holds money stock constant in the face of a fiscal stimulus that leads both to a higher level of income and a higher rate of accumulation of wealth (including additional investment within the private sector as well as net acquisition of public sector obligations) will also require, in principle at least, a continuing rise in interest rates to reconcile savers to the continuing fall in the proportion of money in their asset portfolios. The steady increase will persist, it is argued, so long as the public sector continues to run a (differential) budget deficit (Miller, 1978). In time, interest-sensitive kinds of expenditure will be affected.

Three points may be made in qualification of the above argument. So far, little evidence has been found for a wealth effect on the demand for money in the UK; wealth terms have been tried in demand for money equations in this country but without success, partly perhaps because the data are still rather inadequate. And the evidence for a similar effect in the USA appears to be inconclusive (Currie, 1978b). While it is logical to think that an individual's demand for money should bear some long-run relation to his wealth, it seems implausible that it should be very stable or precise, so that extremely small adjustments in relative yields between money and other liquid assets should be capable of reconciling savers to variations to the composition of their portfolios.

Second, as pointed out earlier in a slightly different context, the enlarged rate of wealth accumulation that accompanies a fiscal stimulus should in time add to consumers' expenditure, if the latter is determined by wealth as well as income. In the long run this should in itself enable the budget deficit to be reduced, thereby bringing a halt to the continuous rise in interest rates.

Third, the interest rate increases themselves can be expected to reduce the market value of the existing stock of wealth, more especially through capital losses on fixed interest securities. (This point will be returned to below.) If the demand for money depends partially on wealth, this reduction in market values should in itself *reduce* the demand for money, and this will also tend to mitigate any longer run rise in interest rates.

Impact of interest rate changes   There remains the issue of the effect of interest rate changes on expenditure in the circumstances of 'practical monetarism'. It now seems fairly generally accepted that the traditional effects operating via the cost of capital are probably rather weak in this country except in the area of housebuilding. Most research in the UK (unlike that in the USA) suggests that company fixed investment is not sensitive to interest rate changes, while the evidence on stockbuilding is inconclusive (Savage, 1978); this may be partly attributable to the comparative openness of the British economy or to the absence of major interest rate changes until quite recently. There is little evidence on the effect of the cost of borrowing on consumers' expenditure, but changes in hire purchase terms are known to have an appreciable if temporary effect and changes in the cost and availability of bank advances also probably have an influence. Housebuilding is affected principally by the flow of mortgage finance, which is in turn highly dependent on differences between rates offered by building societies and competing rates. Since there tends to be more inertia in building society rates than others, a change in monetary policy is likely to produce a considerable temporary effect on housebuilding. And swings in mortgage lending in turn appear to have a detectable impact on consumer durables spending, partly by affecting the extent to which consumers can mobilise their equity in their houses, and partly because the demand for durables is somewhat complementary to that for new houses.

There appears less agreement about the impact of interest rate changes via wealth effects. Such changes have a direct effect on the market values of marketable securities with nominally fixed interest coupons, such as gilts, the prices of which vary inversely with prevailing rates, and are held to have parallel influences on equity and property prices. There is no doubt that the values of these assets plunged violently in the UK between 1973 and 1975, although they have recovered since, and that these changes were to some extent correlated with interest rate swings. It is plausible to think that the capital gains and losses entailed by such swings should affect expenditure, particularly by consumers. The evidence is however mixed. Wealth effects of this kind are thought by some American economists to be the main route by which monetary policy affects activity in the USA, and the evidence there seems reasonably in their favour (Savage, 1978). But the published evidence for the UK is so far relatively sparse and not very encouraging on the whole; as was seen earlier, the inclusion of broader wealth measures in the Bank's consumption function gave disappointing preliminary results (Townend, 1970) but work on the subject is continuing. One possible reason for a lack of impact when prices of longer term financial assets fluctuate is that the capital gains or losses are perceived to be either temporary or not necessarily realisable. It is also the case that the main concentrations of such financial assets in the UK are held by the long-term financial institutions, particularly pension funds, so that even major capital gains and losses on government securities and equities are not readily detectable by most individuals.

There are two other routes by which interest rates may affect activity in the world of the practical monetarist. Net receipts of interest by the private sector naturally rise when interest rates rise, and unless price expectations rise in the same proportion (i.e., assuming the real rate of interest rises) this represents a rise in real income, some proportion of which (but perhaps a relatively small one) will be spent. Quantitatively this is likely to be an important point that tends to be overlooked in discussions of the crowding out issue.

Second, the rise in interest rates that (most would agree) accompanies a fiscal stimulus with unchanged money supply targets is likely to stimulate a capital inflow into the UK (again assuming price expectations do not rise to the same degree) and this will counteract the downward pressure on the exchange rate that would otherwise occur under flexible rates (discussed earlier). This will both mitigate the medium-term inflationary consequences of a fiscal stimulus under flexible rates and reduce the immediate gain to competitiveness that goes with depreciation.

In these particular respects the combination of non-adjusting monetary targets with flexible exchange rates should have implications for activity that fall between those of the optimistic Keynesian world with fixed exchange and interest rates and a situation with flexible exchange rates but fixed interest rates (i.e., adjusting monetary targets).

4. RESULTS OF SOME ECONOMETRIC SIMULATIONS

The foregoing catalogue of effects may help in grappling with the issues but the fact remains that crowding out is essentially an empirical question incapable of resolution by *a priori* reasoning. The practical issues are, moreover, so complex that there is little hope of reaching quantitative conclusions without resort to econometric models capable of incorporating all the potentially important effects discussed above. It is instructive to refer here to a set of macroeconomic simulations taken from a recent comparative study of the Treasury (HMT), London Business School (LBS) and National Institute of Economic and Social Research (NIESR) quarterly forecasting models (Laury, Lewis and Ormerod, 1978).[9]

The first point to note is that the results of the simulations differ very appreciably in some respects as between the three models. This indicates, *inter alia*, the existence of important differences in the way the modellers view the behaviour of the economy, as reflected in the structure of the models and the precise specification of key relationships. A description of each of the models and the way they were used to produce the simulations is given in the Institute paper and is indispensable to a full understanding of the results and why they differ. Only the barest bones can be conveyed here.

Three of the simulations are particularly relevant to the discussion of crowding out in the present paper. Each relates to the consequences of a once-for-all increase in public consumption of £100 million per quarter at 1970 prices, all other independent inputs into the models, including nominal tax rates, being held constant. (All three models are capable of generating endogenous forecasts of earnings, the exchange rate, interest rates and the money stock, and did so as appropriate in the simulations.) The point of simulations is to discover the impact of this change in fiscal policy on the main features of the economy (activity, inflation and the balance of payments) by looking at differences from a base run comprising the actual out-turn of the economy from 1972 to 1977.

Simulation 1 (see Table 4.1) comes nearest to a representation of the set of circumstances characterised above as Keynesian optimism. Both the exchange rate and interest rates are fixed (i.e., held at base run values), representing a situation in which the authorities support sterling and allow money stock to accommodate to demand as the fiscal stimulus proceeds. Earnings are also fixed, suggesting either that wages do not respond to the extra pressure of demand or that they are closely constrained by incomes policy. In these circumstances there is only minor crowding out according to all three models; the increase in GDP after sixteen quarters is only a little different from what it is after four quarters (when most multiplier effects have come through). Inflation is hardly changed, largely by assumption, but the net resource balance (net exports), and thence the current balance, is worse. The money stock is eventually higher in all three, responding to more real income and larger public sector borrowing requirements. The multiplier on public consumption is put at around 1.1–1.2 in the Treasury and LBS simulations but is conspicuously lower in the NIESR simulation. This divergence reflects in part genuine differences of view (including a relatively low long-run marginal propensity to consume in the NIESR model) and in part the absence in the model of known effects that are allowed for in an *ad hoc* way when the model is used for forecasting, etc.

Simulation 2 (see Table 4.2) portrays the same stimulus in circumstances where exchange rates and earnings are allowed to vary from the base run in accordance with model relationships, while interest rates are held unchanged from the base run; it therefore represents the kind of situation discussed under 3(a) above.[10]

In this case the effect of a fiscal stimulus is clearly magnified, for several years at least, in all three models by the gain in competitiveness associated with exchange depreciation. This produces a large improvement in the net resource balance compared with the fixed rate case (although the improve-

TABLE 4.1   *Simulation 1 (A final consumption + £100m, 1970 prices: interest rates, earnings and exchange rate fixed)*

Treasury model

Quarter	£m (1970 prices)							(000s)	% change				£m	
	RPDI	C	I	S	X	M	GDP	E	EARN	CED	ER	MS	GDP	CB
1	46	6	4	1	−1	2	101	190	—	0.1	—	0.1	101	−4
2	38	10	3	15	−2	11	108	204	0.1	0.1	—	0.1	118	−15
3	44	16	4	24	−2	18	116	219	0.1	0.2	—	0.2	133	−24
4	48	23	5	20	−2	24	111	229	0.1	0.2	—	0.3	133	−31
5	49	29	6	18	−2	31	108	235	0.1	0.2	—	0.4	137	−41
6	52	36	6	16	−2	31	112	242	—	0.2	—	0.4	143	−44
7	53	39	7	13	−2	33	110	244	—	0.2	—	0.5	148	−50
8	53	41	7	11	−2	31	112	246	—	0.2	—	0.5	153	−50
16	53	43	1	−1	−2	19	109	246	—	0.1	—	0.9	231	−64
24	39	35	1	−1	−2	18	105	233	—	0.1	—	1.3	262	−86

London Business School model

Quarter	£m (1970 prices)							(000s)	% change				£m	
	RPDI	C	I	S	X	M	GDP	E	EARN	CED	ER	MS	GDP	CB
1	54	36	—	23	−1	39	109	30	—	−0.4	—	0.5	76	−44
2	76	58	1	37	−1	55	123	64	—	−0.6	—	1.0	66	−59
3	95	63	2	42	−1	57	131	101	—	−0.5	—	1.4	75	−68
4	94	66	2	37	−1	60	125	135	—	−0.5	—	1.7	85	−71
5	84	60	5	27	−1	56	119	138	—	−0.4	—	1.9	95	−72
6	84	63	5	21	−1	53	119	136	—	−0.3	—	2.1	101	−71
7	82	64	6	17	—	51	118	131	—	−0.3	—	2.2	106	−73
8	77	61	7	14	—	50	115	127	—	−0.3	—	2.2	105	−77
16	82	65	4	4	—	45	111	120	—	−0.4	—	3.1	141	−114
24	76	60	2	6	—	46	106	107	—	−0.3	—	3.4	158	−163

National Institute model

Quarter	£m (1970 prices)							(000s)	% change				£m	
	RPDI	C	I	S	X	M	GDP	E	EARN	CED	ER	MS	GDP	CB
1	14	5	1	−15	−1	14	65	35	—	—	—	—	84	−16
2	29	13	3	2	−2	24	77	78	—	—	—	0.1	102	−27
3	40	20	5	10	−4	31	84	111	—	—	—	0.5	118	−36
4	52	28	8	9	−4	36	84	135	—	—	—	0.8	121	−43
5	53	33	9	4	−3	40	78	148	—	—	—	1.1	121	−50
6	54	35	10	1	−4	41	76	154	—	—	—	1.3	119	−56
7	53	36	11	−1	−4	41	76	158	—	—	—	1.4	122	−61
8	52	36	12	1	−4	42	76	160	—	—	—	1.5	125	−68
16	37	27	3	−4	−10	40	49	113	—	—	—	1.6	149	−109
24	31	21	10	—	−19	31	61	102	—	—	—	1.4	186	−162

Key to Tables 4.1–4.3:
RPDI = real personal disposable income
   C = consumers' expenditure
    I = total fixed investment
   S = total stockbuilding
   X = total exports of goods and services
   M = total imports of goods and services
GDP = gross domestic product at factor cost 1970 prices and at current prices

TABLE 4.2 *Simulation 2 (A final consumption +£100m, 1970 prices: interest rates fixed, earnings endogenous, floating exchange rate)*

Treasury model

| | £m (1970 prices) | | | | | | (000s) | % change | | | | £m | |
Quarter	RPDI	C	I	S	X	M	GDP	E	EARN	CED	ER	MS	GDP	CB
1	51	7	4	1	−1	2	101	190	0.1	0.1	−0.1	0.1	104	−5
2	53	13	4	16	−2	12	111	206	0.4	0.2	−0.3	0.2	135	−15
3	64	21	5	26	−2	19	122	222	0.6	0.3	−0.5	0.4	158	−36
4	71	31	6	24	−2	27	121	235	0.8	0.5	−0.8	0.6	198	−32
5	70	40	7	23	−1	36	119	244	0.9	0.7	−1.2	0.9	234	−44
6	65	45	8	23	−1	35	124	253	1.1	0.8	−1.4	1.2	281	−38
7	60	45	9	19	—	35	121	257	1.4	1.1	−1.7	1.4	320	−49
8	63	44	9	15	—	30	124	260	1.7	1.4	−2.0	1.7	372	−46
16	17	−14	14	−6	15	−9	112	248	4.1	3.8	−5.2	5.3	1,131	27
24	−24	−68	25	−7	37	−30	119	247	7.3	6.6	−6.5	9.7	2,495	244

London Business School model

| | £m (1970 prices) | | | | | | (000s) | % change | | | | £m | |
Quarter	RPDI	C	I	S	X	M	GDP	E	EARN	CED	ER	MS	GDP	CB
1	78	21	—	22	—	33	106	29	0.8	—	−0.7	0.7	124	−48
2	87	31	1	35	1	43	116	61	1.0	0.1	−1.2	1.2	155	−60
3	101	31	3	39	2	44	122	95	1.2	0.3	−1.8	1.7	199	−73
4	94	34	2	35	4	46	119	128	1.4	0.7	−2.3	2.1	248	−82
5	91	28	4	27	7	42	116	131	1.7	1.0	−2.8	2.6	310	−84
6	89	28	5	20	7	38	115	131	2.0	1.2	−3.1	2.9	354	−83
7	87	21	5	16	9	32	113	127	2.3	1.6	−3.5	3.2	410	−91
8	84	19	7	12	11	31	113	124	2.6	1.8	−3.8	3.4	467	−100
16	117	2	6	3	30	21	122	108	6.4	4.5	−8.7	6.5	1,488	−152
24	171	13	7	17	54	35	152	145	14.6	10.2	−15.0	9.5	4,185	−96

National Institute model

| | £m (1970 prices) | | | | | | (000s) | % change | | | | £m | |
Quarter	RPDI	C	I	S	X	M	GDP	E	EARN	CED	ER	MS	GDP	CB
1	21	7	1	−16	−1	14	66	35	0.1	—	−0.1	0.1	87	−17
2	36	16	3	—	−2	22	81	80	0.1	—	−0.3	0.1	106	−30
3	45	23	6	8	−3	27	91	116	0.1	0.1	−0.6	0.4	123	−42
4	53	30	9	6	−3	29	96	143	0.2	0.1	−0.9	0.7	131	−52
5	52	32	11	4	−1	31	96	161	0.2	0.2	−1.0	1.1	145	−59
6	56	35	13	2	—	32	98	174	0.3	0.2	−1.1	1.4	159	−65
7	58	37	15	—	2	32	103	185	0.5	0.3	−1.4	1.5	176	−76
8	57	37	16	1	3	32	106	193	0.6	0.4	−1.6	1.7	195	−89
16	25	13	3	−2	18	33	80	176	1.8	1.5	−2.9	3.4	539	−11
24	−30	−28	2	−7	12	22	47	121	3.0	2.5	−3.1	4.0	953	−10

E = total UK employment
EARN = average gross earnings per head CED = consumers' expenditure deflator
ER = effective exchange rate
MS = money stock (sterling M3 definition)
CB = balance of payments on current account (£m)
Note Δ nominal GDP = Δ price × level of GDP in base + Δ GDP × price level in simulation (ignoring second-order terms).
Source: National Institute Economic Review, No. 83, February 1978.

ment in the current balance is somewhat conteracted by worse terms of trade).

Simultaneously, exchange depreciation injects inflation into the domestic economy – very substantially in the LBS simulation, very moderately in the NIESR simulation, with the Treasury nearer the NIESR. Wage–price interactions and fiscal drag cause real personal disposable income and thence consumption to fall back progressively in the Treasury and NIESR simulations, eventually counterbalancing much of the expansionary effect from the new resource balance (particularly in the NIESR simulation). The stimulus ultimately remains strong in the LBS simulation because the LBS model generates progressively more depreciation through the influence of the rise in money stock (caused by higher public sector borrowing requirements); although the deterioration in the terms of trade has a dominant effect in worsening the current balance in the early years, the improvement in the resource balance eventually takes over. Despite the extremely large improvement in real personal disposable income, negative wealth effects stemming from inflation keep consumption about as low in the LBS case as in the other.

Simulation 3 (see Table 4.3) switches to a situation in which, with floating exchanges and endogenous earnings, money stock is held at base run levels (at least in the Treasury and NIESR models) and interest rates adjust in accordance with demand for money functions; it accordingly approximates broadly to the situation discussed under 3(b) above. A critical question is how far interest rate changes lead to crowding out as compared with Simulation 2. In the NIESR simulation the interest rate consequences for crowding out are negligible. This is partly because the rise in interest rates in the NIESR model is small (the consol rate being only 0.4 points higher after eight quarters and 0.2 points after twenty-four quarters), so that crowding out through cost of capital effects is small; and partly because the model as used did not include any significant wealth effects on either expenditure or the demand for money.

By contrast, crowding out following from interest rate changes is major in the Treasury model; after twenty-four quarters the GDP multiplier is only 0.3 (compared with nearly 1.2 after four quarters). The rise in long-term interest rates is relatively large (0.9 points after eight quarters and 3.2 points, or 30 per cent, after twenty-four quarters); this reflects the large expansion in the PSBR needed to finance the fiscal stimulus when there is differentially faster inflation. The rise in rates stimulates more consumption compared with Simulation 2, for real personal incomes are boosted by higher net interest income, while in this version of the model there are no interest-generated wealth effects on consumption to offset this boost; but in other respects the effects are deflationary: fixed investment, stockbuilding and housebuilding are all directly affected, but by far the largest impact occurs in net exports,

TABLE 4.3 *Simulation 3 (A final consumption +£100m, 1970 prices: interest rates and earnings endogenous, floating exchange rate)*

Treasury model

	£m (1970 prices)						(000s)	% change				£m	
Quarter	RPDI	C	I	S	X	M GPD	E	EARN	CED	ER	MS	GPD	CB
1	51	7	4	1	-1	2 101	190	0.1	0.1	-0.1	0.1	104	-5
2	53	13	3	15	-2	12 111	205	0.4	0.2	-0.2	0.2	134	-15
3	65	22	4	25	-2	19 120	221	0.6	0.3	-0.4	0.3	168	-23
4	75	32	4	20	-2	26 117	233	0.8	0.5	-0.5	0.5	194	-31
5	77	42	3	17	-2	33 113	241	0.9	0.6	-0.6	0.5	225	-40
6	78	49	—	14	-2	32 115	247	1.1	0.8	-0.4	0.5	259	-42
7	81	53	-2	9	-1	32 109	248	1.4	0.9	-0.3	0.4	296	-45
8	93	58	-6	4	-1	30 108	248	1.7	1.1	-0.2	0.2	237	-44
16	90	60	-19	-22	-16	24 63	209	3.7	2.8	-1.1	1.1	923	-71
24	98	74	-20	-14	-52	41 29	135	6.1	4.7	-2.4	1.9	1,746	-168

London Business School Model

	£m (1970 prices)						(000s)	% change				£m	
Quarter	RPDI	C	I	S	X	M GDP	E	EARN	CED	ER	MS	GDP	CB
1	73	21	1	22	—	33 105	29	0.8	—	-0.7	0.7	123	-47
2	78	29	-2	34	1	42 113	60	0.9	0.1	-1.2	1.2	151	-59
3	89	28	-3	37	2	41 115	93	1.1	0.3	-1.7	1.7	189	-70
4	77	28	-9	31	4	40 106	121	1.3	0.7	-2.2	2.0	226	-76
5	68	19	-15	21	7	32 95	118	1.5	1.0	-2.6	2.4	272	-72
6	62	18	-20	13	7	26 86	111	1.7	1.1	-2.9	2.7	302	-67
7	57	7	-26	7	9	17 77	100	2.0	1.5	-3.2	2.9	332	-69
8	53	3	-30	3	10	14 72	90	2.2	1.7	-3.5	3.1	381	-72
16	111	-8	-13	15	28	19 106	103	5.9	4.2	-8.3	6.5	1,341	-162
24	175	-7	-35	9	57	16 100	110	14.9	10.5	-15.9	19.8	4,173	-67

National Institute Model

	£m (1970 prices)						(000s)	% change				£m	
Quarter	RPDI	C	I	S	X	M GDP	E	EARN	CED	ER	MS	GDP	CB
1	23	8	1	-15	-1	16 66	35	0.1	—	0.1	—	91	-9
2	34	15	3	2	-2	25 78	79	0.1	0.1	-0.1	—	112	-19
3	46	23	4	7	-4	28 86	113	0.2	0.1	-0.4	—	125	-27
4	55	30	6	4	-4	29 90	139	0.2	0.1	-0.8	—	131	-35
5	54	33	7	2	-2	30 91	156	0.3	0.2	-1.0	—	148	-40
6	68	40	9	—	-1	31 96	171	0.4	0.2	-1.3	—	161	-44
7	63	41	11	2	1	32 102	183	0.5	0.4	-1.4	—	188	-52
8	62	41	12	3	2	32 106	195	0.6	0.5	-1.6	—	210	-65
16	34	21	3	1	13	32 89	190	1.9	1.7	-3.4	—	601	-84
24	-38	-32	—	-6	14	21 47	116	3.3	2.7	-3.3	—	1,010	-63

For Key, Note and Source, see Table 4.1.

which are eventually far lower than in Simulation 2. This is by virtue of the higher interest rates and lower money stock growth, which prevent the exchange rate from depreciating enough to maintain competitiveness (domestic inflation being nevertheless faster than in Simulation 1). In addition, higher consumption sucks in imports. By the end of the simulation the current balance is considerably worse than in Simulation 2.

In the LBS simulations, interest rate changes crowd out a good deal of the extra expansion that occurred in Simulation 2, but the end result is not very different from what happens in Simulation 1; most of the fiscal stimulus survives the combination of floating rates and fixed money stock. The rise in the consol rate is rather modest (0.5 points after eight quarters and 1.1 points after twenty-four quarters), in accordance with a 'reaction function' that makes minimum lending rate in part dependent on the behaviour of the current balance. This depresses investment quite strongly but in itself eventually raises personal income through higher net interest receipts. Unlike the approach in the other two models, which took policy to keep M3 unchanged, money stock is allowed to rise freely in the LBS simulation to be consistent with the interest rate changes implied by the authorities' reactions to inflation and the balance of payments. The rise in M3 is eventually large – more, perversely, than in Simulation 1 – owing to the higher current price cost of the fiscal stimulus and therefore a higher PSBR. This in turn brings about an eventually larger exchange depreciation than in Simulation 2, and this produces an improvement in net exports that to some extent offsets lower investment and eventually weaker consumption (the latter deriving from lower employment compared with Simulation 2).

In summary, the Treasury model implies that maintenance of a fixed money stock in the face of a fiscal stimulus leads eventually to very considerable crowding out of the effects of the stimulus. This is primarily because higher UK interest rates relative to overseas rates prevent the emergence of enough exchange depreciation to enable the maintenance of competitiveness in the face of faster domestic inflation: the deterioration in the trade balance is large and more than offsets the effect of higher personal net interest receipts on consumption. Particular doubts must attach in this simulation to the size of the increase in long-term interest rates and its effects on the exchange rate. The NIESR model suggests that interest rate changes from an inflexible monetary policy are small and do not matter much. Particular doubts must arise here about the small size of the long-run GDP multiplier and the total absence of wealth effects on expenditure or the demand for money. The LBS model depicts significant depressing effects on investment from tighter monetary policy, but these are mitigated by the expansionary effects of larger private net interest receipts and, given the relaxed approach to monetary targets in the LBS simulation, by the role of the expanding money stock in precipitating more depreciation, and better competitiveness, than in the case where interest rates were fixed. The implication that money stock will grow faster when interest rates are allowed to vary than when they are held constant seems a somewhat perverse property of the model, and the difference in the approach to control of the money supply means that the LBS results in Simulation 3 are not closely comparable with those of the other two models.

Finally, it has to be borne in mind that none of the three models as they existed at the time of these simulations incorporated any wealth effects of *interest rate changes*, although the Treasury and LBS models did include some wealth arising from saving and from inflation.

5. CONCLUSIONS

It is evident that there is considerable disagreement as to the importance of crowding out in the results of the three models discussed above. The only conclusions that seem fairly firmly established are that crowding out does indeed not look to be a problem in a relatively fixed price, fixed rate world akin to that of the 1950s and 1960s; and that even in the case of the model that is most disposed to see crowding out as a problem when money growth is restrained, two-thirds of the initial stimulus survives for at least four years, admittedly in the company of more inflation and a worse balance of payments than would be expected by the optimistic Keynesian.[11] The evidence accordingly suggests that fiscal policy under a regime of 'practical monetarism' and flexible exchange rates has to work harder to achieve any given increase in activity, and the consequences for inflation and the balance of payments are probably more immediate and more serious. But if the essential role of fiscal policy is counter-cyclical in the old-fashioned sense, this need not matter too much. It obviously matters more if the economy is chronically depressed, as has appeared to be the case in the UK and overseas since about 1974, for then the pressure to stimulate activity becomes endemic and budget deficits are prone to persist and mount seemingly indefinitely (in nominal if not in real terms). This in itself is likely to create problems of confidence in financial markets, which may themselves have a considerable influence on the effectiveness of policy.

Crowding out clearly impinges more heavily if fiscal stimulus is introduced in isolation. The inflation that stems from exchange depreciation appears an important element in the story, and this would obviously be minimised if other countries were simultaneously stimulating their economies – providing the collective effort were not pressed to the point at which overheating emerged or commodity prices took off.

Two of the three models suggest that, in an environment of flexible exchange rates, crowding out would be substantially less if interest rates did not rise in the wake of a fiscal stimulus; there is therefore some evidence that the pursuit of a tight monetary policy in combination with expansionary fiscal policy does make a lot of difference to the resulting change in activity. In this sense at least, monetary policy does matter. It follows that adherence to tight monetary policy should not occur without good reason. There may indeed be good economic reasons for announcing and pursuing monetary targets, but as yet the grounds for selecting one target rather than another are very imperfectly understood – less perfectly perhaps than those for selecting one budgetary stance rather than another, although some would dispute this. At any event, there is a heavy responsibility on the government, the authorities and on the professional economists who influence them, both inside and outside the government service, to contrive that fiscal policy and monetary policy pull together, not in opposite directions. This can only come from having an integrated view of the economy, rather than seeing it as a collection of separate bits and pieces. And this probably requires the construction of econometric models that somehow incorporate all the important relationships, including all the relevant wealth effects (but only if they are *genuinely* important, which only careful research can hope to establish).

Crowding out has been discussed in this paper largely as though it were a problem peculiar to fiscal policy. A moment's reflection shows that this is a mistake. It is equally likely to arise (to the extent that it does at all) if non-adjusting money targets are followed in the face of a spontaneous revival of activity – stemming, say, from an upsurge in private investment or a recovery in overseas activity. The consequences for incomes and savings in the UK private non-investing sector would be broadly similar to those following from a fiscal stimulus of equal size; and although the monetary implications of a spontaneous private sector revival might differ from those of a fiscal stimulus in some respects, the interest rate changes required by pursuit of unchanged money targets would be deflationary in a broadly similar way. The crowding out that arises from interest rate effects is thus properly viewed as a feature of monetary policy. Fiscal policy is innocent in the matter; it simply provides the context in which crowding out happens most usually to be discussed.

NOTES AND REFERENCES

1. Not all economists would agree. Some believe that the present British recession is atypical in that the extent of spare capacity is actually quite small, or much smaller than mechanical calculations would suggest, for there has been a shrinkage in *effective* capacity resulting from the very low profitability of industry in recent years. (The low profitability is attributed to the inability or failure of companies to pass on the cost of much higher commodity prices to consumers, especially in the period 1973–75.) There is almost certainly some truth in these arguments, although the evidence from industrial surveys suggests that industrialists have for some time seen shortage of demand as by far the major factor limiting

output. At all events, the assumption here is that there is more than ample spare capacity in the economy at the present time and that resource crowding out is not a potentially significant problem.

2. It may of course be possible to influence expenditure while planning to keep the budget balance unchanged (through the balanced budget multiplier), but UK governments are rarely content with this.

3. This follows the approach of Blinder and Solow (1974) p. 4, who in turn cite Bent Hansen and Erik Lindahl. Such a definition is intended as no more than an approximation (see below).

4. If the composition of private sector demand for financial assets of different kinds changes when total wealth rises, fiscal policy entails the accommodation of such changes via open market operations.

5. In the present context, this refers to *nominal* rates of interest. That is to say, a change in price expectations following from changing tax rates or public expenditure is seen here as a consequence of fiscal policy.

6. A survey of the now extensive literature can be found in D. A. Currie (1978a) and chapter 3 by P. Burrows in this volume.

7. Some commentators have argued that, separately from the influence through the trade balance, pressure on the exchange rate will follow from a capital outflow reflecting the expansion of money supply that accompanies the fiscal stimulus. If so, this would appear to imply a degree of irrationality or misinformation on the part of international investors – assuming (as we do) that all the authorities have done is to accommodate the extra domestic demand for money – except to the extent that investors are merely anticipating the inflation that they expect to result from more circuitous processes.

8. An alternative way of putting this that may be more acceptable to those accustomed to the behaviour of orthodox consumption functions would be to say that when separate wealth effects are included the marginal propensity to consume income becomes very low in the short run, but it gradually rises to conventional levels in the longer run (after two years). The full effects of a fiscal stimulus on expenditure by this route therefore take a longer time to materialise when wealth effects are substantial.

9. Chapter 8 by Ormerod and Lewis in this volume uses later versions of the National Institute and Treasury models to revise simulations 1 and 2 reported here and extend the range of simulations to incorporate '*ex ante*' and '*ex post*' balanced budget changes.

10. Earnings in the Treasury and NIESR models are endogenised on the basis of 'expectations-augmented Phillips curves', by which nominal earnings eventually respond fairly fully to price expectations, proxied by a lagged distribution of actual prices, and negatively to unemployment, representing the pressure of demand in the labour market. Earnings in the LBS model are determined very differently – essentially by wholesale manufacturing prices, determined in turn by world prices and the exchange rate, and real national disposable income.

11. It is also worth bearing in mind that fiscal drag was an important depressing influence in all the simulations containing inflation. It would be instructive, and perhaps appropriate in an inflationary world, to have parallel simulations from which the element of fiscal drag attributable to inflation had been removed (by revalorising tax rates). This would seem to come nearer to the notion of a once-for-all fiscal policy change.

CHAPTER 5

Stabilisation Policy in an Open Economy

D. Currie

INTRODUCTION

A prominent feature of the international economy in the postwar period has been the general trend towards growing integration of trade, money-capital flows and production activities between the major advanced capitalist countries. While this is generally recognised to have added a major stimulus to the unprecedented expansion in the period of the long boom up to 1973, it is also acknowledged to have reduced the degree of control and scope for independent policy actions by all except one or two dominant national governments. The limited ability of governments to insulate their domestic economy from forces emanating from the world economy has been revealed with greatest clarity in the present world slump, although this tendency was well-established before. And whereas the abandonment of the adjustable peg exchange rate system in favour of floating rates was frequently advocated in the theoretical literature, on the grounds that such a regime would be superior in permitting governments to aim for domestic objectives relatively unconstrained by external considerations, in retrospect it seems that the shift was a forced one that did little to ease the international constraints on domestic policy-making.

Against this background, much current policy debate is concerned to determine the limits within which national policy objectives can be pursued and the best means of securing them. In examining this debate, it is convenient to classify types of policy problems in two separate ways. First, we may distinguish policy changes carried out in the context of concerted international policy-making from those made in isolation from policy changes elsewhere in the international economy. For harmonised policy-making among a sufficient number of major economies, the literature concerned with the closed economy is most applicable, although this abstracts from important questions concerning the appropriate distribution of policy initiatives and effects, and further problems due to the existence of multiple currencies. (These additional questions have generally received limited attention in the literature, despite their importance.) For isolated policy-making, the extensive literature dealing with the small open economy is directly applicable. Second, cutting across this division, we may distinguish policies aimed to shift the time path of the economy permanently (by, for example, raising the level of output and/or its rate of growth, or changing the rate of inflation) from policies aimed to stabilise the economy along some established time path (by designing policy to reduce, for example, the fluctuations in output and/or prices resulting from random shocks to the system).

These two classifications give four types of policy problem to be considered. Many of the interesting current issues of international economic affairs concern the appropriate design of harmonised policy, whether aimed at modifying the short- and longer-run underlying time path of the international economy, or at reducing short-run deviations from this underlying path. However, reasons of space preclude discussion of this set of problems here, and this paper will focus on policy-making in isolation from concerted policy action elsewhere. This case is, perhaps, most relevant for policy-making currently since, with limited prospects of effective international coordination, policy-makers are thrown back on those measures directly under their own control. We focus particularly on the case of floating exchange rates, which has greatest policy interest at the present time.

In the first part of this paper, we review the literature dealing with the effectiveness of monetary and fiscal policy under floating exchange rates. We argue that there are no reasons to suppose that monetary and fiscal policy, used appropriately in tandem, are ineffective in influencing the level of aggregate demand, though their use separately may be ineffective. Differences in policy prescription arise much more from differences over other aspects of the workings of the economy than from differences over the mechanics of monetary and fiscal policy. In the second section, we turn to discuss the appropriate design of automatic stabilisation policy to deal with random shocks arising from different sources in the economy.

MONETARY AND FISCAL POLICY UNDER FLOATING EXCHANGE RATES

The received view of the effectiveness of monetary and fiscal policy under floating exchange rates derives from the work of Fleming (1962) and Mundell (1968). With a low degree of capital mobility, the effectiveness of either policy in expanding output will be enhanced under floating exchange rates, though at the cost of greater inflationary pressures. For an expansion of aggregate demand, whether brought about by monetary or fiscal policy, separately or in combination, will lead to a worsened external trade account and a fall in the exchange rate.[1] By raising net exports, this depreciation will add to the expansionary effects of the initial stimulus. Or, to put it another way, whereas under a fixed exchange rate part of the initial stimulus is exported to the rest of the world via a worsened trade balance, under a floating exchange rate the stimulus is confined to the domestic economy, so that the effects on domestic demand and output are correspondingly greater. But since the fall in the exchange rate raises the price of imports, which may work through to higher domestic costs and wages, the impact on prices is greater under a floating system.

With increased capital mobility, the standard Fleming–Mundell results suggest that the expansionary effects of monetary policy are enhanced, while those of fiscal policy are reduced.[2] In the limiting case of perfect capital mobility, the expansionary effects of fiscal policy are entirely offset. This occurs because an increase in government expenditure tends to raise interest rates, inducing a potential capital inflow to stem this rise, causing an appreciation of the exchange rate. The resulting erosion of competitiveness leads to a fall in net exports, tending to offset the initial stimulus. With perfect capital mobility, interest rates cannot alter, and the appreciation proceeds to the point where the stimulus to demand is entirely offset by a reduction in net overseas demand. The increase in government expenditure entirely crowds out net exports, and the expansionary stimulus is exported to the rest of the world. At the same time, inflationary pressures are reduced by a reduction in import prices because of the rise in the exchange rate. By contrast, monetary policy tends to reduce interest rates, inducing a potential capital outflow. This generates a fall in the exchange rate, which tends to raise net exports and thereby enhances the expansionary effects of monetary policy, while at the same time adding to inflationary pressures. In the case of perfect capital mobility, the depreciation of the exchange rate is such as to ensure that the rise in demand just stems the downward pressure on interest rates.

Recent work has suggested that these results may be of rather limited applicability. Niehans (1975) suggests that trade flows are determined by long-run or 'permanent' exchange rates, so that the short-run effects of exchange rate changes on real domestic income will be limited or even perverse. Thus if the Marshall–Lerner condition is not satisfied in the short run, the exchange rate will depreciate to the point where expectations of a future appreciation induce a capital inflow sufficient to offset the worsened trade account. In this case, real domestic income will fall, and as a consequence real output and domestic employment are likely to decline. Even if the Marshall–Lerner condition does hold in the short run, regressive expectations concerning exchange rates will mean that the change in the exchange rate will be limited by speculative activity, as Dornbusch (1976) emphasises, again limiting the force of the Fleming–Mundell argument.

The argument is further complicated if allowance is made for the impact of exchange rate changes on inflationary expectations. A fiscal or monetary stimulus may be expected to raise inflationary expectations and therefore to generate expectations of depreciating exchange rate. In this case, the domestic currency would go to a forward discount, and with a given level of world interest rates, domestic interest rates would have to rise to maintain foreign exchange market equilibrium. The consequent rise in money velocity would permit an expansion of demand, enhanced by an initial fall in the exchange rate. In this case, the short-run expansionary effects of fiscal policy would be increased, not offset, by capital mobility, contrary to the standard argument.

An explicit analysis of wealth adjustments also casts doubt on the longer run validity of the Fleming–Mundell result. Katz (1977) and Kenen (1978) point to the fact that the short-run equilibrium need not be a long-run one, because of the effects of a current account imbalance on private sector wealth. Thus suppose that the short-run Marshall–Lerner condition is satisfied, so that with perfect capital mobility a monetary expansion leads to a fall in the exchange rate, generating a current account surplus and an expansion of domestic demand. The current account surplus implies an acquisition of wealth by the private sector (assuming a balanced government budget). This increase in wealth tends to place an upward pressure on interest rates, whether directly via a wealth effect in the money market or indirectly via increased aggregate demand in the goods market. The upward pressure on interest rates is stemmed by a potential capital inflow, generating a rise in the exchange rate and a fall in the current account surplus. In the absence of a wealth effect on money demand, and with interest rates fixed at the world level, money velocity does not change: thus the level of income does not change and wealth adjustments simply eliminate asymptotically the current account surplus. If, however, the wealth effect on money demand is significant, the increased wealth will lower money velocity, and so the adjustment towards a balanced external position will be accompanied and speeded by some fall in the level of income.[3]

The longer run analysis of fiscal policy depends very much on the nature of the fiscal stimulus in question. If, following the Fleming–Mundell argument, a balanced budget fiscal stimulus generates an initial current account deficit via an appreciation of the exchange rate, then a drain of private sector wealth will ensue via the external deficit. As wealth falls, the decline in the demand for money places a downward pressure on interest rates, which induces a potential capital outflow and a decline in the exchange rate, thereby raising income via an increase in net exports. In the long run, the level of private sector wealth will be lower, and income will be higher than initially, in such proportions as to maintain money market equilibrium. Private sector expenditure falls, but since income rises in the long run, this crowding-out is only partial. Since the current account must balance in the long run (so that wealth is not changing) despite the rise in income, the exchange rate must be lower in the long run than its initial position.[4]

Katz (1977) demonstrates that an implication of this is that it is quite possible for increased capital mobility under floating exchange rates to augment the long-run effectiveness of balanced budget fiscal changes, while it reduces that of monetary policy. This reversal of the Fleming–Mundell result depends on the existence of a significant wealth effect in the money demand function. Indeed, if there is no wealth effect on expenditures, but a positive one on money demand, monetary policy is entirely ineffective in the long run under perfect capital mobility. For then, given a fiscal policy and an interest rate set at the world level, there exists a unique exchange rate and level of income that gives equilibrium in the goods market with a balanced current account; the level of wealth then adjusts in the longer run to equate money demand to whatever level of the money supply is established by the monetary authorities. Conversely, balanced budget fiscal policy has enhanced effect for this special case. Thus the standard textbook results can be entirely reversed in the longer run.

However, this analysis of the longer run effects of fiscal policy is specific to balanced budget policy, and is not applicable to bond-financed fiscal deficits. Indeed, for this latter case, the short-run Fleming–Mundell result concerning the ineffectiveness of fiscal policy under perfect capital mobility carries through to the longer run. For since an increase in government expenditure leaves the level of income unchanged in the short run, the resulting budget deficit is equal to the full increase in government spending. Since the current account deteriorates by the same amount to offset the stimulus to demand, the short-run equilibrium is characterised by a position where the current account deficit is entirely matched by the budget deficit. Hence no ensuing private sector wealth adjustments occur, so that the short-run equilibrium persists. The government deficit is financed by the issue of bonds that are taken up by the overseas sector as the counterpart to the current account deficit. Presumably this cannot persist indefinitely, for sustained borrowing by the government can be expected to lead to a decline in international credit-worthiness (although this may depend on the nature of the government expenditures in question). The consequent rise in the differential between domestic and foreign interest rates will disturb private sector equilibrium. Whether adjustment towards a long-run equilibrium (which must be characterised by a balanced current account) will in fact occur is somewhat problematic, and it seems probable that the authorities will be forced to initiate some shift in fiscal policy to restore equilibrium.

So far, our analysis suggests a rather pessimistic conclusion concerning the effectiveness of monetary and fiscal policy for demand management purposes in an open economy under floating exchange rates. For we have argued that in both the short and the longer run, monetary policy may be less effective than the standard analysis suggests; while we have suggested that fiscal policy is only effective in the form of balanced budget fiscal changes, which most economists would regard as a relatively weak instrument (measured in terms of demand impact per pound of extra government outlay).

However, such a conclusion would be unwarranted, and stems from our way, in common with the literature, of discussing the effects of monetary and fiscal policy in isolation from one another. While this is of interest analytically, it is not helpful for policy design, since in practice, of course, the two policies are likely to be used jointly. It is relatively straightforward to show that, using monetary and fiscal policy in combination, effective demand management packages may be devised. Suppose, for example, that the authorities aim for a certain target level of demand, and suppose that fiscal policy is changed in such a way as to yield a balanced budget if this target level of income is attained.[5] Then there exists some stance of monetary policy that will yield the level of the exchange rate that ensures balance of payments equilibrium at the target level of demand. (Import tariffs or controls may, of course, be used instead of exchange rate changes to secure balance of payments equilibrium.) This yields the appropriate policy package. No wealth effects disturb this equilibrium, since both the balance of payments and the government budget are in balance.

Of course, policy design is not as simple as this argument suggests, since many additional problems intrude. There may, for example, exist real constraints on the extent of possible domestic expansion and effective devaluation (we consider these problems briefly in a moment); and lags in response and uncertainties concerning the structure of the economy make the correct policy mix hard to determine. But these are familiar problems in any policy context. The essential point to be noted in the context of our discussion of stabilisation policy is that sustained domestic expansion may be obtained by an appropriate combination of monetary and fiscal policy. This reinforces the traditional, and rather eclectic, view on policy-making that monetary and fiscal policy should work in tandem.

The emphasis placed on wealth adjustments and considerations of portfolio adjustment in recent theoretical analyses of the effectiveness of monetary and fiscal policy is also to be found in recent developments of macroeconometric forecasting models of the UK economy. All the large models now incorporate the financing aspects of government budgets and the financial implications of the balance of payments in a more or less complete form, thereby specifying the stock/flow relationships governing the supply side of financial markets. The London Business School model, the Treasury model and the National Institute model all include some form of liquidity or wealth effect on consumption, while implicit wealth effects on money demand are also common. The characteristic result of the Cambridge Economic Policy Group (CEPG) model, concerning the interrelationship between the budget deficit and the current account of the balance of payments, also results from an implicit, and relatively rapid, wealth adjustment mechanism for private sector behaviour.[6]

Indeed, it is not stretching things too far to suggest that there has been a considerable convergence in the modelling of these financial effects. Thus, for example, the analysis of the international monetarists, with their emphasis on the interrelationship between domestic credit expansion and the overall balance of payments, does not differ greatly in these matters, certainly in the medium to longer run, from that of the CEPG, with their concern for the fiscal deficit and the current account of the balance of payments. (All that is required to reconcile the two is the recognition that policy-induced changes in the capital account are not likely to be sustained so that the current account balance acts as a longer run constraint on policy. For a discussion of the similarities of the two schools, see R. Smith, 1976.) This argument for convergence may appear perplexing, for the rival forecasting groups appear to reach markedly differing policy prescriptions for the UK economy. However, these differences arise principally from the alternative specifications of the supply and balance of payments constraints on policy actions, and not from the modelling of monetary and fiscal effects. Thus the CEPG advocacy of import controls on competitive imports used in conjunction with expansionary fiscal policy is based on the view that the fundamental constraint on domestic expansion in the UK comes from the loss of world markets and consequent balance of payments difficulties, together with the view that the pricing behaviour of domestic manufacturers is little influenced by the prices of competitive imports. By contrast, the Treasury model incorporates a long-run vertical Phillips curve (through this is often overwritten in practical forecasting) so that the basic constraint is located on the supply side. On this view, monetary and fiscal policy is constrained by the need to avoid excessive domestic expansion. A similar, though not identical, mechanism is incorporated in the London Business School model: using what amounts to a purchasing power parity theory of exchange rates, expansionary policy is seen as inducing simply higher inflation via a depreciating exchange rate, with little real effect. These issues, and not the intricacies of the interrelationships between monetary and fiscal policy, lie at the heart of current policy debates.

However, convergence of view on these issues seems very distant. Consider, for example, differences of view on inflation. The views incorporated in the Treasury and London Business School models necessarily places considerable limits on the scope for domestic expansion. (Thus the only form of expansionary policy that makes sense in such a framework is to reduce unemployment from a level above the natural rate towards it: since such a movement is predicted to occur anyway, even in the absence of discretionary policy, the only purpose of such action is to speed up the process of adjustment.) The National Institute model incorporates a steep, but non-vertical, long-run Phillips curve, so that the standard Keynesian prescriptions stand (though the trade-off between inflation and unemployment is seen as being much less favourable in the long run). By contrast, the CEPG model bases itself on a bargaining view of the inflationary process; within such a context, domestic expansion eases the conflict over distributive shares, and thereby reduces inflationary pressure. On this view the fundamental constraint is external, situated in the erosion of the UK share of world markets, which therefore represents the fundamental inflationary force operating on the economy (though presumably operating at least partly through monetary mechanisms).

The evidence to discriminate between these theories is, perhaps inevitably, rather poor. The long-run vertical Phillips curve is largely imposed on the models, not estimated freely from the data, so that its claim as a basis for policy-making seems rather weak. (This seems to be acknowledged by policy-makers: see Laury, Lewis and Ormerod, 1978, and Posner, 1978.) And while the bargaining view of the inflationary process seems to work well up to 1975, the precipitate fall in real incomes since then seems to contradict this position. Whether this is indeed a shift structure, or rather the result of a draconian incomes policy that has been successful (in terms of driving down real wages) because of the socio-political climate created by inflation itself, seems likely to be an issue of debate for some time to come. The possibilities of these issues being satisfactorily resolved seems slight, yet as the author has argued elsewhere (Currie, 1978b), it is on these questions that debates over crowding out and the appropriate choice of monetary and fiscal policy centre. While our understanding of the effects of monetary and fiscal policy in an open economy has advanced significantly over the past decade, the policy debate remains as alive as ever.

THE DESIGN OF AUTOMATIC STABILISATION POLICY

So far we have considered the appropriate stance of instruments to achieve a desired underlying time path for the economy. We now turn to a different concern: the appropriate design of automatic policy responses to keep the economy as close as possible to this underlying time path.

It is sometimes argued, most prominently by M. Friedman (1953), that the authorities should not seek to engage in stabilisation policy, since given the lags in the system and possibly inadequate information such interventions are likely to add to, rather than reduce, economic fluctuations. This argument has some force for discretionary policy changes, although it seems unlikely that the problems of information and lags are so great as to leave no scope for reducing price and output fluctuations. However, it has no force when applied to automatic policy changes. Random fluctuations in the economy that result in unanticipated changes in realised tax revenues necessarily require some governmental response simply because of the government budget constraint. The government may respond by changing fiscal parameters (though the scope for this in the short run is slight) or money creation or bond issues, each of which responses has different effects. The one choice it does not have is to do nothing. Fluctuations in financial markets require the monetary authorities to respond, either by offsetting the effects on the money supply by suitable interventions, or by maintaining interest rates by intervention in the markets for public sector liabilities. Intervention of some form or other cannot be avoided. And while in foreign exchange markets the authorities can respond to shifts in supply and demand conditions by permitting changes in the exchange rate without intervention, it is not at all clear that such a response results in smaller fluctuations in the economy than a more interventionist policy of allowing some of the disturbance to be reflected in the foreign exchange holdings of the authorities.

The simplest analysis of this policy problem for the closed economy is provided by Poole (1970). In the face of shocks arising from the money demand function or (though Poole does not consider this case) from the money supply process, he argues that a policy of pegging interest rates will prevent these shocks feeding through to aggregate demand, output and employment. If the shocks are on the real side, by contrast, a policy of fixing the money supply will be superior, for then the disturbance to output will be reduced by an offsetting induced rise in interest rates. In the face of simultaneous shocks from both sources, a mixed policy, whereby the money supply is permitted to vary with the prevailing rate of interest, will be superior, but the appropriate choice of this policy requires accurate knowledge of both the slopes of the *IS* and *LM* curves and the relative variances and covariance of the shocks to the two curves.

This analysis may readily be generalised to the open economy, where a greater multiplicity of disturbances need to be considered. Thus we can consider shocks to aggregate demand, whether arising from internal or external sources; shocks to the money market, whether arising from money demand or the money supply process within the banking sector; shocks to aggregate supply; external shocks from capital flows, whether of an autonomous nature or arising from changes in overseas interest rates; and shocks arising from changes in the foreign price level. The policy options that we consider are: (1) to peg interest rates or fix some monetary aggregate in the short term; (2) to peg the exchange rate in the short term or to allow it to float freely.[7] It should be emphasised that the fixing of any particular instrument refers only to the short period, and is therefore compatible with large discretionary changes over the longer run. To emphasise this in what follows, we shall refer to the exchange rate options as being either a managed or a freely floating exchange rate. Thus the distinction is not between an exchange rate fixed for all time and an exchange rate able to change freely, but rather between whether the authorities allow the immediate effect of balance of payments disequilibrium to be on foreign exchange reserves or on the exchange rate, irrespective of the longer run time path of the exchange rate.

The time period for the analysis under consideration is usually taken to be relatively short. This is because the focus is the automatic policy response to unanticipated shocks: with the elapse of time, the authorities are able to respond by discretionary policy changes to continuing disturbances, and may tailor the policy to the particular type of disturbance in a way that is not possible in the very short term. (Parkin, 1978, provides another motivation, which is that with rational expectations the economy is self-stabilising: the only purchase that policy has is within the decision period of the private sector, when the automatic response of the authorities to unanticipated shocks may act to dampen or amplify their effects on output or prices. In this author's view, this greatly overstates the equilibrating nature of the macroeconomy, but the value of Parkin's analysis is in demonstrating the robustness of the results even under quite extreme assumptions concerning private sector behaviour and expectations.)

Two problems arise within a very short period of analysis. First, the dampening influences under consideration may be very limited in the short run, so that the differences between policies in terms of stabilisation may be very small. Second, certain policies may simply not be feasible. Thus Goodhart (1975) argues that very short-run control of the money supply may be impossible in the face of random shocks to the economy because of lags in the collection of data on the growth of monetary aggregates from the banking system. To the extent that this is valid, it is more appropriate to follow Parkin by taking the alternative to a policy of pegging interest rates to be maintaining constant the reserve base of the monetary system (or, if this includes privately supplied assets, that component of the reserve base supplied by the authorities). However, even this policy may be ruled out by Goodhart's second objection, that lags in the response of private sector portfolios to interest rates may induce wild fluctuations in interest rates if officially supplied reserve assets are maintained constant in the face of disturbances. The weight that one gives to this objection depends on one's faith in the lags estimated in money demand functions, but to the extent that this argument is valid, it inclines policy towards pegging interest rates, rather than a monetary aggregate, in the short run.

Despite these qualifications, the following analysis is useful in illustrating the appropriate type of policy response, whether automatic or discretionary, to different sources of disturbance to the economy. This is of particular importance in the context of current policy debates. The present inclination of policy towards monetary targets, for example, means that, to the extent that random disturbances impinge on the money market, their impact is on interest rates rather than on the money supply. The appropriateness of this depends very much on the nature of the disturbance under consideration, as we see in the following.

With these points in mind, we can now proceed with the analysis. Consider first the effect of shocks to aggregate demand whether arising from the foreign sector or domestically. In this case, following the analysis of Poole (1970), it is generally inferior in terms of stabilising both prices and output to fix the interest rate, for in this case the full multiplier effects on demand come through with no offset via a change in interest rates. If interest rates are pegged, the smaller disturbance to prices and output occurs if the exchange rate is pegged in the short run, so that part of the disturbance is exported and absorbed in changes in foreign exchange reserves. If a monetary aggregate, such as the money supply or reserve base, is fixed, a freely floating exchange rate will generally be superior. For then an increase in demand will tend to raise interest rates, inducing a potential capital inflow and an appreciation of the exchange rate, which will dampen the rise in demand.[8] If, however, the degree of capital mobility were low enough, then the rise in demand and consequent deterioration in the trade account could induce a fall in the exchange rate despite the rise in interest rates, thereby amplifying the disturbance to aggregate demand. In this case, pegging the exchange rate will prove superior. But it seems more relevant for current policy-making to assume a fairly high degree of capital mobility, so that the most appropriate policy is to fix the monetary aggregate and float the exchange rate. The ranking of policies, in descending order of optimality, is recorded in Table 5.1.

Disturbances originating in the monetary sector in the form of a shock to money demand are best dealt with by a policy of pegging interest rates, so that the shock results in an accommodating expansion of the money supply, which neutralises the output and price effects of the disturbance. Any disturbances in the money supply process are also neutralised by such a policy. If the inferior policy of fixing a monetary aggregate is adopted, it is better, in terms of stabilising output fluctuations, to manage the exchange rate, for an increase in money demand tends to lower aggregate demand and raise inter-

TABLE 5.1 *Ranking of alternative stabilisation policies*

Policy	1	2	3	4
Exchange rate:	Managed	Freely floating	Managed	Freely floating
Monetary target:	Interest rate	Interest rate	Monetary aggregate	Monetary aggregate
Source of disturbance:				
Aggregate demands	3	4	2	1
Monetary sector	1	1	3	4
Money-capital movements	1	4	1	3
Foreign price level	4	2	3	1
Aggregate supply:				
a low price elasticity	1	2/3	2/3	4
a high price elasticity	4	2/3	2/3	1

est rates, which under a freely floating regime with a fair degree of capital mobility will induce an appreciation of the exchange rate, amplifying the disturbance to output.[9]

If the disturbance arises from international capital markets, whether in the form of autonomous fluctuations or as a result of changes in foreign interest rates, the effects on output are, in principle, entirely offset if the exchange rate is managed, irrespective of the monetary policy followed. However, the feasibility of such a policy is in question with a high degree of capital mobility. While it may be possible to peg interest rates in the face of a random outflow of money-capital, with highly mobile capital it will be impossible for the authorities to withstand a change in foreign interest rates without enormous loss of foreign exchange reserves. Similarly, the ability of the authorities to fix a monetary aggregate, sterilising the effects of capital movements, will be slight. In these circumstances, there may be no choice but to float the exchange rate in the short run. In this case, it is better to fix a monetary aggregate, so that the disturbance can be partly offset by a rise in interest rates. Thus a capital outflow generates a fall in the exchange rate, raising prices and output. If a monetary aggregate is maintained constant, then the induced rise in interest rates tends to attract money-capital from overseas, helping to offset the initial disturbance. Thus the ordering of policies is as in the table, with the proviso that the top-ranked policies may not be feasible with too high a degree of capital mobility.

Disturbances arising from the foreign sector in the form of changes in the foreign price level are best dealt with by means of a freely floating exchange rate, so that the impact via the trade account on demand is partly offset. Greater dampening is also provided by a monetary policy defined with respect to a monetary aggregate rather than an interest rate, so that the induced change in interest rates provides further dampening.

The analysis is rather more complex if the disturbance is from the supply side domestically. In the first place, whereas for the disturbances considered up to now the twin objectives of reducing fluctuations in price and output are not in conflict, this is not so for supply shocks. For, if the authorities seek to stabilise output in the face of supply-side disturbances, sharp fluctuations in prices will result, while price stabilisation will be at the expense of marked output changes. We assume here that the authorities seek to stabilise output, leaving the reader to work through the case of price stabilisation, which simply results in a reversal of the ranking of alternative policies.

For this case, the choice between a free and managed float depends very much on the reduced form price elasticity of aggregate demand. If this elasticity is low, the effect of an increase in aggregate supply is to cause a large fall in prices and a small increase in output, thereby reducing the demand for money and placing a downward pressure on interest rates. This leads to a potential capital outflow and a fall in the exchange rate, stimulating output still further. If the demand schedule is elastic, however, the result is a large increase in output and a small fall in prices, increasing money demand and thereby tending to raise interest rates. With a sufficiently high degree of capital mobility, the result will be an appreciation of the exchange rate that tends to dampen the shock to output. Thus with a low price elasticity of aggregate demand, a managed exchange rate is preferable to a pure floating one, while the converse holds for a high elasticity. A policy of fixing a monetary aggregate tends to incline policy towards a pure floating exchange rate, since it adds to the price elasticity of aggregate demand by allowing interest rates to fluctuate (though a policy of managing the exchange rate can still be superior even with a policy of fixing a monetary aggregate). It would seem, therefore, that the choice is between a policy of operating on interest rates and managing the exchange rate and one of determining monetary aggregates and letting the exchange rate float freely. If output stability is the goal, the former is preferable if aggregate demand is price inelastic; while the converse applies if price stabilisation is the goal.

From our analysis, it is clear that the optimum choice of stabilisation policy depends very much on the empirical question of what the source of the disturbance is, or is expected to be. It is not surprising, therefore, that widely differing types of policies are advocated. For it is a very difficult exercise to determine empirically the relative importance of alternative shocks, say over the past ten years.[10] If this disagreement occurs over past developments, much wider disagreement must be expected over the likely relative strength of shocks in the future, on which optimal policy design depends. Nonetheless, our analysis does clarify the issues on which policy disagreements are likely to hinge. The table shows that no single policy design dominates the others, so that the choice of policy must be based on an implicit or explicit view of the significance of different types of shock.

So far our analysis has been confined to the short run, and has, therefore, been able to neglect the concern of the first section of this paper, namely the effects of changes in asset stocks, whether arising from the budget deficit (via changes in the level of demand and hence tax revenues) or from the balance of payments.[11] It may be argued that this neglect is valid, since our concern is with the appropriate design of short-run policy, not with longer run effects. However, this is not correct, for a consistently implemented short-run policy may have longer run effects that are not at all evident from an analysis of the short run. Thus, for example, asset flows resulting from random disturbances to the budget deficit or the balance of payments may build progressively more fluctuations into the system as time proceeds, resulting in asymptotic destabilisation.[12] In the longer run, therefore, it is important to select short-run policies, the asymptotic properties of which are such that asset flows tend to dampen, rather than amplify, shocks to the system. What is not yet clear at this stage is whether monetary targets (which, given relatively inflexible fiscal parameters in the short run, put the burden of residual financing on bonds issues) are, in fact, dampening in this sense. The answer to this question is clearly vital for current policy formulation in the UK. The long-run properties of short-run stabilisation policies should, therefore, assume much greater importance in the formulation of policy than perhaps they do at the present time.

Unfortunately, for any realistically specified model the resulting dynamics are probably too complex to permit analytical solution, and this would appear to explain the lack of analysis of this type for the problems that we have been discussing. There would, therefore, appear to be scope for simulation studies of small empirically estimated models to focus on these types of questions. In the absence of such studies, it is fair to say that our understanding of the appropriate design of short-run policy is still rather limited.

CONCLUSIONS

In the first section of this paper, we reviewed the literature dealing with wealth and portfolio adjustments resulting from monetary and fiscal policy. We argued that there is no reason to suppose that monetary and fiscal policy, suitably designed, is ineffective, whether in the short or longer run, in influencing the level of aggregate demand. The severe constraints on policy-making, which we noted in the Introduction, occur elsewhere, and it is from differences in the analysis of wage and price behaviour and of the forces operating on the balance of payments that the markedly different policy prescriptions of the rival schools arise. In the second section, we looked at the question of stabilisation policy along a given time path, and concluded that the appropriate design of policy centres on the issue of what is the source of the major shocks operating on the economy, on which disagreement seems equally great. The growing convergence that we have noted in the analysis of the monetary and fiscal interactions in an open economy therefore seems unlikely to reduce the wide disparity of viewpoint on the appropriate design of stabilisation policy in an open economy.

NOTES AND REFERENCES

1. We must assume that the Marshall–Lerner (or more generally the Bickerdike–Robinson) conditions are satisfied, so that a depreciation of the exchange rate improves the current account. Otherwise, in the absence of significant capital movements, the foreign exchange market will be unstable.
2. Throughout this paper, we define monetary policy to be changes in the money supply, while fiscal policy is taken to be changes in fiscal parameters financed in such a way as to leave the money supply unchanged. The characteristics of such policies may, of course, be dependent on the choice of definition of the money supply.
3. Wealth effects on money demand are likely to be of greater importance the wider the definition of the money supply adopted. See Currie (1978b).
4. The argument of this paragraph, as elsewhere in the paper, assumes that the import content of government expenditure is the same as that of private sector expenditures. For a discussion of other cases, see Currie (1978b).
5. This assumes a static, non-inflationary economy. In practice, the government budget must be unbalanced to the extent required to meet the flow demand for government liabilities resulting from growth and inflation.
6. For very helpful comparisons of the existing models, see Laury, Lewis and Ormerod (1978) and Posner (1978).
7. The following analysis is based heavily on that provided by Parkin (1978), to which the interested reader is referred.
8. This is simply the Fleming–Mundell result, noted in section 1, in a different form.
9. Again this is simply the Fleming–Mundell result that monetary policy or monetary disturbances are highly effective under a floating exchange rate regime.
10. It should be noted that the covariances between shocks are just as relevant as the variances, though this has not been discussed here. See, for example, Poole (1970).
11. If the period of analysis is long enough, this neglect may not be appropriate, but it seems unlikely that an explicit consideration would overthrow our conclusions.
12. See, for example, Currie (1976). With optimal policy, instrument instability, rather than price or output instability, is the outcome. However, if we assume, rather more realistically, sub-optimal policy-making, progressive destabilisation of prices and output will result. With rational expectations, no cumulative destabilisation of output will result, since the financing effects will be anticipated by the private sector; instead instability will manifest itself in the price level.

CHAPTER 6

Endogenous Government Behaviour: Wagner's Law or Götterdämmerung?

A. Chrystal and J. Alt

INTRODUCTION

No economist working in the employment of government needs to be told that it has long been the concern of governments to understand and influence the workings of the economy. Rather more recent are the attempts systematically to analyse the economic behaviour of governments. The empirical work reported in the second half of this paper is a first shot at what we hope will be a contribution to the latter line of analysis. But first, by way of background, it is useful to review some of the implications for macroeconomics of the fact that government economic policy is systematically related to the state of the economy. The public sector is, on the whole, an endogenous sector.

We have become involved in this area because we were dissatisfied with attempts both to test for political influences on economic policy and to estimate government reaction functions *per se*. It has become clear to us that equations that treat the policy instrument as the dependent variable and the state of the economy as the independent variable cannot be estimated, as is almost universal in the existing literature (e.g., Pissarides, 1972; Frey and Schneider, 1978), by single equation techniques. Similarly, it would be dangerous to assume, as has typically been the case, that, in the context of macroeconomic models, policy instruments can be regarded as exogenous when in fact they change in a systematic way in response to changes in the state of the economy.

Many economists will not be surprised at the assertion that the government is endogenous. Indeed, there are many specific examples of analyses that incorporate reaction functions in specific contexts (see, for example, Hutton, 1976; Sheen and Sassanpour, 1976). However, it is clear that the full implications of even endogenous stabilisation policies have not been taken on board by the bulk of the economics profession. The implications are quite far-reaching and may well underlie some of the important controversies arising from estimates of policy effects. There has to our knowledge been only one major rigorous attempt to analyse the implications of endogenous policy. This is the study by Stephen Goldfeld and Alan Blinder (1972). They are concerned only with endogenous stabilisation policy and especially with the context of the US economy. Section 1, therefore, contains a review of Goldfeld and Blinder (G and B), section 2 presents some evidence on the nature of the underlying government expenditure function for the UK economy, and section 3 presents some international comparisons from a cross-section of different countries.

1. GOLDFELD AND BLINDER ON ENDOGENOUS STABILIZATION POLICY

The approach adopted by G and B is to ascertain the likely extent of bias involved in the estimation of the multiplier effects of instruments upon targets. It is presumed that the true structural model is known and the question is what the effects are of estimating multipliers under the mistaken assumption that policy instruments are exogenous. Their broad conclusions depend crucially upon the purpose for which the estimates are required and upon the institutional framework within which stabilisation policy is conducted. First, for a *genuinely unified* stabilisation authority (i.e., all instruments – fiscal and monetary – are perfectly harmonised to achieve the optimum policy) there need be no cause for concern so long as it builds structural models and deduces multipliers from these. However, even the unified authority could get a very distorted picture if it were to compute multipliers directly from reduced forms. Second, if stabilisation involves some division of responsibility, say between fiscal and monetary policies or taxation and expenditure, then it is vital for each policy division to anticipate the reactions of the other. Failure to do this may lead each division seriously to overestimate the potency of its own instrument. This argument would, of course, also apply to, say, the fiscal authority if it were to omit, say, the monetary sector from its model. It would be failing to anticipate an endogenous feedback.

The final general conclusion is of importance for the outside economist, particularly if he wishes to study the effects of macroeconomic policy in the past. He is likely to arrive at dangerously erroneous conclusions about the effects of stabilisation policies if he estimates models on the assumption that the policy instruments were exogenous variables. Reduced form estimation is particularly dangerous when endogenous policy is ignored. The only correct way to proceed is to specify the structural equations of the model, appending to these the likely reaction functions of the policy-makers, and then estimate by simultaneous equation techniques. Thus it is clear that no researcher in macroeconomics can ignore the problem posed by the existence of systematic policy responses without taking the risk that his estimates may be entirely erroneous.

The G and B paper is extremely long and disorganised in parts, but their analytical results lead to a number of simple propositions. We shall proceed by stating the gist of their propositions in a somewhat different form. Some attempt will then be made to offer an interpretation of their results.

Proposition 1: In the case of a unified stabilisation authority the existence of estimation bias depends upon the feedback rule adopted. There do exist a number of feedback rules that would validate reduced form estimation of multipliers.

Proposition 2: If stabilisation policy is dichotomised and the authorities are imperfectly offsetting a stochastic disturbance, reduced form estimates of both policy multipliers are likely to be biased toward zero, with the larger bias being associated with the more efficient stabiliser.

Proposition 3: Should an authority overestimate its multiplier or react too weakly to random fluctuations, this will result in a larger bias than would 'correct' reactions. Conversely, underestimating the multiplier or reacting too vigorously to random shocks will reduce the bias.

Proposition 4: If the monetary authority predicts fiscal policy and changes its behaviour as a result, then (a) the bias in estimating the money multiplier shrinks but it grows again as the monetary authorities' forecasts of fiscal policy become more accurate, and (b) the bias in estimating the fiscal multiplier becomes more negative than previously.

Proposition 5: If both authorities are imperfectly offsetting both a stochastic error and an exogenous variable, then reduced form estimates of all coefficients are likely to be biased toward zero. The multiplier associated with the more astute forecaster will have the larger bias.

In order to understand the problem introduced by endogenous stabilisation policy, consider the reduced form of a simple national income determination model

$$Y = a + bX + cP + e \tag{1}$$

where Y is national income, X represents the set of truly exogenous variables and P represents the set of policy instruments. A necessary condition for unbiased estimation of (1) is that $E(Xe) = E(Pe) = 0$. This is what the assumption of exogeneity really amounts to. However, if P responds in a systematic way to Y, this assumption will be violated. The proof is identical to the demonstration that bias exists if an equation of a simultaneous system is estimated by ordinary least squares. Since the disturbance, e, affects Y and Y affects P, e and P cannot be statistically independent, as a general rule.

There are a number of policy rules that, if adopted, would permit unbiased reduced form estimation. These rely on a policy feedback rule being adopted that ignores the effects of the random disturbance. One such rule would be the Theil certainty equivalence principle. According to this rule, policy-makers should assume that X takes on its statistical expected value and that e takes on a value of zero. The policy solution would be

$$P = \frac{Y^* - bE(X) - a}{c} \tag{2}$$

where Y^* is the target value of Y. Reduced form estimation of (1) would be unbiased because P is, in effect, endowed with the properties of the in-strumental variable required for estimating the second stage of two-stage least squares. In general, of course, it would be most surprising if the forma-tion of stabilisation policy were so sophisticated that random disturbances could be filtered out. So it would be safer to assume that the problem exists rather than that it does not.

The structure of the problem becomes slightly more complex if some partition of the policy instruments is introduced

$$Y = a + bX + c_1 P_1 + c_2 P_2 + e. \tag{3}$$

P_1 may be thought of as fiscal policy with its associated multiplier c_1, and P_2 could be monetary policy with a multiplier c_2. It is quite likely here that the relationships between P_1, P_2 and e will differ considerably. Fiscal policy typically changes rarely, whereas monetary policy adjusts almost contin-uously. But, in addition, fiscal and monetary authorities have to make some presumption about the other's behaviour. In other words, in order to react optimally each needs to anticipate the reactions of the other. It is from an examination of the range of possibilities open within this framework that propositions 2–5 emerge.

One useful insight that G and B stress as emerging from their analysis is a simple interpretation of the famous results obtained by Anderson and Jordan. The latter estimated a reduced form very similar to (3) except that X was excluded and lags were permitted. It appeared that the results were consistent with the existence of a significant monetary policy multiplier but the fiscal multiplier ended up negligible. G and B offer a number of reasons why the fiscal policy multiplier may be more biased than the money multi-plier. The ones they favour are simply that the fiscal authority could be a more cautious stabiliser or the monetary authority may try to forecast and react to fiscal policy while the fiscal authority does not do likewise for monetary policy. Proposition 2 offers another simple explanation, which is that the fiscal authority is the better stabiliser.

A simple example should help to provide an intuitive feel for why it is that these results emerge. Consider a world in which investment is the only exogenous expenditure and government expenditure is the fiscal instrument. Assume for simplicity that the multiplier is the same for investment and government expenditure, and that fluctuations in income are caused solely by fluctuations in investment. Ignoring lags, in the absence of policy responses, the path of income will be linearly related to the path of investment (see Figure 6.1a). An optimal fiscal stabilisation policy would be such that

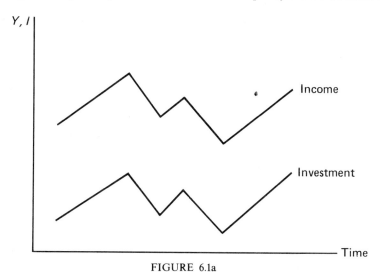

FIGURE 6.1a

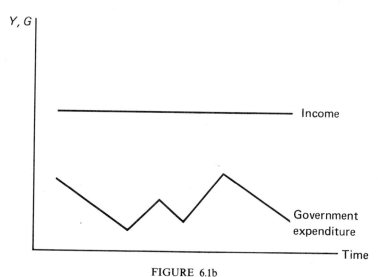

FIGURE 6.1b

government expenditure mirrored investment (see Figure 6.1b). Income would thereby become perfectly stable. A regression of income on government expenditure would undoubtedly reject the existence of a significant fiscal policy multiplier despite the fact that there is certainly a significant coefficient. Indeed, fiscal policy has worked perfectly but reduced form methods would discover it to be ineffectual. Furthermore, if fiscal policy is too weak so that income still has its original direction of change, though damped, the fiscal multiplier may even come out negative. A rise in income will appear to be associated with a fall in government expenditure and vice versa. Only if the fiscal authority over-reacts will income and government expenditure move together.

The final contribution of G and B is to illustrate the implications of endogenous reactions by reference to a Monte Carlo study of a hypothetical economy. They discover that, in their example, the simultaneity problem *per se* is not very serious, so long as structural estimation methods are pursued. However, reduced form estimation as expected produces a grossly distorted picture. Their general conclusion is that '. . . the severity of the various problems posed by reaction functions is strongly dependent on the character of the functions employed. It is thus extremely important to get at least a crude handle on both the qualitative and quantitative nature of the reaction functions that have characterized US policy making.' It is to this issue that we now turn.

2. THE GOVERNMENT EXPENDITURE FUNCTION

Elsewhere we have reviewed what we regard to be the principal contributions to the UK literature on reaction functions (Alt and Chrystal, 1977), though we have concentrated mainly on work looking for political motivation. The literature suffers to a large degree from the methodological problems highlighted above, i.e., single equation methods applied to 'quasi-reduced form' equations. It should by now be clear that the only safe way to proceed is to specify a more or less complete macroeconomic model within which the behavioural equations of the public sector can be explicitly set out. Identification issues can easily be handled and exogenous elements of government behaviour can be separated from endogenous ones. As a first step in this task, the remainder of this paper examines the nature of one particular public sector behavioural relation – the government expenditure function.

Most previous approaches have used the assumption either that government expenditure is exogenous to the economy or, the reverse, that policy instruments respond to an exogenous economy. Of greater importance than the methodological point that both assumptions are incorrect is the empirical observation that both approaches convey an entirely misleading picture of what government economic behaviour, and especially government expenditure, is actually like. The reason for this is that excessive attention is paid to the stabilisation function of government and none at all to its dominant continuing role as provider of public goods and services. The primary explanation for changes in government expenditure has nothing to do with stabilisation policy (or election cycles) but is rather a growing demand for the services that governments provide.

The existence of a government expenditure function is not a novel suggestion. In fact, it is probably the second earliest documented relationship in economics, second only to the quantity theory of money. Indeed, through the writings of Adolf Wagner, the relationship came to have the status of a law – known, of course, as Wagner's Law. This was stated by Wagner, himself, as the law of increasing expansion of public, and particularly state activities'. He justifies the relationship in the following manner:

> That law is the result of empirical observation in progressive countries, at least in our Western European civilisation; its explanation, justification and cause is the pressure for social progress and the resulting changes in the relative spheres of private and public economy, especially compulsory public economy. [Musgrave and Peacock, 1967, p. 8]

Wagner's Law has been widely interpreted as predicting a growing *share* of government expenditure in national income. There may well be some such statement in Wagner's work but it is not at all clear that he would have continued to endorse that view. Indeed, he prefaces his statement of the law with the following:

> There is thus a proportion between public expenditure and national income which may not be permanently overstepped. This only confirms the rule that there must be some sort of balance in the individual's outlays for the satisfaction of his various needs. For in the last resort, the State's fiscal requirements covered by taxation figure as expenditure in the household budget of the private citizen. [Ibid., p. 8]

The sense of this statement is clearly that, at least when some level has been reached, government expenditure will grow in proportion to national income. This can be thought of in terms of elasticities that express the proportional change in one variable with respect to a proportional change in another. Thus if G was always a fixed proportion of Y the elasticity of G with respect to Y would be 1. Wagner's Law has been taken to mean that in fact the elasticity of government expenditure with respect to national income exceeds 1, though Wagner himself would seem to be saying that it is close to 1. There is, of course, no reason *a priori* why any particular number should be true. It is not hard to believe that certain publicly supplied goods, such as education and health, could be 'luxury goods', so that demand increases more than in proportion to income. However, the issue has taken on a different complexion in recent years as a result of a prolonged campaign in certain quarters against the alleged increase in state activity (see, for example, M. Friedman, 1962). The best contribution we can make to this latter debate is to present the evidence. It is to this that we now turn.

There already exists one major study of the growth of public expenditure in the UK, that by Peacock and Wiseman (1961). They reject Wagner's law, as interpreted, and suggested that the true picture was dominated by a 'ratchet effect'. Government expenditure would run broadly in line with national income between wars but after a war it would never fall back to its prewar level. Nonetheless, a student of theirs working on the same data did estimate income elasticities both for the whole sample and for interwar periods (Gupta, 1967). He found that the vast majority of such estimates exceeded unity, both for the UK and other countries. We wish to argue that there is good reason to question the existence both of a ratchet effect and of an income elasticity in excess of unity. Rather, we shall demonstrate that there is more truth in Wagner's above statement than has previously been recognised. There are, however, a number of preliminary comments to be made.

The first point is that previous studies have looked at public expenditure *including transfers*. We propose to deal with transfers in a separate paper, since we expect their explanation to be very different from the growth of *real* government output. Many authors have made the mistake of talking in terms of the share of government expenditure in national income while measuring G to include transfers. The nonsense of this is clear when it is realised that the maximum of such an expenditure/income ratio exceeds 100 per cent. Imagine, for example, an economy where all output is produced by civil servants. Any redistribution in this system would make G so defined exceed Y. Most importantly, since Y excludes transfers it makes no sense to include them in G.

The second point is that Peacock and Wiseman only looked at data up to 1955. We have the benefit of observations over an extra two decades. The importance of this is quite considerable, because it is clear that times of war must be treated separately. We are interested in modelling peacetime behaviour. However, before 1955 there are less than twenty years this century that could not be considered biased by war, its anticipation or its aftermath. This is because allowance has to be made not only for the two world wars but also the second Boer War of 1901–2 and the Korean War of 1950–52. The expansion of expenditure after 1935 is almost entirely for defence in anticipation of war (see Figure 6.2). Thus the 'normal' times we have to work on are limited to the periods 1907–13, 1922–34 and 1955–76, with the latter being by far the longest continuous period. Nonetheless, we do present some results for the century to date, excluding only the periods most severely affected by world wars, as well as results since 1955.

A final preliminary concerns estimation techniques. First, all the estimates of government expenditure functions we have seen use ordinary least squares regression techniques. Since Y is known to be an endogenous variable, i.e., Y is affected by G as well as vice versa, this introduces a certain bias into the estimated coefficients. Secondly, it is clear that positive first-order autocorrelation is present in the regression residuals. This invalidates the t-ratio as a test of significance for the regression coefficients. We bypass these problems by using two-stage least squares (2SLS) methods and correcting for autocorrelation by the Cochrane–Orcutt iterative technique. The 2SLS estimates are achieved by adding exports and investment as exogenous expenditures to generate an instrument for national income. The results are presented in Table 6.1.

The first three equations are fitted for the period 1900–76 excluding only 1914–20 and 1939–47. The second three equations are for the period 1955–76 only. Looking first at the long period, it is clear that despite the distortions of war, the overall fit is remarkably good. This is true for both the simple linear form and the log linear version. The income coefficient in the log linear version is an estimate of the elasticity and this is significantly *less than*

TABLE 6.1   *Estimates of government expenditure*

	Dependent variable	Constant	Income (Y)	Logged income $(\log(Y))$	Expenditure $t-1$ (G)	$\bar{R}^2$	ρ
			Period: 1900–76, excluding major wars				
(1)	G	3884	.11			.993	.98
		(2.0)	(3.4)				
(2)	$\log(G)$	3.5		.53		.991	.98
		(1.4)		(2.3)			
(3)	G		.009		.97	.998	.56
			(.8)		(15.1)		
			Period: 1955–76				
(4)	G	453	.17			.974	.76
		(.6)	(7.8)				
(5)	$\log(G)$	−.61		.90		.977	.73
		(.6)		(8.8)			
(6)	G		.04	.79		.9997	.32
			(1.7)	(6.1)			

Note: G = government expenditure on goods and services; Y = GDP at factor cost; ρ is the Cochrane–Orcutt first-order autocorrelation coefficient. Estimation is by two-stage least squares, adding exports and investment to generate an instrument for Y. All data are in constant prices. Bracketed numbers are t-statistics.

Source: for annual data 1900–76, excluding 1914–20 and 1939–47 *Key Statistics 1900–1970* (London and Cambridge Economic Service) plus recent issues of *Economic Trends*.

unity. However, the dominant feature of the first two equations is the high value of the autocorrelation coefficient, ρ. The addition of G lagged one period in equation (3) confirms that the dominant feature of the time series of government expenditure is its autoregressive nature. The growth of government expenditure is in fact remarkably stable. G this period is almost entirely explained as a linear function of G last period. The interpretation of this is quite clear if one looks at the interwar period in Figure 6.2. National income fluctuates quite dramatically but G carries on along a smooth growth path. Similarly through the boom of 1973 and the depression of 1974–76 government expenditure carries on the growth along a fairly stable trend. The only dramatic change in G, in normal times, comes with an excessive expansion in 1967 followed by a cut back in 1968–69.

The most remarkable feature of Figure 6.2 is that the trend in expenditure from 1958 to 1976 is an exact extrapolation of that established in 1907–13. Moreover, interwar developments are parallel to *but below* this long-term 'normal' trend, just as income is below its trend in the interwar period. This evidence suggests strongly what might be called a 'permanent income' hypothesis of government expenditure.

Governments plan expenditure to grow in proportion to expected national income. These plans are sticky and are only revised when it is clear that trend income has changed. There will, however, be random deviations of G from plan, and of Y from its expected level, but these deviations will be uncorrelated. This formulation is exactly that invented by Friedman (1957) to explain the relation between aggregate consumption and disposable income. The expected or permanent level of income is generated by a distributed lag on past levels with exponentially declining weights. This is simplified by means of the Koyck transformation, which, in effect, substitutes a lagged dependent variable for all but the current value of income. Thus equation (6), applied to the post-1955 data, is a direct test of this hypothesis (as indeed is equation (3) but for periods including abnormal data). The fit is probably better than when applied to personal consumption. The coefficient on income is not strongly determined but we would expect it to improve with a longer run of 'normal' data. We shall ourselves retest with quarterly data.

The interpretation of the coefficients in equation (6) is simple. A £100m increase in GDP in the current year would increase G in the current year by £4m, and ultimately by £18m *if sustained*. It is reassuring that this long-run propensity implicit in equation (6) is almost exactly equal to the linear coefficient in equation (4). And also it should be noted that the elasticity estimated in equation (5) is not significantly different from unity.

The conclusions that we draw from this evidence, limited though the data may be, are quite simple. There is neither reason to accept the existence of a ratchet effect nor reason to believe that the elasticity of government expendi-

Government
and GDP
(log scale)

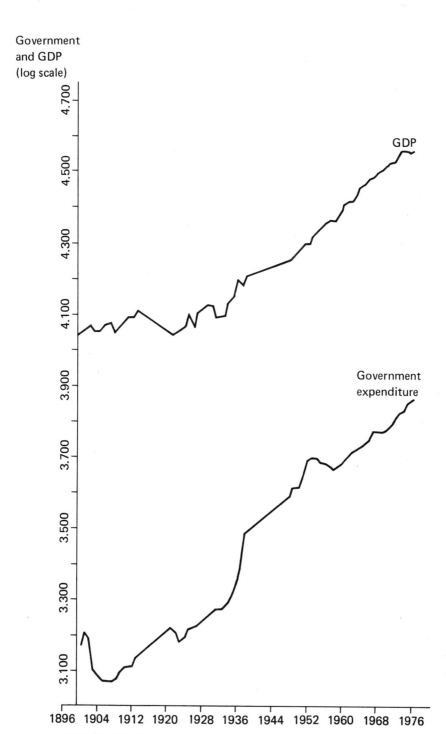

FIGURE 6.2   *Government expenditure and national income 1900–1976.*

ture with respect to national income exceeds unity. Indeed, we are impressed by the strength of the evidence in favour of Adolf Wagner's original contention that 'there is a proportion between public expenditure and national income'. In the UK that proportion is something approaching 20 per cent.

It is hard to avoid a brief comment on the recent UK experience in the light of the above evidence. There has been great concern expressed in some quarters about the excessive growth in public expenditure since 1973. It is true that the ratio of G to Y has risen in recent years. However, it is quite clear that the reason for this is not a major upward deviation of G from its trend. Rather, the explanation is to be found in the downward deviation of Y from trend. Our permanent income formulation would forecast exactly such a pattern in the event of temporary depression. The evidence from the interwar period is ample testament to that.

3. International Comparisons

We can confirm some of the conclusions of the previous sections with reference to cross-sectional data from a variety of countries. These cross-sectional estimates of the relationship between government expenditure and national income will give us a sense of how Britain stands relative to the rest of the world. Furthermore, we can use this approach to illuminate from another perspective the question of the income elasticity of government expenditure. Data from forty-nine countries are involved:[1] figures (in current dollars) were obtained for government consumption (i.e., expenditure) and gross domestic product. Expenditure was regressed on income, with the intercept constrained to zero (so that there should be no expenditure where there was no income),

$$G = bY + e$$

and the logarithm of expenditure was regressed on the logarithm of income

$$\log G = \log a + b \log Y + e$$

which is a test of the alternative form

$$G = aY^b + e.$$

The latter equation can be interpreted as test for the adequacy of the assumption of linearity in the first equation, with the assumption satisfied if b is not significantly different from unity. More importantly, b in the latter equation is an estimate of the income elasticity of expenditure. The results are shown in Table 6.2, with each of two equations estimated for both 1955 and 1974, and in each case over a variety of subsets of nations.

TABLE 6.2. *Cross-section estimates 1955 and 1974*

| | | $G = bY$ | | | | $\log G = \log a + b \log Y$ | | | | | |
| | | 1955 | | 1974 | | 1955 | | | 1974 | | |
	Countries (*n*)	Coef.	R^2	Coef.	R^2	*a*	*b*	R^2	*a*	*b*	R^2
(1a)	All (50)	.186	.99	.200	.97	−.99	1.051	.97	−.932	1.047	.97
		(96.6)		(38.6)		(43.6)	(39.6)		(25.2)	(39.9)	
(1b)	All bar USA (49)	.138	.97	.147	.91	−.990	1.037	.96	−.926	1.038	.97
		(39.2)		(22.4)		(43.4)	(35.6)		(24.4)	(37.0)	
(2a)	Industrial (24)	.186	.99	.201	.97	−.972	1.051	.99	−.834	1.023	.97
		(69.7)		(27.1)		(27.3)	(41.2)		(11.3)	(24.9)	
(2b)	Industrial bar	.139	.98	.148	.92	−.940	1.030	.98	−.810	1.008	.96
	USA (23)	(29.5)		(15.4)		(32.7)	(35.0)		(10.3)	(21.8)	
(3)	Non-industrial	.109	.82	.096	.99	−1.023	.958	.93	−.910	.932	.96
		(10.6)		(49.6)		(32.9)	(17.3)		(25.0)	(23.2)	
(4)	12 industrial	.186	.99	.210	.99	−.958	1.073	.99	−.760	1.007	.98
		(53.9)		(34.9)		(26.0)	(40.3)		(7.1)	(20.0)	

The results can be interpreted readily as follows. The fitted average share of GDP in government expenditure (equation (1a)) is 20.0 per cent in 1974, up from 18.6 per cent in 1955. The elasticity is 1.047, not significantly greater than unity, and apparently unchanged since 1955. However, these results are heavily distorted by the inclusion of the United States, with much larger values of G and Y than any other country. When the USA is excluded (equation (1b)), the average shares drop to 14.7 per cent in 1974 and 13.8 per cent in 1955. The elasticities remain insignificantly different from unity. An interesting effect is uncovered by splitting the sample roughly in halves between 'industrial' and other countries. The best-fitting equations for industrial countries are essentially the same (see equations (2a) and (2b)) as those just discussed, with the results again varying according to whether the USA is included. Non-industrial countries, however, clearly spend smaller proportions of GDP (9.6 per cent in 1974 down from 10.9 per cent in 1955) and the elasticity of expenditure, while perhaps not less than unity, is very clearly not greater than unity (equation (3)). This suggests that any evidence in equations (1) and (2) that the elasticity of expenditure is greater than unity probably derives from the difference between these two disparate groups of countries. It could also suggest that industrialisation involves a once-for-all upward shift in government consumption, but the elasticities in rows (2b) and (3) make it clear that, within groups, there is no evidence at all that expenditure grows disproportionately with income.

Not only do industrial countries spend relatively more, but they maintain their relative positions more consistently than do the non-industrial countries. Thus, the correlation between the two sets of residuals for the unlogged equation (3) in 1955 and 1974 is .190; for the two corresponding sets of residuals in equation (2b) it is .540. While some might find surprising amounts of change in a correlation as low as .54, it nevertheless implies that industrial countries are far more likely than non-industrial countries to maintain their positions as relatively big or small spenders.

In view of the fact that there is some change among countries with respect to the extent of their spending out of GDP, it is natural to inquire whether systematic variations can be found. Elasticities close to unity suggest that income, while clearly a determinant of government expenditure, will not explain expenditure as a proportion of income. Ideology presents a further possible source of variation. Hibbs (1976) has suggested that twelve countries show a sort of cross-national 'Phillips curve' with respect to the extent of recent socialist government: countries where socialist parties have been in power more have relatively high inflation and low unemployment rates. If we consider these twelve countries (see equation (6)) we see that they are similar to the larger set of industrial countries, save that the elasticity estimate was significantly greater than 1 in 1955, and has clearly fallen, implying that the fastest rates of growth of G/Y in these years must have been in the comparatively smaller of these countries.

It is, however, also the predominantly socialist countries where the growth has been fastest: Denmark, Finland and Sweden all had the share of government consumption in GDP grow by about half over the twenty years we are considering. The fit is by no means excellent, though; Canada saw the share of consumption grow by a similar amount, and growth in the Netherlands, for instance was much smaller. Intriguingly, much of this correlation arises through a negative correlation between socialism and spending in 1955, which could imply that low government spending earlier served to motivate socialist voting as much as the reverse.

Britain was a relatively big spender in 1955, with 17 per cent of GDP going to government consumption; in 1974, the figure was 20.5 per cent, smaller than in Denmark, Sweden and the United States, and similar to that of West Germany. Moreover, growth of the government share in GDP was comparatively slow in Britain over these two decades, outstripping only the expenditure growth rates in Italy, the Netherlands, France and the United States. Two separate cross-sections twenty years apart are not appropriate data for pursuing hypotheses about comparative rates of growth of expenditure very far, however, though even these modest results do suggest that the British experience is not unique and that there are clearly no grounds for assuming that government expenditure in Britain has grown atypically fast or takes an atypically large share of national income.

CONCLUSION

The message of this paper should be clear and simple. Macroeconomic estimation, for whatever purpose, is a hazardous pastime if the systematic responses of government, or indeed any sector, are blindly ignored. Structural estimation reduces the problems but even here omission of reaction functions will introduce specification error. Reduced form estimation is a particularly misguided procedure the outcome of which should usually be ignored. We suggest a procedure dependent upon specifying the public sector as endogenous to a macroeconomic model. Preliminary evidence is presented supporting the existence of a stable government expenditure function. Indeed the function fitted would appear to be as stable as any of the more popular aggregate expenditure functions.

NOTE

1. The countries are: Australia*, Austria*, Belgium**, Bolivia, Canada**, Chile, Colombia, Costa Rica, Denmark**, Dominican Republic, Ecuador, El Salvador, Finland**, France**, West Germany**, Greece*, Guatemala, Honduras, Iceland*, Ireland*, Israel*, Italy**, Jamaica, Japan*, Korea*, Luxembourg*, Malta, Morocco, Netherlands**, New Zealand*, Nigeria, Norway**, Panama, Paraguay, Peru, Philippines, Portugal, South Africa*, Spain, Sri Lanka, Sweden**, Switzerland*, Thailand, Trinidad and Tobago, Turkey, UK**, USA**, Uruguay, Venezuela (* = industrial, ** = industrial and used in Hibbs, 1976). Source: *International Financial Statistics*.

PART II

Fiscal Policy Simulations

CHAPTER 7

Theory, Policy and Macroeconomic Models

P. A. Ormerod

There are several large economic models of the UK economy, estimated by econometric techniques, that are in regular current use. The Cambridge Economic Policy Group, the London Business School, the National Institute and the Treasury all have large models, the former constructed using annual data and the latter three using quarterly data. The main purpose and the main use of such models is in providing the framework in which to develop forecasts of future developments of the economy. There are, however, two other interrelated uses to which the models are put. First, to explain the past behaviour of the economy and the effects of past policy changes[1] and, second, to analyse the effects of possible changes in current government policy. The concern of this paper is with the use of models of this type in this latter way and principally with the limitations of models when used to analyse the effects of changes in fiscal policy. The paper first discusses briefly how macroeconomic models are typically used in this context, and then goes on to examine certain limitations of models that are relevant to all three of their uses, and finally considers limitations that are more specific to the analysis of policy.

In very small models of the economy, policy analysis can be carried out by analytical solution of the model. For example, consider the following simple model given by the national income identity

$$Y \equiv C + G + X \tag{1}$$

where Y is total income, C is consumption, G government expenditure, and X all other components of national income. Given a simple consumption function

$$C = a + bYD \tag{2}$$

$$YD = Y - T \tag{3}$$

where YD is disposable income and T, taxes. For this model, Y and C are endogenous variables, that is they are determined within the system, and G, T and X are assumed to be exogenously determined outside the system. The effects of a unit change in one of the exogenous variables, G say, is first to increase Y (equation (1)), which increases YD (equation (3)), then C (equation (2)), which leads to a further increase in Y in equation (1). This increase then feeds into equation (3) again, further increasing YD, etc. The final effect on Y is easy to obtain analytically by writing Y as a function of the exogenous variables only.

$$Y = \frac{a}{1-b} + \frac{1}{1-b} \cdot G - \frac{b}{1-b} \cdot T + \frac{1}{1-b} \cdot x. \tag{4}$$

Thus the effects on Y of an increase in G can simply be read off from equation (4) as $1/(1-b)$ times the increase. Given a base set of data such as a forecast, the effects of changing the exogeneous variables in the system by specified amounts over specified periods can then be read off from equation (4), and these effects are simply the differences in the values of the endogenous variables, C and Y, from their levels in the base set of data.

In practice, however, it is extremely difficult to obtain model solutions analytically since this involves the multiplication and inversion of extremely large matrices, and in practice simulations are carried out using the method of numerical simulation. Moreover, there is a further problem connected with the non-linearities of most models. In equation (4), Y is a linear function of the exogenous variables in the system and the effects of changes in the exogenous variables are independent of the levels of the variables. However, even a simple extension of the above model rapidly involves non-linearities as the following example taken from Wallis (1973) shows. Consider the following model in which real and current price variables are distinguished.

$$C = a + bY \tag{5}$$

$$Y \equiv C + I \tag{6}$$

$$p_c C + p_k I = pY \tag{7}$$

$$p_c = \lambda + \mu p \tag{8}$$

where p_c is the price of consumption, p_k the price of capital goods and p the overall price index, and where C, Y, p_c, p are endogenous, and I, p_k exogenous. Unless all price indices are equal, the effect on current price income of changes in current price investment is a function not simply of the parameters of the model, but also of the price of capital goods and real income. In other words, the effect on current price income of a change in current price investment is dependent on the levels of the variables in the system, so that the effects may be different at different states of the economy.

The problem of non-linearity is in fact an important qualification to the use of simulation results generated by large macro-models, for in general the results will depend to some extent upon the initial conditions of the base run and so cannot be used directly in other contexts.

An example of this is a simulation of a sustained devaluation of 5 per cent reported by Laury, Lewis and Ormerod (1978). In the National Institute model, when the base set of data was chosen to start with the first quarter of 1972, the devaluation did not improve the current balance of payments relative to the levels of the base run (which in this case comprised actual historical data) until the 13th quarter of the simulation. Using a base run starting in the first quarter of 1976 however, led to an improvement in the current balance after only four quarters. The difference between the two runs is in the main attributable to the different levels of domestic capacity utilisation in the first few quarters of the base run. During 1972 capacity utilisation rose very sharply and remained high during 1973, whilst in 1976 and 1977 utilisation was very low.

The inclusion of capacity utilisation terms in equations, such as the volume and price of exports and the volume of imports, which are important in the above example, is the main way in which supply effects enter into existing UK macro-models. Supply problems are not modelled explicitly, but implicitly by variables such as capacity utilisation in demand equations. There is an obvious weakness of this approach. At full employment, an increase in demand must be met entirely by imports, or be absorbed in price increases, or a combination of the two factors. Yet although, in the example given above, the level of utilisation does have an effect on the impact of policy in the National Institute model, increases in demand could still reduce unemployment and not spill over completely into imports or prices even if unemployment were way below its full employment level. These factors can, of course, be allowed for judgementally when models are used in forecasting, but the models themselves do not capture these properties in a satisfactory way. Klein (1978) has recently drawn attention to another problem that arises from the use of models that are mainly demand-oriented. Bottlenecks in individual industries might arise when the overall level of demand is well below full employment, and unless the intermediate flows in the economy are modelled as well as the demand for final transactions, the models will not be able to describe these problems adequately.

Perhaps the most obvious limitation of such simulations, however, is that the models are only highly imperfect representations of reality. Indeed, one of the purposes of carrying out simulation exercises is to reveal properties of the model that seem unreasonable according to one's *a priori* view of the world; the individual equations may seem perfectly plausible, but when combined together in a simultaneous model the overall properties might seem quite unrealistic. Again, taking an example from the experience of the

National Institute, during 1974/75 a model was constructed that was quite separate from the model in regular forecasting use, and that was constructed on a consistent theoretical basis. When this model was programmed in the autumn of 1975 however, policy simulations revealed that the model had certain properties that were not felt by the Institute's forecasting team to be plausible descriptions of the real world. The pricing and investment equations were accordingly changed, at a loss of theoretical consistency, but at the gain that the overall properties proved more acceptable to the forecasting team.[2] There is a delicate balance here between three factors. How far the data are allowed to determine freely the parameters of the individual equations and hence the overall properties of the model; how far the *a priori* views of the model operators are allowed to change the individual equations when the overall properties are disliked (these views not necessarily being derived from a rigorous theory); and how far the properties of the model are directly imposed to satisfy a particular theoretical viewpoint. All three factors need to be taken account of by model builders, and all three have advantages and drawbacks. The approach of allowing the data to determine the parameters freely, for example, is on the face of things a scientific approach to follow. Of course it cannot be carried out in complete isolation from some theoretical notion of what are the appropriate explanatory variables in an equation, otherwise the exercise simply deteriorates into meaningless data mining. It is of particular advantage in determining the lag structure of equations, since although we may have an *a priori* view of the long-run coefficient on an explanatory variable, we may not have such a view on the particular lag structure. Thus, in a simple consumption function relating consumption to disposable income and to the lagged dependent variable, it may be felt that the long-run coefficient on disposable income should be unity, since if it is different from this there is an implication that the personal sector is willing to accumulate or run down indefinitely its stocks of assets as income rises. However, no such firm views may be held about the lag structure of the equation. The problem with following this approach completely, however, is that data often reveal parameter values that do seem to be at odds either with theory or with simple casual empiricism. It seems plausible, for example, that the marginal propensity to consume out of current grants (pensions, social security payments, etc.) is higher than out of other components of income, yet attempts to test this is in the National Institute have frequently led to estimates of the long-run marginal propensity to consume out of current grants well in excess of unity, so that in the end the coefficient has been imposed.

The idea of changing a particular equation because of a simple dislike of either its individual properties or its properties combined in a large model may seem quite unsound. Yet this is done implicitly by almost every single forecaster in the world when the residuals on equations are changed to modify the forecast in a judgemental way. This is done for a number of reasons. For example, there will inevitably be explanatory variables omitted from the estimated relationship either because their influence in the past has been too weak to be detected or because of the complete absence of any suitable data. Second, there may often be explanatory factors that are not readily quantified, such as 'confidence', and so cannot be explicitly written into an econometric relationship. Thus, the spring budgets of 1968 and 1973 seem to have affected anticipations of expenditure in the first quarter of those years before the actual budget changes were announced. These effects can be proxied by a dummy variable in estimating equations over the past but are extremely difficult to model explicitly, so that it is only possible to introduce these effects in other situations (in forecasts or in policy simulations) judgementally. Third, economic relationships may themselves change over time in a way that it is again difficult to model explicitly. For example, if a forecast or policy simulation gave rates of inflation that had not been experienced over the sample period of the model, a strong element of judgement would be required to evaluate the possible consequences. It is inescapable, then, that the mechanical output of econometric models often has to be modified by judgement and that judgement is an integral part of any forecasting process. It does seem less acceptable, however, to impose policy simulation properties upon a model purely by judgement and without reference to any theoretical model.

As an example of the direct imposition of theoretical properties, the London Business School explicitly imposed the properties of the 'Scandinavian' model of inflation upon their macro-model (Ball and Burns, 1976), which implies the equalisation across countries of traded goods prices, although with longer lags than suggested by the theory. In this theory, export prices are determined by world prices and so, for a given level of world prices in foreign currency, UK export prices will change only with the exchange rate. Domestic manufactured prices are determined by export prices as well as by unit labour costs, and in turn are a determinant of earnings in manufacturing, and earnings in the rest of the economy are related to those in manufacturing. Thus, the property that in the long run a given percentage change in either the world price of manufacturers or the exchange rate will lead to an equal (but opposite in the case of the exchange rate) increase in the domestic price level, is imposed upon the London Business School model. This is a perfectly acceptable procedure in principle, provided that it is actually made explicit by the modeller. Otherwise, users of the results of the model might be led to think that the model provides empirical support for a theoretical hypothesis, when the results have in fact been imposed to satisfy that hypothesis. A model constructed in this way provides empirical evidence on a particular theory only in the event of the data completely contradicting the theoretical imposition. This approach, however, does have the advantage of focusing upon policy multipliers at the very beginning of model construction, and a general criticism of UK models is that the multipliers have tended to emerge in exercises carried out after the models have been put together. This reflects the fact that their main use is as tools in short-term forecasting, but it is perhaps time that the policy aspects of their use is recognised as being as at least as important.

A problem with the above approach of imposing properties according to theory is that economic theory actually provides relatively few clear-cut results to impose. For example, in the context of fiscal and monetary policy the short-run quantity of money theory indicates that the nominal GDP multiplier with respect to an expansionary change in fiscal policy unaccompanied by a monetary expansion should be zero in a relatively short time period, say four to five quarters. Yet economic theory in general gives little guide as to even the size of the GDP multiplier with respect to fiscal policy. In the case of a fiscal expansion accompanied by a monetary expansion, theorists agree that this has an unequivocably expansionary effect upon GDP, but there is no such agreement on the effects of fiscal expansion that is financed by bond sales, in other words not accompanied by monetary expansion. A substantial and interesting literature has developed in recent years analysing this particular problem, following the seminal work of Blinder and Solow (1973). Currie, in a recent survey (1978a), concludes that under a number of restrictive assumptions such as a fixed price level in the case of a closed economy the literature points to the conclusion that fiscal policy has significant and lasting effects on GDP, whether it is financed by bonds or by money. Even in this case, however, theory suggests that in the case of bond-financed expansion the effects may be perverse. In the case of an open economy, which is obviously the relevant case for the UK, theory gives less guidance, particularly when assumptions such as a fixed price level are relaxed. Because of the complexity of the analysis, Currie suggests that further theoretical advance in this area may be rather difficult.

Even the sign of the long-run effect on GDP of fiscal expansion then is theoretically unclear. Moreover, even in cases where the long-run sign of the effects of fiscal policy on GDP is theoretically unequivocal, theory has very little indeed to say about the timing of these effects. We have effectively no guidance on such questions as the size of the multiplier in the current quarter relative to its long-run value, or even what its long-run value actually is, and certainly no guidance as to whether the GDP multiplier, with respect to a tax cut say, should be 0.5 or 1.5 after ten quarters. This means that the strength of the tests modellers can apply to test the validity of their models is accordingly reduced, for if clear-cut and undisputed theoretical results existed the overall properties of each model would have to satisfy these results. As it is, the multipliers obtained from macro-models can only occasionally be subject to direct verification from theory.

A further important qualification to the use of the models relates to the time horizon over which it is possible to obtain meaningful results. The models are principally designed to make a conditional forecast up to two or three years ahead, and do not make allowance for the effects of changes in variables that can plausibly be represented as exogenous in the short run but that are endogenous in the longer run. An example of this is the underlying trend growth of productivity in the economy. The precise determinant of this has been by no means established empirically, but variables such as the capital stock, the associated level of technology and the education level and the skills of the labour force are clearly important. In the short run, it is reasonable to assume that these are exogenous, for any addition to investment will be small in relation to the total capital stock. Such an assumption, however, becomes less valid the longer the time period that is considered. If the underlying growth of productivity is changing during a forecast or a simulation, there are implications for the movements in other variables such as output and employment. It is difficult to be exact about the effects of factors such as this, except to note that in practice the operators of models have been very reluctant to use them over a period of more than five or six years.

There is, however, a more fundamental qualification to the use of the models over long time periods. For although results obtained with them are almost invariably presented as point estimates, there is inevitably a margin of error associated with each estimate. There are three main components of this margin of error. First, the fact that estimated equations have error terms that are subject to random disturbance. In the context of the simple linear regression model, Johnston (1973) proves that the variance of the predicted values of an endogenous variable will increase the further the values of the explanatory variables lie from the mean of the sample values employed to compute the estimated values of the parameters in the equation. Second, the explanatory values themselves may be exogenous to the system and hence appear to be non-stochastic, but in fact there will also be margins of error associated with their values. This could easily be seen in the context of the forecast in world trade, the level of which is usually taken to be determined exogenously in UK models. But in fact world trade is simply the sum of each individual country's exports, which are forecast endogenously within each individual country, so that their sum is clearly subject to a margin of error. The third main source of margins of error is perhaps more relevant in a simulation context, namely that the estimated parameters themselves are not determined precisely, but have standard errors associated with them. Relatively small changes in key parameters can have substantial effects upon the policy simulation properties of models, yet these parameters are rarely identified with any great degree of precision. The marginal propensity to import with respect to domestic expenditure is a crucial parameter for the

UK economy, for example. Yet the potential margin of error associated with estimates of this is usually quite large. In the National Institute model, for example, aggregate goods imports are related *inter alia* to domestic expenditure. The coefficient on the expenditure variable gives the short-run marginal propensity to import (the equation is in log form), and there is a lagged dependent variable amongst the other regressors that imposes a distributed lag on this coefficient, giving the long-run marginal propensity to import as the coefficient on expenditure divided by 1 minus the coefficient on the lagged dependent variable. Even assuming that the coefficient (1.01) on domestic expenditure is known with certainty, simply varying the value of the coefficient on the lagged dependent variable by one standard error on each side of its estimated value yields a long-run marginal propensity to import of either 1.24 or 1.78. Varying the coefficient on the expenditure variable by one standard error each side as well, and ignoring covariance terms, gives a range of estimates for the long-run marginal propensity to import of between 0.98 and 2.15.

Klein (1974) focused on the above problems at a very early stage in the development of macroeconomic models, presenting forecasts for GNP in the USA for the fiscal year 1947 to which potential margins of error were attached. Working with very small models, Klein was in fact able to quantify in a rigorous way the confidence intervals of the predictions that arose from the existence of error terms on the estimated equations and from the standard errors associated with the estimated parameter values. Even though this was done, allowance could not be made for margins of error associated with forecast values of the exogenous variables for the simple reason that these were not known. The development of larger models in the 1950s and 1960s meant that the technique of calculating confidence intervals in a precise way rapidly became impractical, even though these models are themselves regarded as small by the standards of today. Interestingly, the tremendous developments in computing technology in recent years may mean that we shall once again be able to obtain such confidence intervals even for large models, although this will be a very difficult task indeed. Yet it is clearly one that should be carried out, for if each figure that emerged from the model had an associated confidence interval some of the apparently different properties of models and shapes of forecasts may well prove to be statistically indistinguishable. Modigliani (1977) has recently argued that even the widely differing GDP multipliers for fiscal expansions unaccompanied by monetary expansion given by St Louis models and the more orthodox macro-models give values around 2; it is obviously important to know whether this is in fact the case.

The above points are qualifications that apply to the use of models in whatever context, whether it is for forecasting or for simulation of policy analysis. This section of the paper concentrates on qualifications that are more specific to simulations of models, and most of these arise from the fact that the models are essentially designed for short-term forecasting rather than for simulation purposes. For example, in applied macroeconomics it is often very difficlt to distinguish between alternative hypotheses, yet for the purposes of short-term forecasting this is not necessarily a problem. Very simple consumption functions, in which consumption depends upon disposable income and the lagged dependent variable, proved successful in explaining movements in consumption until the savings ratio rose sharply in the early 1970s. Although several hypotheses have been put forward to explain the rise, such as the reduction in real personal sector wealth and the consequent building up of assets, inflation itself and the increase in contractual savings, the exact contribution of these factors has not yet been empirically established. So a very simple consumption function can still be useful in short-term forecasting, provided that the forecaster uses judgement to allow for the factors that are thought to be missing in the equation. However, in simulation work this is obviously less acceptable and the feedback onto the consumption from whatever factors are thought to have caused the rise in the savings ratio needs to take place within the model.

This example raises a further problem, which is perhaps more fundamental. Even if the simple specification of the consumption function discussed above had not run into recent empirical difficulties, the problem would remain that this specification is consistent with a number of underlying theoretical hypotheses. For example, the inclusion of the lagged dependent variable can be justified by Friedman's permanent income theory in which permanent income is represented by a distributed lag on actual income. And alternatively, by an extension of Duesenberry's 'ratchet effect' in which the lagged value of consumption proxies the previous peak value of consumption. Yet these two theoretical structures can have quite different implications in simulations of fiscal policy. For example, if there is a tax increase that is expected to be permanent, the permanent income hypothesis implies that consumption is immediately reduced because a tax change is seen as lowering the level of permanent income. Under the ratchet effect theory, however, consumers attempt to maintain their consumption at its previous peak value despite the fall in disposable income and only adjust gradually to the new lower level of income. For practical short-term forecasting it might well be unimportant that these two theories are not distinguished in the equation's specification, for again judgement will be used in this context. For simulation purposes, however, the distinction clearly is important and the existence of problems such as this are a weighty qualification to the fiscal policy results of existing models.

A further problem that arises in carrying out simulations is the relevance of the estimation period to the simulation. This statement covers a number of points, such as the fact that simulations that are carried out are usually rather artificial, serving to illustrate the partial differentials of a model rather than what would necessarily happen if such policies were continuously pursued over the simulation. As an example, the large UK models all show a continuous negative effect on the current balance of payments with respect to a sustained increase in current government expenditure under the assumption of fixed exchange rates. Yet such a deterioration in the current balance would either lead to a devaluation in an attempt by the authorities to eliminate the induced deficit, in which case one of the assumptions of the simulations would be violated, or the expectation of a devaluation amongst decision-making units would modify their behaviour from that described by the equations in the model. Of course, these complicating factors can also be simulated at the same time as the expenditure increase and their combined effects analysed. Indeed, in simulations carried out for actual policy analysis, factors like this are taken into account, but in the mechanical simulations reported in the literature they are not.

A more general problem arises from the fact that the simulations presented often include policies that were not observed during the period over which the equations of the models were estimated. Thus the estimated parameters are not necessarily applicable to the assumed conditions of the simulation. For if different policies had been carried out over the sample period the data would be different and in consequence so would the estimates of parameter values. An obvious problem arises if very large shocks are administered to the model, so that if income tax were abolished, for example, the short-run marginal propensity to consume might well be different from that observed from actual data. Yet it is not necessarily the size of such shocks that causes problems. Cleanly floating exchange rates have been assumed in recent UK policy simulation exercises, yet where the exchange rates are freely estimated they include the effects of dirty floating. In fact we have virtually no data with which to model the behaviour of the exchange rate under a clean float and so the estimated parameters are not necessarily applicable to the assumed conditions of the simulation. Although we obviously cannot know how the parameters change quantitatively, it is often possible to obtain qualitative prediction of the way they will probably change. Using an example from a recent article by Gordon (1976) suppose a constant rate of growth of the money supply were simulated on a model. If such a policy had actually been carried out and the incidence of periods of credit restriction and tight monetary policy thereby reduced, economic agents might have become less afraid of bankruptcy and hence have smoothed their spending more. Such behaviour would have led to the interest elasticity of spending being lower than that observed with the actual sample data.

Lucas, in a recent article (1976), has developed the above points into a fundamental attack upon the validity of simulations carried out with existing macro-models, in which he states that 'simulations using these models can, in principle, provide *no* useful information as to the actual consequences of alternative economic policy'. Lucas argues that although the short-term forecasting accuracy of the models is good, they can provide no evidence as to the long-term effects of simulated policy. This is essentially because the simulations are based upon a single set of fixed parameters estimated from the sample period, whereas the true parameters may not in fact be fixed but may vary with each alternative policy. There are clearly circumstances in which this point is valid and in which the parameters of a model might vary substantially with respect to a particular policy or set of policies. For example, the speed and extent to which the domestic price level responds to a devaluation will obviously depend upon the experience that economic agents have had of devaluation. Workers and employers can be expected to learn from devaluation that prices will subsequently increase and will, therefore, modify their behaviour if a subsequent devaluation takes place. In particular, the lags in the wage–price system will presumably shorten if a rapid series of devaluations occur, and simulations based upon a fixed lag structure may provide little evidence as to the effect of a policy that entails a series of devaluations. Lucas, however, surely presses his point too far by stating that the models can ultimately 'in principle provide *no* useful information' on long-run effects of policy changes. As mentioned above, if actual policies had been different in the past, the data would have been different and parameters estimated from this data different also. So, if a particular policy were simulated over a long time period, we would certainly expect it to have an impact upon the parameters of any given model. Such an impact may be strong, as in the case of a series of devaluations, but it seems doubtful whether the effect of an extra £1 billion a year in public expenditure, for example, would have quite the same impact. More importantly, there is the old question of how long is the long run. Even if a particular policy had a substantial effect on the parameters of the model in the long run, if the long run were more than five or six years say, this problem would be irrelevant to an analysis of policy options by model simulations. Over the period of time relevant for policy choice, the model would provide an adequate description of the properties of the economy. Lucas, in fact, dismisses this possibility and simply asserts that 'the hope ... that changes in [parameters] induced by policy changes will occur slowly ... is both false and misleading' (p. 39). It is difficult to test his assertion precisely, but the ability of forecasters to predict short-term movements in the economy reasonably accurately using fixed parameter models suggests that the changes in policy that have actually taken place have not induced rapid changes in the underlying structure of the economy.

The critique by Lucas is part of a wider discussion in which the relevance of existing macro-models has been questioned because of their failure to model adequately the mechanism by which economic agents form their expectations of future economic variables. The alternative approach that is proposed is not to model expectations arbitrarily, such as by autoregressive schemes, but 'rationally'. Rational in this context is used in the sense that expectations so formed are true mathematical expectations of the future variables, conditional on all variables in the model that are known to economic agents at time t.[3] In other words, it is postulated that economic agents have knowledge of the latest economic data at any given time, and form their expectations about future values of variables according to the mathematical expectation of these values, given the information that is available. Apart from the general problem that this type of analysis raises for macro-models, there is a point that is particularly relevant to the use of models for policy simulation. For according to rational expectations, if a policy rule is followed for long enough, rational individuals will learn how the policy rule affects the economy and will adjust their behaviour in the light of this knowledge. The effect of the policy on the economy becomes part of the set of information available to the general public, and they accordingly adjust their expectations and behaviour to take account of this. It seems doubtful, however, whether the rational expectations approach can be of widespread use in formalising the perception of economic agents of the effects of government policy on the UK economy. For over the last twenty years or so actual policies tended to be very short lived and have lacked continuity.[4] Given the fact that most econometricians require at least fifteen to twenty observations before being willing to run a regression, and given that policies have only occasionally continued unchanged over that number of quarters, it appears to be very difficult for economic agents to discover the effects of a policy rule and use it in a rational way, unless of course they all have far greater insight into the workings of the economy than practising econometricians! There are other problems associated with rational expectations, and the topic is discussed in detail in a recent paper by Shiller (1978). His conclusion is that the concept of rational expectations has drawn attention to an important area of model development, but that it is very unlikely that future macro-models will be rational expectations models in the strictest sense. In some areas of the economy such as the stockmarket, agents clearly do have easy access to the large amounts of information required to model expectations rationally, and the concept will probably be more useful here than in, say, explaining the behaviour of unemployed workers who equally clearly do not have access to such large amounts of information. This seems to be sensible, although it should be noted that the reason why modellers have previously used few expectational variables is not because they failed to realise the importance of expectations but because expectations have proved extremely difficult to model in a satisfactory way.

A further criticism that is made of the treatment of fiscal policy in existing macro-models is that government activity ought to be entered explicitly into the structural equations explaining private sector behaviour. It is argued, for example, that increases in government expenditure directly displaced equal or smaller amounts of private expenditure, and that existing models only allow for indirect displacements via the change in wealth, interest rates, etc., that follow from any increase in government expenditure. There are several strands to this type of argument, which is known in the literature as 'ultrarationality'. If the personal sector sees the public sector as an instrument of the private interests of the personal sector for example, then personal and public saving are by definition perfect substitutes, and thus increases or decreases in public saving will be offset completely by equivalent decreases or increases in personal saving. This is an extreme statement of the ultrarationality position, and one does not have to be a Marxist to regard this hypothesis as being sociologically very dubious indeed. A more subtle approach is to argue, as does Barro (1974), that if future tax liabilities are accurately foreseen the level at which total tax receipts are set at any given time is immaterial. For the behaviour of the private sector will be exactly the same as if the budget were continuously balanced, since if taxes are cut or government expenditure increased the private sector will perceive that the level of taxes in the future will be higher in order to pay the increased interest charges on public sector debt. Private sector saving will, therefore, rise, nullifying the effect of the immediate reduction of public sector saving. There has been a recent theoretical interchange on the conditions under which this type of effect could possibly take place.[5] The main criticisms relate to the fact that individuals may not have to face all future tax liabilities. They will be passed on to their decendents, and individuals will vary in the way in which they include the welfare of future generations in their utility functions. Again, the imperfection of capital markets might mean that there may be a divergence between the rate of interest on government debt and the social rate of time preference at which future tax liabilities are discounted. Further, if the government undertakes productive capital formation and not simply current expenditure, the proceeds of this will help to service future debt. Essentially, however, the ultrarationality concept needs to be subjected to empirical testing, since there are obvious examples of cases where public expenditure might well be at least a partial substitute for private expenditure. If the system of government grants for postgraduate courses were replaced by loans, for example, many postgraduates would presumably be willing to take up loans. It does seem intuitively plausible, however, that the size of such examples relative to total public expenditure is very small. Buiter (1977a) has recently referred to US empirical evidence on the existence of ultrarationality as being 'inconclusive', and particularly given the theoretical problems associated with this concept, strong evidence is needed before it can be accepted as being quantitatively important.

In conclusion, then, it is clear that there are a number of substantial qualifications that have to be made to the use of existing macro-models in the analysis of fiscal policy. Apart from the basic problem that the models are imperfect representations of reality, their results are sensitive to the initial conditions of the base run, and the time horizon over which they can be taken seriously is quite short although possibly adequate from a policy point of view. Results of models are almost invariably presented as point estimates, but in fact there are confidence intervals associated with them that at the present level of technology are very difficult to obtain for large models. A further problem is that the data often make it hard to discriminate between alternative hypotheses. Particular difficulties are caused for the analysis of fiscal policy by the fact that similar specifications of important equations such as the consumption function are consistent with a number of different theoretical hypotheses. The simulations presented in the literature are usually artificial, serving to illustrate the partial differentials of models rather than to illustrate what would happen if certain policies were carried out over the period of the simulation. Also, certain policies that are simulated have not actually been carried out during the sample period so there is a question as to the relevance of the parameter estimates obtained to these particular simulations. An important extension of this point is the argument that the parameters of the model are not fixed but are themselves functions of the particular policies being analysed. This is almost certainly correct, for example, in the analysis of a series of devaluations, since the lag structure of the wage–price system would be modified by experience. It does seem of little relevance, however, to relatively small changes in fiscal policy over the short run. A related point is that expectations might well be changed by policies and, whilst not accepting that it is sensible to construct models that have complete rational expectations, the development of this concept has drawn attention to a weakness in the specification of existing models.

These problems point to a number of developments in model construction. Modellers ought to pay as much attention to the policy properties of their models as to their short-term forecasting ability, and this means focusing on policy multipliers from the very start rather than viewing them as a byproduct of a forecasting model. In particular, more use should be made of theoretical restrictions of model properties, although it must be admitted that theory often gives little relevant guidance. The inclusion of more expectational effects would further strengthen the use of models in policy simulation. It must, however, be emphasised that it is only by confronting the data and attempting to establish empirical relationships that economists can understand how the economy works and what the effects of the policy are. Further, in the practical analysis of the effects of alternative policy, the models are used as just one (very important) input into the procedure, much in the same way as they are used in forecasting. So despite their imperfections, existing econometric models are valuable tools of analysis, if only to remind us of how little we do actually know.

NOTES AND REFERENCES

1. See Blinder and Goldfeld (1976).
2. For a discussion of this see Worswick in Fane (1977).
3. The seminal article was written by Muth (1961).
4. See, for example, Blackaby (1978).
5. See, for example, Feldstein (1976), Buchanan (1976) and Barro (1976).

CHAPTER 8

Policy Simulations and Model Characteristics

G. R. Lewis and P. A. Ormerod

INTRODUCTION

This paper first discusses the use of the macroeconomic models of the UK of the National Institute and the Treasury in fiscal policy analysis, and then goes on to report on the effects of fiscal policy using simulations of the two models. The article by Laury, Lewis and Ormerod (1978; referred to below as LLO) describes a number of simulations with the quarterly econometric models of the London Business School, the National Institute and the Treasury, using the versions operative in mid-1977. This paper uses versions of these two models as they stood in March 1978, and is concerned only with those simulations relevant to fiscal policy, although the exercise is extended in one respect by including the case of the 'balanced budget' multiplier.

FISCAL POLICY AND THE USE OF ECONOMIC MODELS

Although forecasting and policy analysis are conducted by separate divisions within the Treasury, cooperation between the two is inevitably very close, with the work of both revolving around the Treasury's macroeconomic model.[1] Apart from the production of the forecast itself, the major contribution of the econometric model to the policy-making process consists in providing a set of simulations very similar in nature to those reported here, known as 'ready reckoners'. These simulations show the effect on output, unemployment, the balance of payments and prices, etc., of changing various fiscal policy instruments by some convenient conventional amount. The 'ready reckoners' will usually cover a wide range of alternative fiscal instruments, such as public authorities current expenditure, nationalised

156

industries investment expenditure, changes in both personal tax allowances and the standard and higher rates of tax, changes in corporation tax, and changes in each of the more important indirect taxes such as VAT, petrol, beer or tobacco duty.

The Treasury's pre-budget short-term forecast will usually be based on the assumption of the continuation of existing policies. Combinations of 'ready reckoners' can then be constructed by the policy analysts to illustrate the effect on the forecast of any particular combination of policy changes. In this way the individual 'ready reckoners' provide the building blocks by means of which a large range of alternative policy options may be evaluated without the need for endless computer runs. Alternatively, 'ready reckoners' can be used to calculate what policy changes are necessary to produce some desired time path for certain target variables. In this sense the model simulations are being used to achieve an elementary kind of open-loop optimal control.

The latest forecast will usually form the base from which the simulations are run. The differing economic effects of changing different fiscal instruments are made comparable by expressing the results in terms of some standard revenue change, e.g. per £100m full year yield. While the simulation results do depend to some extent upon the base forecast from which they were computed, as a first approximation they can be used more generally. Hence the term 'ready reckoner', for they can be pro-rated to model larger or smaller tax changes, or applied to different points in time. The 'ready reckoner' approach has the disadvantage that the economic effects of a tax change are not necessarily linear so that raising £200m through a particular tax instrument may not have twice the economic effects of raising £100m. Second, combining two or more tax changes using the 'ready reckoner' ignores any interaction effects. The element of approximation involved will depend on the size of the fiscal change considered, being much less for fairly small changes. Since the 'ready reckoners' only approximate the models' properties, the final choice between the small number of alternative fiscal packages that remain under consideration will be made using a series of complete model runs.

It is worth emphasising that in contrast to the rather mechanical unconstrained use of the models reported here, in actual forecasting and simulation work the results are only partially determined by the formal properties of the model. The Treasury model is programmed in a flexible way so as to allow additional economic judgements to be incorporated within the equation system, most commonly by residual or intercept adjustment, although it is also relatively easy to change the equations themselves. In the case of the economic effects of policy changes, these *ad hoc* adjustments are discussed and agreed by a working party of forecasters, policy analysts and fiscal experts, including representatives from the Inland Revenue and Customs and Excise. As an example of the type of adjustment that is made, the short-run marginal propensity to consume assumed for changes to the higher rates and bands is lower than that for changes to the main allowances and basic rate since typically the short-run marginal propensity to consume declines as income rises.

Estimates of the direct effects of a tax change are not produced by the equations in the tax sector of the Treasury model, but instead are provided off-the-model by the two revenue departments (i.e., Inland Revenue and Customs and Excise).

The tax equations included on the model are too aggregative to distinguish all the parameters of the tax system that are of interest. In forecasting, they are normally used for iteration purposes only, since initial tax forecasts are provided by the revenue departments on the basis of forecasts of incomes, employment and other variables taken from some model base. These departments estimate the initial effect on tax revenue of changing any particular allowance or rate. In other words, their estimates exclude the income–expenditure feedbacks that occur when changes to rates or allowances are made. The eventual change in total tax revenue will in general, therefore, be different from the initial estimate of the direct effect. In constructing the 'ready reckoners', the direct revenue effects for each tax change will be fed in turn into the Treasury model as a series of residual adjustments to the relevant tax equation, and the full economic effects computed.

This system of operation has the advantage that in working out the direct revenue effects of, say, a 10 per cent increase in the single and married personal tax allowance, or a 2 per cent reduction in the standard rate of value added tax, the revenue departments will be able to employ fully their expert knowledge of the tax system. This is especially important for the purpose of short-run demand management in relation to the timing of the effects of a given tax change. The existence of lags between tax accruals and receipts means that the short-run impact will often differ from the full effect, which occurs only after the new tax regulation has been in operation for some time. Another advantage of this approach is that in assessing the effects of a change in the income tax provisions the Inland Revenue employ a highly disaggregated tax simulation model based on cross-section data for the distribution of personal incomes. A model of this size would be too cumbersome to incorporate directly into any macroeconomic model, but can be expected to produce a much more accurate assessment of the effects of a tax change than the aggregate equations used in the Treasury model. The Inland Revenue tax simulation model allows the tax revenue for each group in the income distribution to be calculated in much the same way as a tax inspector would calculate an individual's tax. This is then grossed up by the number of tax units in each income group to give total tax revenue.

Estimation by Customs and Excise of the direct revenue yield for a change in indirect taxes is rather more complicated, since associated with each tax change there will be a price effect. Raising an indirect tax will increase the price of the goods bearing that tax relative to other goods and this will lead to substitution by consumers away from those goods towards goods not bearing the tax. If these goods have a lower tax content the yield will be lower than it otherwise would have been, e.g., spirits in particular exhibit a large substitution effect and a substantial rise in duty leads to only a small increase in revenue. Furthermore, there is the income effect of the tax-induced price change to consider: since consumers have to pay more for the taxed goods, they will have less income to spend on other goods and this will also change total revenue. Consequently, the direct revenue effects for a change in any single indirect tax are calculated to include the effect on all Customs and Excise taxes, so a change, for example, in beer duty will lead to a change in the receipts of VAT and other duties.

The use of the National Institute model in policy analysis is similar to that of the Treasury in that it involves the construction of 'ready-reckoners', but it is inevitably carried out with less disaggregated detail. Having constructed the central forecast for the UK economy, which appears in the quarterly *National Institute Economic Review*, the model is then used for two main purposes. First, for the construction of alternative forecasts under different assumptions from those of the central forecast; these are sometimes reported in the *Review*, and are sometimes carried out by the forecasters as a check on the sensitivity of the forecast to their assumptions. Second, the model is used in the analysis of the policy recommendations that appear in the Appraisal in each *Review*. As is the case with the Treasury model, both these uses involve the construction of genuine alternative forecasts, whose results are again only partially determined by the formal properties obtained by a mechanical use of the Model.

The Models

Only a brief description of the models is possible in a paper such as this, although full listings are available on request to the model proprietors. The version of the Treasury model reported here is considerably larger than that of the National Institute, the models containing 810 and 237 variables respectively of which 230 and 87 are exogenous. This difference in size, however, to some extent reflects the different uses to which the models are put rather than different views about the desirable level of aggegation in a macro-economic model. In particular, the Treasury forecasters are required to produce a detailed set of accounts for the public sector and much of this takes the form of exogenous data input. The main economic structure of the

Treasury model is contained in a much smaller subset of key equations, making comparison with the National Institute model somewhat easier. Both the models have developed from the mainstream tradition of income–expenditure macroeconomic models, although there are a number of important differences between them, which have increased in recent years.

Both models employ an income–expenditure framework for the determination of effective demand in real terms. The main determinant of the expenditure components of GDP by volume are real output, real personal disposable income, world trade, relative trade prices, the exchange rate and interest rates. The consumption function plays a key role in any income–expenditure model and both models relate consumption to real personal disposable income with a lag. The National Institute allows for a higher short-term marginal propensity to consume out of current grants than out of other income and for the effects of changes in bank advances and hire purchase. The consumption sector of the Treasury model has recently been completely respecified, and the old aggregate equation, which included the stock of liquid assets as an important explanatory variable, has been replaced by separate equations for durable and non-durable consumption. The new non-durable equation contains a term in the price level and another in the level of past savings that together can be interpreted as an implicit real wealth variable. A rise in the inflation rate will, therefore, have quite a powerful depressing influence on consumers' expenditure via this negative wealth effect. There is also an unemployment term, when a reduction in the general level of unemployment is held to improve consumer confidence, reducing the need for precautionary savings. While the cumulative effect of savings of wealth implies an eventual long-run marginal propensity to consume of unity, the build up is very slow. After a few years the MPC is only a little higher than the 0.73 shown by the National Institute consumption function.

Investment and stockbuilding are determined along familiar flexible accelerator and stock adjustment lines, but in addition to lagged output the Treasury investment equations also feature nominal interest rates, price expectations and real corporate cash flow as explanatory variables. The National Institution stockbuilding equations include the value of stock appreciation as a proxy for the cost of holding stocks. Both models employ a comparable degree of disaggregation in the exports sector. Here, export volumes are related primarily to world trade and to a measure of competitiveness (relative prices for NIESR and relative wage costs for the Treasury). There has been another important structural change in this sector of the Treasury model. The old split-period demand and supply model for UK exports of manufactured goods has been replaced by a single equation reduced form model, which includes relative wage costs rather than relative prices as the measure of competitiveness, and which produces a rather more powerful devaluation effect. Import volumes are related to output or expenditure, capacity utilisation and relative prices. In the Treasury model, imports are disaggregated into seven main categories of goods, while the National Institute model contains a single equation. This makes any comparison difficult, though the average elasticity with respect to domestic activity is probably close to the National Institute estimate of 1.5. The relative price elasticity of imports for the National Institute is -0.3, while the corresponding weighted sum of elasticities for the Treasury model is -0.6.

The composition of output by industrial sector is determined as a function of the expenditure components of GDP. Employment in turn is a function of current lagged output and productivity trends, with the National Institute including real labour costs as an additional argument. For manufacturing employment the National Institute model has a long-run output elasticity near unity, whilst the comparable figure in the Treasury model is 0.6. A coefficient below unity is not necessarily inconsistent with constant returns to scale in production, since the data on employment do not include any adjustment for the substantial number of part-time workers contained in the total. Average earnings are determined by an expectations-augmented Phillips curve in both models, with the long-run coefficient on prices being imposed at unity.[2] The Treasury Phillips curve also contains a retention ratio (i.e. the ratio of net wages to gross wages) whereby a reduction in income tax has a moderating effect on wage demands. Price deflators for the main expenditure categories are determined by mark-up equations on labour costs, import prices, indirect taxes and productivity, with the National Institute also including capacity utilisation.

The National Institute model contains an option to determine either the real money stock (M3 definition) or the consol rate endogenously, with the consol rate feeding through to a very simple term structure of interest rates. Privately held government bonds are determined residually via the government financing identity. The exchange rate is determined by a single equation reduced form relationship, and is a function of relative export prices, the visible trade balance and the covered differential between UK and US interest rates (see Batchelor, 1977). There is no explicit capital flows model, but a stock adjustment model is implicitly assumed so that changes in the covered differential only affect the exchange rate temporarily. In contrast to the National Institute, money is the residual asset in the monetary sector of the Treasury model, which consists of equations for bank lending together with demand and supply functions for gilts, where supply depends upon the divergence of sterling M3 from the authorities' desired path and demand on interest rates and inflationary expectations.[3] Demand and supply are brought into balance by varying long-term rates of interest to clear the market. External capital flows are determined by changes in interest rates and exchange rate expectations, the valuation effects of exchange rate movements on inward and outward investment flows and movements in current price exports and imports. The expected exchange rate depends partly on relative UK/US money supplies adjusted for different real growth rates, and partly on recent actual exchange rates. The actual exchange rate adjusts each quarter in order to balance the supply and demand for sterling.

SIMULATION RESULTS

The simulations reported here are as follows:[4]

(1) Public authorities' current expenditure on goods and services increased by £100m at 1970 prices in each quarter relative to the level in the base run. Average earnings, the exchange rate and interest rates held at the level of the base run.
(2) As (1), but with average earnings and the exchange rate allowed to vary.
(3) Personal income tax reduced by £100m at 1970 prices in each quarter relative to the base run. Average earnings and the exchange rate allowed to vary, and interest rates fixed at the level of the base run. The appropriate current price reduction in personal income tax was calculated using values of the consumer price index in the base run.
(4) Public authorities' current expenditure and personal income tax both increased by £100m per quarter at 1970 prices. Interest rates fixed and average earnings and the exchange rate allowed to vary. This is referred to as the 'ex ante' balanced budget case, since the initial stimulus is accompanied by a first-round tax increase of equal magnitude.
(5) As (4), but with personal income taxes being adjusted so as to leave the level of the public sector borrowing requirement unchanged from the base run. This is referred to as the 'ex post' balanced budget case.

The base run commenced in the first quarter of 1972 and comprised historical data up to the end of 1977. An accommodating monetary policy was assumed to accompany each fiscal action so that interest rates remained unchanged at their base run levels in each simulation. The effects of fiscal expansion unaccompanied by monetary expansion are discussed for slightly earlier versions of these models by Taylor (see chapter 4 in this volume). It should be emphasised that there are a number of qualifications that must be borne in mind when interpreting these results and these qualifications are discussed by Ormerod (see chapter 7 in this volume). A comparison with the earlier results indicates that in some cases there have been substantial changes in overall model properties due to recent changes in model specification, the most notable of which is undoubtedly the new Treasury consumption function with its strong emphasis on the role of wealth in consumer behaviour. These changes in the properties of the models over a fairly short period of time serve to remind us of the continually evolving nature of most econometric models. The numbers that emerge at the end of the day as 'model multipliers' should not be regarded as a set of constants. They are liable to change over time because of continuing efforts to improve the specification of different sectors of the model as new theories, data or estimation techniques become available, or as the structure of the economy itself changes. Second, the results are themselves to some extent dependent upon the initial conditions of the control solution on which the simulations were based. For example, the influence of capacity constraints will imply different multiplier effects at different stages of the economic cycle.

Simulation 1

Public authorities' final consumption increased by £100m at 1970 prices in each quarter; interest rates, earnings and exchange rate fixed (see Table 8.1 and Figures 8.1 and 8.2, Simulation 1).

This simulation is probably closest in nature to those carried out in the early 1970s to illustrate the properties of previous versions of the models. In the article by LLO it was noted that the GDP multipliers were of a similar order of magnitude to those previously reported in the UK literature. (The GDP multiplier in any quarter is defined to equal the ratio of the change in constant price GDP in that quarter, measured at factor cost, to the change in the initial expenditure or tax stimulus.) In a symposium of UK models held in 1972, Bispham reported a GDP multiplier of 0.98 after eleven quarters for the National Institute model with respect to a sustained shock in current government expenditure; Ball, Burns and Miller reported a real multiplier of 1.11 after twenty-four quarters for the LBS model, and Evans and Riley 1.33 after sixteen quarters for the Treasury model (see Renton, 1975). The corresponding multipliers reported by LLO were 0.68, 1.06 and 1.09 respectively, the lower multiplier values for the 1967 versions of the National Institute and Treasury models being mainly attributable to the higher import propensities that are obtained when the estimation period is extended to include more recent experience.

Although there are many differences in detail, the general picture that emerges from the Treasury model is similar to that described by LLO. The National Institute model produces multipliers that, except for the first few quarters, are much lower than any that have been previously reported for the UK with this particular simulation. The main reason is the reduction in exports from the level of the base run, which becomes particularly large towards the end of the simulation period. The lower level of exports reduces the GDP multiplier not only directly but also indirectly through the consequent lower level of employment, and hence via real disposable income to

TABLE 8.1 Simulation 1 (Public authority consumption +£100m per quarter, 1970 prices; interest rates, earnings and exchange rate fixed)
National Institute model

Quarter	£m (1970 prices)							(000s)	% change				£m	
	RPDI	C	I	S	X	M	GDP	E	EARN	CED	ER	MS	GDP	CB
1	19	7	—	-14	1	17	68	76	—	—	—	—	87	-16
2	36	16	2	5	—	30	80	122	—	—	—	—	106	-29
3	51	26	4	14	-3	39	86	158	—	—	—	0.4	117	-43
4	59	33	6	13	-8	46	82	182	—	—	—	0.8	122	-54
5	62	38	7	5	-12	49	72	194	—	—	—	1.0	115	-66
6	62	40	7	—	-20	47	63	197	—	—	—	1.2	109	-73
7	59	41	6	-4	-23	45	58	193	—	0.1	—	1.3	112	-75
8	58	40	4	-2	-28	45	34	188	—	0.1	—	1.3	114	-82
12	44	32	-6	-5	-56	34	18	134	—	0.1	—	1.1	106	-122
16	21	18	-17	-6	-82	18	-13	66	—	0.1	—	0.7	70	-167
24	8	5	-15	—	-89	-6	1	21	—	-0.1	—	-0.4	47	-242

Treasury model

Quarter	£m (1970 prices)							(000s)	% change				£m	
	RPDI	C	I	S	X	M	GDP	E	EARN	CED	ER	MS	GDP	CB
1	38	66	1	3	-2	7	142	201	0.1	0.1	—	—	161	-12
2	46	18	7	23	-2	19	117	213	0.1	0.1	—	0.1	128	-26
3	49	21	8	29	-2	26	122	225	0.1	0.2	—	0.1	140	-32
4	51	19	11	19	-2	29	109	230	0.1	0.2	—	0.2	130	-36
5	52	19	12	16	-1	29	106	233	—	0.2	—	0.3	130	-40
6	54	35	11	12	-2	27	116	238	—	0.1	—	0.3	143	-41
7	56	29	11	9	-2	28	108	235	—	0.1	—	0.3	137	-45
8	52	29	10	5	-2	24	106	233	—	0.1	—	0.3	139	-45
12	48	26	—	-1	-1	12	102	220	—	0.1	—	0.4	169	-37
16	43	21	-1	—	-1	13	98	218	—	0.1	—	0.8	205	-45
24	32	24	1	—	-1	15	99	215	—	0.2	—	1.0	259	-72

Key to Tables 8.1–8.5:

RPDI = real personal disposable income
C = consumers' expenditure
I = total fixed investment
S = total stockbuilding
X = total exports of goods and services
M = total imports of goods and services
GDP = gross domestic product at factor cost

E = total UK employment
EARN = average gross earnings per head
CED = consumer's expenditure deflator
ER = effective exchange rate
MS = money stock (sterling M3 definition)
CB = balance of payments on current account (£m)

Note: Δ nominal GDP = Δ price × level of GDP in base + Δ GDP × price level in simulation (ignoring second-order terms)

165

a lower level of consumption. The lower level of exports is due to the fact that, although the consumer price index is barely affected by the simulation, the increased level of capacity utilisation leads to the export price of manufactures rising by a maximum of 1.6 per cent compared to the levels of the base run. With the assumption of a fixed exchange rate, this implies a loss of competitiveness that, given a price elasticity of -1.6, has a substantial effect upon the volume of manufactured exports.

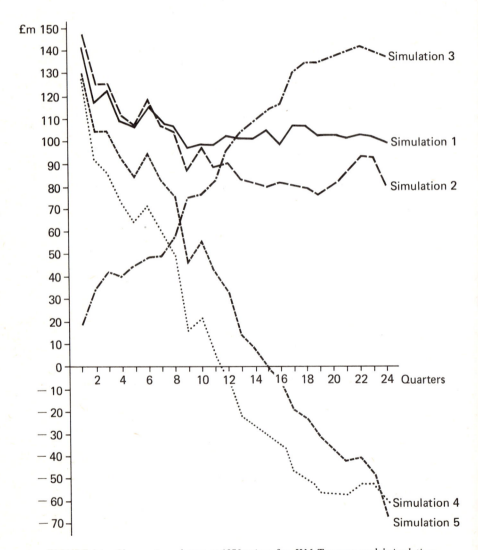

FIGURE 8.1   *Changes in real* GDP *at 1970 prices, £m, HM Treasury model simulations.*

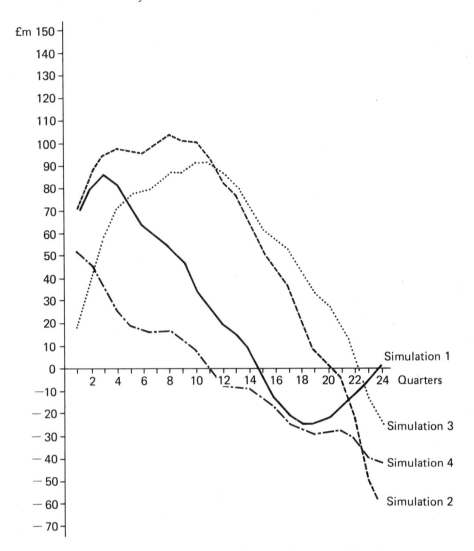

FIGURE 8.2   *Changes in real* GDP *at 1970 prices, £m,* NIESR *model simulations.*

The National Institute multipliers are lower than those of the Treasury for a number of additional reasons, some of which reflect what might be termed genuine differences of view and some of which reflect factors that are not explicitly modelled but that are corrected for when the National Institute model is used in actual policy analysis. There are two main examples of the latter. First, average hours worked rise due to the increase in output and utilisation rates, but this does not feed through onto earnings and then onto real disposable income because, under the conditions of the simulation, the average earnings variable is fixed exogenously at its base run values. Second, public consumption in its first-round effect has a lower import content than other components of final expenditure, but this is not explicitly modelled so the increase in imports is higher than it ought to be, which reduces the value of the multiplier.

There are further reasons for the lower National Institute multiplier. On average, a high proportion of public authorities' current spending arises from employment in public services, and the simulations in both models reflect this, with an immediate increase in public sector employment thereby raising the total income of the personal sector. In the National Institute model, however, the increase is only 40,000 compared with 170,000 in the Treasury model. Of course, in practice, the employment content of public spending is very sensitive to the precise nature of the goods and services that are purchased, and if the higher Treasury estimate was applied to the Institute model, the multiplier in the latter model would exceed unity in the early part of the simulation period. The Treasury figure is, in fact, a more accurate estimate of the average employment content of current spending, since only a part of public sector employment is endogenous in the National Institute model. Further, the National Institute equation for manufacturing stock-building implies a fall in the stock–output ratio as output rises, which is reflected in the fact that the permanently higher level of output in the simulations leads to almost no long-term increase in the level of manufacturing stocks. Manufactured stocks invariably fall in the first quarter when any expansionary shock is administered to the model, implying that not all the increase in demand can be met by increased output in the first quarter. The fall in manufactured exports referred to above, combined with an increase in imports over much of the simulation period due to the higher level of domestic activity, leads to an eventual deterioration in the current balance of £242m by quarter 24. Finally, the money stock (M3) follows the movement of real GDP, the long-run elasticity of demand with respect to real GDP being 2.5. The elasticity of demand with respect to prices is imposed at unity, but the relevant price level hardly changes.

Again, the GDP multiplier in the Treasury model approaches an asymptotic value of about unity from the third year. But the short-run profile over the first few quarters has changed with the peak impact on GDP now occurring in the current rather than the third quarter. One reason for this is that the new consumption function for non-durables possesses a higher short-run income response, but the main reason is due to the addition of an employment term to the consumption function. A reduction in the level of unemployment is held to improve consumer confidence and to reduce the need for precautionary savings. In this instance, the high employment content of public consumption causes a sudden fall in unemployment, so that the confidence effect is large.[5] The increase in employment also increases real personal disposable income, which is further increased by a rise in the number of hours worked. And these higher incomes lead, after tax and savings leakages, to higher personal consumption. Over the middle years the GDP multiplier· is rather lower than before, reflecting both a lower medium-term marginal propensity to consume in the new consumption function, and the reduction in the long-term output–employment elasticity from unity to 0.6. One apparently puzzling factor is that although the Treasury employment response is initially some 100,000 per quarter higher than in the National Institute model, the resulting increase in real disposable income looks low relative to real output. The reason for this is that consumer prices rise slightly because of an increase in local authority rates following the increase in local authorities' consumption, tending to reduce real incomes. The effect on imports is relatively small because of the low direct marginal propensity to import out of public consumption and because of the low reponse of real personal disposable income relative to real output. The deterioration in the current balance of payments reaches £72m by the end of the period, of which £42m relates to goods and services, the remainder representing lower interest receipts from abroad arising from the cumulative loss of foreign currency reserves.

Simulation 2

Public authorities' consumption by £100m at 1970 prices in each quarter; interest rates fixed, earnings endogenous, floating exchange rate (see Table 8.2 and Figures 8.1 and 8.2, Simulation 2).

Many of the model properties in this simulation depend upon the respective wage–price feedbacks and, as was pointed out above, this is an area of considerable uncertainty. Since the simulation assumes a freely floating exchange rate, the way in which this is determined is also of importance. Simple economic theory suggests that monetary and fiscal policy will, *ceteris paribus*, be more expansionary under a floating than under a fixed exchange rate regime. This is essentially because, in a floating regime, the addition to imports resulting from higher expenditure will bring down the exchange rate, thus improving competitiveness and hence improving the *real* trade balance relative to the fixed rate simulation. The 1977 versions of the models had this property, the Treasury model over the whole of the simulation period and the National Institute model for all except the last few quarters. The National Institute model retains this property as a comparison of Simulations 1 and 2, although in the Treasury model the multiplier in Simulation 2 is higher than in Simulation 1 only over the first six quarters of the simulation.

The main reason for the smaller expansionary effect in the floating rate

TABLE 8.2 Simulation 2: (Public Authority Consumption +£100m per quarter, 1970 prices; interest rate fixed, earnings endogenous, floating exchange rate)

National Institute Model

| | £m (1970 Prices) | | | | | | | (000s) | % Change | | | | £m | |
Quarter	RPDI	C	I	S	X	M	GDP	E	EARN	CED	ER	MS	GDP	CB
1	28	10	1	−16	1	17	69	77	0.2	—	−0.1	0.1	90	−17
2	46	21	2	3	1	29	85	125	0.2	—	−0.3	0.1	117	−33
3	61	32	5	10	—	36	94	163	0.3	0.1	−0.7	0.6	138	−50
4	67	39	8	9	—	41	97	191	0.4	0.2	−1.1	0.9	158	−64
5	71	43	11	4	2	45	96	210	0.6	0.4	−1.3	1.3	185	−77
6	79	48	13	—	—	45	95	223	0.9	0.5	−1.5	1.6	211	−89
7	81	50	13	−5	5	44	99	231	1.3	0.8	−1.9	1.7	250	−102
8	78	48	14	−3	6	44	103	237	1.6	1.0	−2.4	1.9	296	−124
12	41	29	10	−5	2	38	83	234	2.9	2.3	−4.1	3.4	575	−203
16	−8	−10	−6	−3	−5	25	45	166	4.8	3.7	−6.0	4.9	1054	−182
24	−147	−122	−37	−1	−23	−12	−60	18	8.9	6.5	−6.1	7.8	2070	−91

Treasury Model

| | £m (1970 prices) | | | | | | | (000s) | % change | | | | £m | |
Quarter	RPDI	C	I	S	X	M	GDP	E	EARN	CED	ER	MS	GDP	CB
1	48	73	1	4	−3	7	148	202	0.3	0.2	−0.2	0.1	176	−14
2	69	28	7	25	−2	21	125	217	0.7	0.3	−0.5	0.2	162	−30
3	74	24	8	33	−2	27	125	229	0.8	0.4	−0.8	0.3	173	−49
4	78	19	10	22	−1	30	111	234	1.0	0.6	−1.0	0.5	198	−39
5	75	17	10	19	−1	28	106	237	1.1	0.7	−1.3	0.8	221	−43
6	72	31	9	15	−1	24	117	241	1.3	0.9	−1.4	1.0	267	−32
7	73	23	8	10	−1	23	107	237	1.6	1.1	−1.5	1.2	291	−37
8	75	20	7	6	−1	17	104	234	1.9	1.2	−1.5	1.4	329	−31
12	57	1	−2	−2	—	—	90	213	2.9	2.1	−2.6	2.4	574	−23
16	52	−10	−1	−5	−2	−3	81	198	4.1	3.1	−4.1	4.4	936	−15
24	37	−50	8	−1	6	−16	80	195	7.3	5.6	−5.0	9.0	2163	179

For Key and Note, see Table 8.1.

simulation in the Treasury model is the increased importance of real wealth in the consumption function as the following analysis shows. The rise in public consumption produces a balance of payments deficit on current account, and the spot rate must fall sufficiently to generate expectations of an appreciation that will attract a matching capital inflow. The rise in the domestic price level occasioned by both the increase in earnings and the fall in the exchange rate is much the same as before. However, an increase in inflation now has a much greater depressing effect on the economy on account of the implicit wealth variable in the consumption function. This wealth effect is the predominant factor in reducing the value of the multiplier over quarter 9 to quarter 12, but thereafter the most noticeable difference concerns exports. In LLO the exchange rate fell in absolute terms by more than the rise in domestic prices, leading to an improvement in export competitiveness averaging $\frac{3}{4}$ per cent and a consequent increase in UK export volume. But on the current version of the Treasury model, the simulation causes the exchange rate to depreciate by nearly 2 per cent less, so that there is no longer any significant gain in UK export competitiveness. The main explanation for this change in the behaviour of the exchange rate is readily apparent. The response of consumers to the fiscal stimulus now diminishes more rapidly over time as inflation erodes the real value of personal sector wealth, reducing the demand for additional imports. A smaller balance of payments deficit in reponse to fiscal expansion means that the spot rate now has less far to fall under a floating regime in order to attract a matching capital inflow. But many of the changes in model specification made during 1977/78 will impinge on the exchange rate in one way or another, and it is very difficult with such a highly endogenous variable to determine all the factors that are at work. At a purely intuitive level the results of the present simulation do appear to be more acceptable, in that it always seemed unlikely that a sustained fiscal expansion by government should lead in the long run to substantially higher export volumes.

The long-run coefficient on prices in the Phillips curve in this version of the model is imposed at unity rather than at its estimated rate of 0.82. The wage–price spiral is thus more explosive than before with earnings and prices increasing by 8.9 per cent and 6.5 per cent respectively by the end of the simulation period, compared to 6.8 and 5.3 per cent in the Treasury model. The high earnings levels in this simulation have important implications for the value of the multiplier because of the progressivity of the tax system in the National Institute model. Personal income tax revenue increases by 1.6 per cent for every percentage increase in personal incomes, so that 'fiscal drag' operates powerfully to reduce real disposal income in this simulation.

Fiscal drag explains why the GDP multiplier in Simulation 2 falls away towards the end of the simulation period, below the levels of the multiplier obtained in Simulation 1. This fall is very much an artificial phenomenon, since in practice the authorities would almost certainly carry out some form of indexation of the tax system. (Indeed, under current legislation they are effectively committed to the indexation of personal tax allowances.) The higher multiplier over much of the simulation period compared with Simulation 1 is mainly due to the visible trade balance terms in the exchange rate equation. The current balance worsens as imports increase due to the rise in expenditure, which lowers the exchange rate. The exchange rate falls faster than the domestic price level rises, so that there is a gain in trade competitiveness. This reduces the increase in imports below what they would have otherwise been and, more importantly, prevents the fall in exports that occurred in Simulation 1 due to the lack of competitiveness. The *real* trade balance is consequently improved, which enhances the value of the GDP multiplier. But towards the end of the simulation period this process is reversed and exports are reduced. The fall in consumption due to fiscal drag leads to lower imports, which reverses the deterioration in the current balance, whereupon the exchange rate begins to fall by less than the rise in domestic prices, so that competitiveness is lost.

Simulation 3

Income tax reduced by £100m at 1970 prices in each quarter; interest rates fixed, earnings endogenous, floating exchange rate (see Table 8.3 and Figures 8.1 and 8.2, Simulation 3).

The results for both models are not much changed from those reported earlier. Compared to Simulation 2, the National Institute model results are fairly similar for the first two years except that the effects are somewhat muted because of the greater direct leakage with the tax stimulus: the whole of the spending increase goes directly onto total final expenditure, whilst the tax cut increases total final expenditure through consumption via real disposable income, and there is a substantial leakage into savings. The tax multiplier also starts from a much lower level than the expenditure multiplier, primarily because there is no direct increase in public sector employment in the tax simulation, and also because of the lag between an increase in disposable income and an increase in consumption. The tax multiplier falls away towards the end of the simulation, and as in the case of the expenditure multiplier this is largely due to the progressivity of the tax system. (Although the initial adjustment in the simulation is to reduce taxes by £100m per quarter at 1970 prices, taxes remained endogenously determined in this simulation so that the final changes in taxes will in general be different from the initial adjustment.)

The Treasury results are somewhat different from those of the National Institute model. The tax multiplier is initially lower than the expenditure

TABLE 8.3 Simulation 3 (*Income tax – £100m per quarter, 1970 prices: interest rates fixed, earnings endogenous, floating exchange rate*)

National Institute Model

Quarter	£m (1970 prices)							(000s)	% change				£m	
	RPDI	C	I	S	X	M	GDP	E	EARN	CED	ER	MS	GDP	CB
1	107	37	2	−11	2	5	18	9	0.1	—	—	—	23	−4
2	115	58	5	−4	5	13	39	28	0.1	—	—	—	51	−10
3	125	73	10	6	7	22	57	52	0.2	—	—	0.1	78	−18
4	132	82	16	12	9	30	70	78	0.2	0.1	−0.1	0.3	96	−28
5	139	89	22	13	11	37	76	102	0.2	0.1	−0.1	0.6	108	−10
6	149	96	26	8	10	39	78	120	0.2	0.2	−0.3	0.8	113	−52
7	156	101	29	4	13	41	81	134	0.4	0.2	−0.4	1.1	125	−62
8	163	106	30	4	13	43	86	145	0.6	0.2	−0.7	1.2	145	−77
12	155	106	27	5	20	45	87	166	1.4	1.0	−1.9	2.3	307	−131
16	125	85	13	−2	18	37	58	146	2.6	1.9	−3.4	3.3	593	−81
24	26	7	−15	−8	2	9	−22	12	5.2	3.7	−3.5	3.8	1211	+10

Treasury Model

Quarter	£m (1970 prices)							(000s)	% change				£m	
	RPDI	C	I	S	X	M	GDP	E	EARN	CED	ER	MS	GDP	CB
1	94	25	—	1	−1	2	19	6	—	—	—	—	24	−4
2	106	43	1	5	−1	7	33	15	—	—	—	0.2	39	−11
3	109	54	2	10	−1	12	42	24	—	—	—	0.4	36	−31
4	106	56	3	12	—	19	40	31	−0.1	—	−0.2	0.7	42	−28
5	97	61	5	12	1	22	44	38	−0.3	—	−0.5	1.0	37	−38
6	92	60	7	12	2	21	47	44	−0.5	—	−0.8	1.3	36	−32
7	89	57	8	11	5	20	49	48	−0.7	−0.1	−1.2	1.5	19	−40
8	91	56	10	10	8	16	57	53	−0.7	—	−1.4	1.7	23	−34
12	90	51	13	16	32	4	95	85	−0.6	0.3	−1.6	2.6	111	−13
16	115	56	15	10	55	5	116	120	−0.2	0.4	−1.7	2.8	239	45
24	101	45	15	5	87	1	137	156	0.8	1.3	−2.9	7.2	745	202

For Key and Note, see Table 8.1.

173

multiplier, but catches up with the expenditure multiplier by quarter 11, and thereafter rises steadily to reach a long-run value of 1.4. There are two main reasons for this. Firstly, the Treasury Phillips curve contains a retentions ratio (the ratio of gross to net wages). The reduction in income tax raises the retention ratio, which significantly reduces the effects of the wage–price spiral, so that at the end of the simulation period prices are only 1.3 per cent above those of the base run, compared with 5.3 per cent in Simulation 2. (Experiments with the National Institute model suggest that the inclusion of such a retentions ratio has a similar impact on the relative effectiveness of expenditure and taxation policies.[6]) The smaller price rise reduces the negative effects on the GDP multiplier via real wealth and fiscal drag on consumers' expenditure, which now increases throughout the period. This result rests largely on the influence of a single parameter in what is undoubtedly one of the most difficult relationships to model in the UK economy. It must be admitted that there are few satisfactory empirical wage equations in existence for the UK, and the econometric evidence that wage bargaining is significantly affected by changes in direct taxation is not completely conclusive. The second reason is that tax cuts produce a considerably lower revenue feedback initially than do expenditure increases, so that there is a bigger rise in the PSBR and an appreciably faster growth in the money supply. This in turn causes faster depreciation of the exchange rate. But because the tax cuts also reduce wage demands and hence home costs there is little increase in the domestic price level, despite the fall in the exchange rate. Hence there is a substantial gain in trade competitiveness, which leads to a substantial increase in the volume of exports and reduction in imports. Thus in the Treasury model the tax cut policy produces more favourable economic conditions in later years, both higher GDP and less inflation.

Simulation 4

Ex ante balanced budget simulation. Public authorities' final consumption increased by £100m at 1970 prices in each quarter and income tax initially increased by an identical amount. Interest rates fixed and average earnings and exchange rate endogenous (see Table 8.4 and Figures 8.1 and 8.2, Simulation 4).

and

Simulation 5

Ex post balanced budget simulation. Public authorities' final consumption increased by £100m at 1970 prices in each quarter and income taxes adjusted so as to leave the public sector borrowing requirement unchanged from the

TABLE 8.4 Simulation 4 (Ex ante balanced budget (taxes and public authority consumption +£100m per quarter, 1970 prices): interest rates fixed, earnings and exchange rate endogenous)

National Institute Model

Quarter	£m (1970 prices)							(000s)	% change				£m	
	RPDI	C	I	S	X	M	GDP	E	EARN	CED	ER	MS	GDP	CB
1	−78	−27	−2	−5	−1	11	51	68	0.1	—	−0.1	—	67	−13
2	−69	−38	−3	7	−3	16	46	97	0.1	—	−0.3	—	65	−23
3	−63	−41	−5	5	−7	14	36	111	0.2	—	−0.6	0.3	60	−32
4	−66	−44	−8	−3	−10	11	26	113	0.3	0.2	−1.0	0.6	61	−36
5	−67	−46	−11	−9	−10	8	19	108	0.5	0.3	−1.2	0.7	77	−37
6	−69	−48	−14	−8	−10	6	17	102	0.7	0.5	−1.3	0.8	99	−37
7	−75	−51	−15	−9	−9	3	17	96	0.9	0.6	−1.6	0.8	126	−41
8	−95	−57	−16	−7	−8	1	17	91	1.1	0.8	−1.8	0.8	152	−47
12	−115	−79	−17	−11	−17	−6	−7	66	1.6	1.4	−2.3	1.3	268	−73
16	−135	−96	−20	−3	−23	−11	−17	29	2.2	1.8	−2.6	1.5	447	−68
24	−173	−131	−23	−4	−25	−20	−41	−1	2.3	2.6	−2.6	1.7	806	−40

Treasury Model

Quarter	£m (1970 prices)							(000s)	% change				£m	
	RPDI	C	I	S	X	M	GDP	E	EARN	CED	ER	MS	GDP	CB
1	−53	47	1	2	−2	5	128	196	0.3	0.2	−0.2	0.1	151	−9
2	−37	−16	6	19	−1	14	92	202	0.6	0.3	−0.1	—	123	−19
3	−35	−28	7	22	−1	15	85	205	0.8	0.4	−0.1	−0.1	128	−28
4	−27	−35	7	11	−1	12	73	204	1.1	0.6	—	−0.2	159	−9
5	−20	−40	6	7	−1	8	64	200	1.4	0.7	0.1	−0.2	188	−4
6	−17	−23	2	3	−4	6	71	199	1.8	0.9	0.3	−0.3	237	5
7	−12	−28	—	—	−7	6	60	191	2.2	1.1	0.3	−0.4	268	−2
8	−13	−29	−3	−4	−10	6	49	183	2.5	1.2	0.2	−0.4	298	−6
12	−34	−47	−14	−19	−34	−2	−6	128	3.4	1.8	−0.1	−0.3	441	−25
16	−69	−70	−16	−16	−56	−10	−37	79	4.3	2.6	−1.1	0.9	680	−57
24	−98	−103	−8	−6	−81	−19	−60	40	6.3	4.2	−2.5	1.0	1320	−61

For Key and Note, see Table 8.1.

175

TABLE 8.5 Simulation 5 (Ex post balanced budget (public authority consumption +£100m per quarter, 1970 prices: income tax adjusted to leave PSBR at levels of base run): fixed interest rates, endogenous earnings, floating exchange rate).

National Institute Model

Quarter	£m (1970 prices)							(000s)	% change				£m	
	RPDI	C	I	S	X	M	GDP	E	EARN	CED	ER	MS	GDP	CB
1	-69	-24	-1	-6	—	12	53	69	0.1	—	-0.1	—	69	-14
2	-59	-32	-2	6	-3	17	49	99	0.1	—	-0.2	—	69	-24
3	-58	-36	-4	6	-7	16	41	115	0.2	0.1	-0.6	0.4	66	-33
4	-63	-41	-7	-2	-9	13	30	118	0.3	0.2	-1.0	0.6	66	-38
5	-68	-45	-10	-8	-10	9	21	113	0.5	0.3	-1.2	0.7	80	-39
6	-67	-47	-12	-9	-11	6	18	106	0.7	0.5	-1.3	0.9	100	-39
7	-72	-50	-14	-10	-9	3	18	99	0.9	0.6	-1.6	0.8	128	-42
8	-82	-55	-15	-7	-7	2	18	94	1.1	0.8	-1.8	0.9	156	-49
12	-125	-82	-18	-10	-17	-7	-9	65	1.6	1.4	-2.4	1.3	271	-72
16	-148	-105	-23	-4	-23	-13	-25	18	2.3	1.9	-2.6	1.5	441	-41
24	-141	-113	-19	-2	-24	-15	-26	11	3.4	2.6	-2.5	1.6	815	12

Treasury Model

Quarter	£m (1970 prices)							(000s)	% change				£m	
	RPDI	C	I	S	X	M	GDP	E	EARN	CED	ER	MS	GDP	CB
1	-42	49	1	3	-2	5	130	197	0.3	0.2	-0.2	0.1	154	-10
2	18	—	6	20	-1	16	104	206	0.6	0.3	-0.3	0.1	137	-21
3	25	-3	8	26	-1	19	104	24	0.8	0.4	-0.5	0.1	150	-36
4	25	-7	9	16	-1	19	92	217	1.0	0.6	-0.5	0.2	180	-23
5	20	-16	8	13	-2	19	84	218	1.2	0.7	-0.6	0.3	202	-22
6	25	3	5	9	-3	14	74	219	1.5	0.9	-0.6	0.3	251	-13
7	27	-3	5	5	-4	14	83	213	1.9	1.1	-0.6	0.4	277	-19
8	21	-8	3	1	-6	11	75	208	2.2	1.2	-0.6	0.5	309	-18
12	-14	-34	-8	-12	-17	-3	33	165	3.1	1.9	-1.1	0.9	492	-15
16	-64	-67	-12	-17	-32	-13	-6	117	4.2	2.7	-1.5	1.8	750	-9
24	-84	-94	-12	-13	-74	-11	-66	50	6.8	4.3	-1.6	1.3	1387	-47

For Key and Note, see Table 8.1.

base run. Interest rates fixed, average earnings and exchange rates endogenous (see Table 8.5 and Figures 8.1 and 8.2, Simulation 5).

One of the most well-known properties of the simple Keynesian *IS/LM* model that is presented in most intermediate economic textbooks is that known as the 'balanced budget multiplier theorem'. In such models it is easy to show that an increase in government spending that is financed by an equivalent increase in taxation will lead to a multiplier equal to unity, i.e., total spending increases by an amount equal to the initial rise in government spending. For example, given the national income identity

$$Y = C + I + G + X - M \tag{1}$$

where Y is total income, C is consumption, I is investment, G is government expenditure, X is exports and M is imports, and given the simple consumption function:

$$C = a + bYD \tag{2}$$

$$YD = Y - T \tag{3}$$

where YD is disposable income and T is taxes, it follows that:

$$Y = \frac{a - bT + I + G + X - M}{1 - b} \tag{4}$$

$$YD = \frac{a + I + X - M + G - T}{1 - b} \tag{5}$$

The government expenditure and tax multipliers are thus $1/(1 - b)$ and $-b/(1 - b)$ respectively, and since the model is linear while taxes are exogenous, the balanced budget multiplier is simply the sum of the two separate multipliers, i.e., unity. Few, if any, texts suggest that such deductions from a highly simplified abstract theoretical model provide a good guide to real world behaviour. In fact, this very simple model excludes a large number of leakages and income–expenditure feedback so that in practice the balanced budget multiplier need not be equal to unity at all. This result has been known for many years, and was demonstrated, for example, by Baumol and Peston (1955), who pointed out that in practice there is very little assurance that unity is even a rough approximation to the balanced budget multiplier. They considered the simple model result to be misleading in that it 'appears by a feat of magic to be able to determine an empirical magnitude ... without the use of any empirical material'.

One factor working in favour of a positive balanced budget multiplier is the fact that public authorities' current spending is thought to possess a much lower marginal propensity to import than private consumer spending. The current version of the Treasury model shows that of a direct increase of

£100m in aggregate demand at factor cost brought about by additional public procurement of goods and services some £24m would be met by imports. But to achieve a similar increase in total demand by raising private consumption would lead to an increase in imports of some £42m, nearly twice as much. Moreover, the total governmental marginal import propensity in the simulations reported here will be much lower than 24 per cent. In constructing the simulation, the additional government spending was assumed to be distributed pro rata over the main categories of expenditure, so that some 60 per cent took the form of extra public employment, which by definition has no direct import content. However, it should be stressed that the increase in employment indirectly increases consumption, which then increases imports.

Another empirical complication that the simple theoretical model ignores is that each category of final demand will have a different indirect tax content. This is another factor that will tend to produce a positive balanced budget multiplier, since the factor cost content of public expenditure is much higher than that of consumers' expenditure. For example, to raise final demand by £100m in 1970 prices at *factor cost* would require an increase in the volume of private consumption at *market prices* of about £125m, whereas public procurement expenditure would only have to rise by some £109m.

Empirical studies have revealed values for the balanced budget multiplier that are quite different from unity. In the US, Duggal (1975) used the November 1969 versions of the Brookings model and obtained a balanced budget multiplier whose peak value was 2.43 after seven quarters, and that actually exceeded the value of the expenditure multiplier from quarter eight to quarter 10. This was due to the very large revenue feedbacks arising from the increases in output. Although actual simulations of balanced budget multipliers with more recent versions of US models are not reported in the literature, Fromm and Klein (1976) note that the real GNP tax multipliers for a number of US models are significantly lower than the corresponding expenditure multipliers by a range of 0.3 to 0.9 after two to three years (most of the real expenditure multipliers being between 2.0 to 3.0 over this period). After twenty-four quarters, however, the range is considerably widened, with the tax multiplier being greater than the expenditure multiplier for some of the models. Similar results for the short-run balanced budget multiplier are obtained for the models reported here. After eight quarters, the *ex ante* and *ex post* balanced budget multipliers in the National Institute model are 0.18 and 0.17 respectively, and in the Treasury model 0.49 and 0.75. After twenty-four quarters, however, the respective figures are −0.26 and −0.41 for the National Institute and −0.60 and −0.66 for the Treasury. In Simulation 4, the *ex ante* case, we have simply increased the volume of public authorities' current spending on goods and services by £100m per quarter, while adding a residual at current prices to the equation for taxes on employment incomes equivalent to £100m in constant prices when deflated by the level of the consumer price index in the base run. Although the initial tax and spending change are the same, the results will not be exactly 'balanced budget' since in the absence of a lump sum tax system the level of taxes in the simulation will also vary with whatever changes take place in the level of activity.[7] Nevertheless, it may be of some interest to consider the effects of a policy change specified in this manner. One could, in fact, argue that this cruder specification of the balanced budget change is the more practical alternative. It turns out that the sophisticated version of the balanced budget simulation produces such an uneven quarterly path for taxes that it is unlikely that any existing tax instrument possesses the flexibility to achieve it.[8]

In both the National Institute and the Treasury models the *ex ante* and *ex post* balanced budget multipliers are very similar, and are not very far different from what one obtains by simply adding the expenditure multiplier to the tax multiplier with sign reversed. The *ex ante* multiplier is smaller in the early part of the simulation, reflecting the fact that the initial stimulus to the economy from the increase in public spending produces a further rise in taxes in addition to the initial exogenous increase. But since the GDP multiplier declines over time, this profile of an initial expansion in activity followed eventually by a large fall is reflected in the PSBR, which falls at first, but later rises. Consequently, in the *ex post* balanced budget case, taxes need to be raised by rather less over the first three years but rather more thereafter. For the Treasury simulation the *ex post* rise in GDP exceeds the *ex ante* almost throughout, although for the National Institute this only holds over the first two years.

In the National Institute model the separate expenditure multiplier is initially larger than the tax multiplier, and it then falls in value due to the progressivity of the tax system. The tax multiplier builds up more slowly, and although not reaching the peak levels of the expenditure multiplier, remains above the expenditure for the last eighteen quarters of the simulation. In the balanced budget case, the positive GDP multiplier in the early quarters is sufficient to set off the wage–price spiral in the model, principally due to the effect on the exchange rate of the deterioration in the current balance of payments. Subsequent reductions in the pressure of demand below the levels of the base run as the GDP multiplier becomes negative are not sufficient over the simulation period to reverse the feedback growth of earnings and prices. Thus, the increase in the price level over that of the base run means that not only does public expenditure in current prices increase by the increment in 1970 prices multiplied by the deflator, but the deflator itself increases so that the current price value of the whole of current public expenditure is increased. Thus, in order to produce an unchanged PSBR, substantial increases in taxation are required, which serve to depress the real disposable income of the personal sector and hence consumption.

In the Treasury model the path of the balanced budget multiplier is also effectively explained by combining the factors operating in the separate tax and expenditure multipliers. It should be noted that the favourable long-term effects shown for the tax reduction are now operating in reverse. The effect of the retentions ratio in the Phillips curve is to accelerate the wage-price spiral, which both increases fiscal drag and erodes personal sector net worth. Again it is worth emphasising the importance of the accompanying earnings and exchange rate assumptions in determining the long-run outcome. Under the 'conventional' assumptions of a given money wage and fixed exchange rate the results would have appeared more favourable to the balanced budget theorem, in that a positive multiplier would have emerged, approaching a reasonably stable value of 0.8 compared with unity in simulation. But even in this case, by quarter 8 it is the exogenous addition to public sector output (which by convention equals the constant price wages and salaries of the additional public sector employees) that accounts for the whole of the remaining increase in gross domestic product. The multiplier effects of the extra government procurement spending would have been more or less offset by falling consumer demand, with consequently no net stimulus to private sector output. In other words, the lags in the output–employment relationship are such that the initial procurement multiplier is fairly weak and is overwhelmed by the exogenous increase in taxes, so that real personal disposable income and hence consumption falls. This provides a good example of the importance attached to the correct determination of lag structures in any practical application of economic models to fiscal policy, something that a theoretical approach to policy-making is likely to ignore.

The National Institute and Treasury models both indicate a value for the balanced budget multiplier for the UK of well below unity even on the assumption of an accommodating monetary policy. Indeed, after four years both models indicate a negative value for this multiplier, mainly for reasons connected with the impact of inflation on the models. However, results must be treated with caution over this time period, particularly given the artificial nature of the simulations. Even over a period of two to three years, where the results are probably more reliable, the balanced budget multipliers are well below unity.

It was stressed above that the use of mechanically generated model results as a guide to policy recommendations can be full of pitfalls. Nevertheless, a considerable degree of overwriting of the results of both models would be required in order to escape from the conclusion that over a period of some two to three years it is difficult to stimulate domestic economic activity by a policy of balanced increases in public expenditure and taxation. Equally, for the models are approximately linear with respect to small shocks, the results indicate that a policy of tax and expenditure cuts would have little effect on domestic activity over this period, although this effect would be negative.

CONCLUSIONS

The paper by LLO concluded that there was rather less disagreement between the models that were analysed than one might have been led to expect from similar US studies, and that as far as the pattern of fiscal policy impact is concerned the UK models were telling similar stories. Over a period of two to three years this conclusion still holds broadly for the National Institute and the Treasury models, with neither model showing the very large impact on economic activity observed in US models from policies of public expenditure increases or taxation cuts, whether carried out separately or in combination. But the impact over this period in the UK models is by no means negligible; at end-1977 prices, for example, the value of the increase in public expenditure in Simulation 2 is about £1100m per annum, which creates 230,000 extra jobs in both models.

The multipliers in the two models over longer periods diverge quite considerably, although as in the LLO simulation we believe that we have been able to explain many of the differences between the models, and that therefore these differences are potentially reconcilable. One possible extension of research along these lines is to undertake a programme of model combination, so that variables or equations that have been potentially revealed as being important determinants of the properties of a particular model, such as the retentions ratio or the consumption function, could be tried out in another model to see if the properties of other models became more similar. In this way we might hope to isolate more clearly the fundamental areas of disagreement between models, although, to end on a somewhat pessimistic note, this procedure in itself is no guarantee that either model provides an accurate reflection of reality.

NOTES AND REFERENCES

1. A good description of both the forecasting and policy-making processes within the Treasury can be found in Chapters 3 and 4 of the *Report of the Committee on Policy Optimisation* (HMSO, 1978).

2. It should be stressed, however, that there is little faith in the existence of a stable Phillips curve for the UK.
3. As in Laury, Lewis and Ormerod (1978) the Treasury simulations employ a small set of provisional monetary relationships. The full-scale monetary model that has been developed in recent years has yet to be fully integrated with the rest of the system.
4. Simulations 1, 2, and 3 correspond to Simulations 1, 2, and 5 respectively in the Laury, Lewis and Ormerod (1978) paper.
5. In the context of the present simulation this effect may be exaggerated if increased deficit spending itself has adverse effects on consumer confidence.
6. For a discussion of this point see Ormerod (forthcoming).
7. In this case there is not a great deal of difference over the short run. The initial and final changes in personal taxes were as follows:

	Treasury		NIESR	
	Initial	Final	Initial	Final
Q1	112	126	112	118
Q4	119	156	119	137
Q8	130	215	130	169

8. In Simulation 5, spending is again increased by £100m per quarter at constant prices, but now personal income tax is used as an instrument in order to achieve zero change in the public sector borrowing requirement. The personal income tax function is altered in such a way that the change in income tax plus any induced changes in other tax receipts or reduction in transfer payments just equals the increase in public spending at current prices.

PART III

Making Fiscal Policy

CHAPTER 9

The Economics and Politics of Demand Management

F. T. Blackaby

INTRODUCTION

It is not fashionable, at the moment, to speak well of demand management. Indeed, we are confronted on all sides – or at least on many sides – with those who encapsulate Britain's economic experience of the past two decades in the following syllogism:

(a) Economic policy in Britain has been a failure. It has failed to improve our economic performance.
(b) Economic policy has consisted of 'Keynesian demand management'.
(c) Therefore 'Keynesian demand management' has been a failure.

The burden of this paper is to suggest that this syllogism is incorrect, and to suggest the following rather less succinct, less simplistic, and rather more laborious set of alternative propositions:

(a) The British economy has not performed well (compared with continental competitors) during the last two decades. Its wage-driven inflation has been worse than that of other countries; and its manufacturing industry has been inadequately competitive.
(b) 'Keynesian demand management' is not an appropriate way of dealing with wage-driven inflation or with lack of competitiveness.
(c) Further, the effect of 'Keynesian demand management' methods on employment in this country is limited, but not eliminated, by a high import propensity and, to a lesser extent, by the tendency for reflationary measures to push the exchange rate down.

However,

(d) The proponents of 'Keynesian demand management' have recognised most of these limitations for a long time.

In defence of Keynesis (handwritten margin note)

(e) It does not follow that, because 'Keynesian demand management' fails
to do everything, therefore it does nothing. The economy is not self-
righting, nor is it self-righting with any simple fiscal or monetary rule.
Consequently new fiscal judgements have constantly to be made.

(f) It may be more difficult than it used to be for a small country like Britain
to reflate alone. This makes it more important than it used to be that the
industrial countries as a whole should, at appropriate times (such as now),
reflate together. National Keynesianism may not rule as it once did; so
now it should be international Keynesianism that rules.

This paper is addressed to the defence of this set of propositions.

THE ATTACK ON REFLATION

Throughout the postwar period, up to the end of the 1960s, successive
governments practised demand management confidently – confidently, that
is, in the sense that they believed that it was the government's job to make
appropriate adjustments from time to time to the level of demand, predominantly through fiscal policy. The confidence of that period is expressed –
indeed perhaps exaggerated slightly – by Sir Douglas Wass in a lecture given
in 1978:

> For twenty-five years the industrialised Western economies, following
> their emergence from the chaos and destruction of the War, had experi-
> enced an era of steady and indeed rapid expansion. A Keynesian prescrip-
> tion of maintaining aggregate demand at a high pressure mainly by the
> counter cyclical use of fiscal policy seemed to have reduced the economic
> cycle to almost trivial dimensions. If the problem of inflation had not been
> disposed of, it did not seem to be much more than a mild irritant to those
> who had to take economic decisions. Here and abroad there was a mood
> of almost Victorian optimism among business men, bankers, consumers
> and Government officials ... [Wass, 1978]

There were certainly arguments about the appropriate frequency of intervention, and in the early 1960s there was the move to introduce instruments
of control that could be used between budgets – for example, Selwyn Lloyd's
regulator. Practitioners conceded that their quantifications of the effects of
tax changes were not precise (Hopkin and Godley, 1965; Shepherd and
Surrey, 1968). There were certainly arguments about whether the right stimuli had been applied at the right time. But it was not generally disputed
that a good part of economic policy was concerned with: 'The practical
application ... the broad rule – to stimulate demand when it is deficient and
to restraint it when it is excessive' (R. L. Hall, Introduction to Dow, 1965).

From fairly early on the practitioners became increasingly aware that demand management was not the whole story. For example, Harold Mac-Millan in his memoirs (1973, p. 85) describes how, back in 1962, he became disillusioned with demand management as a way of dealing with wage-driven inflation – though he preferred to use medical metaphors rather than technical economic phraseology to describe his disillusionment:

> During the previous twelve months the conventional and lowering regime had been conscientiously applied; yet the pressures were by no means reduced ... one of the usual symptoms of a boom, that is unjustified wage demands, continued unchecked ... this unexpected persistence of high fever in spite of a low diet [led to] my growing conviction that some better and more effective methods should be devised.

This is only one of a long list of possible examples, to show that the realisation of the limitations of demand management is no new thing. However, this did not mean that it was rejected *in toto*.

What one might call the root and branch attack on demand management – and, as I shall point out later, particularly on 'reflation' – came mainly during the last five years, and it came much more from the City journalists than from academics. So far as politicians are concerned, this particular route of influence is an important one; politicians do not read academic journals, but they do read the papers. The consequence has been that the root and branch critiques have had a disproportionately large influence on the way in which economic policy is discussed, so that it is much easier to find economic journalists than it is to find academic economists who will put forward these basically critical views. The main result has been to produce a magnificent confusion in the political statements on the matter. The great public relations achievement of the critics was to get a root and branch dismissal of demand management (again referring particularly to reflation) into the Prime Minister's speech to the Labour Party conference in 1976:

> We used to think that you could spend your way out of a recession, and increase employment by cutting taxes and boosting Government spend-ing. I tell you in all candour that that option no longer exists, and that insofar as it ever did exist, it only worked by injecting a bigger dose of inflation into the economy, followed by a higher level of unemployment as the next step. Higher inflation followed by higher unemployment. We have just escaped from the highest rate of inflation this country has known; we have not yet escaped from the consequences: high unemploy-ment. That is the history of the last twenty years. [Callaghan, 1976]

Mr Callaghan must have found that quotation something of an embarrass-ment in his attempts since that time to persuade the German and Japanese governments to reflate.

1976 was, I think, the high point of the influence of 'anti-reflationary' doctrine. Since then, of course, we have had the 1978 budget; and we are back in the old mode of deciding on the appropriate size of demand stimulus, and quantifying its effect on output: 'I have, therefore, concluded that it would be right to give the full year stimulus to the economy of £2½ billion – or about £2 billion in 1978/79. The measures should raise output by another three-quarters per cent in the next twelve months . . .' (Healey, Budget Speech, 1978). It is also interesting that it is not easy to find the critics of demand management going on record in advance of the 1978 budget to say that there should be no tax reductions at all. This is partly because, in the bowdlerised form of anti-demand management doctrines, it is reflation by increases in public expenditure that are considered to be particularly damaging; the criticism of reflation by tax reduction is much more muted. And, of course, reflation by reducing taxes on higher income groups is positively beneficial, because of the consequent release of entrepreneurial activity. (We should all pause from time to time to recognise the unconscious bias by which we tend to select for approval the economic doctrines most likely to bring benefit to the group to which we happen to belong.)

This issue of whether reflation 'works' is not just an academic question. Indeed, it is tempting to say that it is too serious a question to be left to academics. The Western industrial world is performing very badly. Up to 1973, its trend growth rate – that is, the average annual rise in aggregate real national product of the members of OECD – was 4–5 per cent. Now we have had five years in which that growth rate has been halved. Increasingly a number of large firms – whose assumptions about the medium-term future always tends to be simple extrapolations of the recent past – are coming to the conclusion that the period of rapid growth for the industrial world is over, and are basing their forward plans on a very much slower rate of growth in future. It is a great pity if all this is unnecessary. If there proves in fact to be little substance in the criticisms of the effectiveness of reflation – at least on an international scale; if, collectively, the Western industrial world could, by using fiscal policy, move back to its previous trend rates of growth without worsening the prospects for inflation; if, in short, we are simply suffering from a collective failure of Keynesian nerve – then it is a matter of some importance to clarify whether or not that is the case.

There are three fairly separate hypotheses that lead up to the conclusion that 'reflation does not work'. The first two imply that no reflation, whether national or international, works; the third essentially amounts to a caution about any nation trying to reflate alone. One of the main problems of certainly the first two of these hypotheses is that they face a confrontation with common sense. For there is a certain intrinsic plausibility in the proposition that, if there is a large number of persons unemployed, then if the government employs some of them, the number of those unemployed will fall. Equally, there is an intrinsic plausibility in the proposition that, if the government allows some of its citizens to keep more of their money, they will spend at least some of it, and so increase employment. To that extent the counter-hypotheses have something of an uphill task.

The first counter-hypothesis is built round the concept of the 'natural' rate of unemployment. Starting from the assumption that the economy is running at that 'natural' rate, it then considers the consequences of some reflation. It concedes that this will initially induce a faster rise in output than would otherwise have occurred; but after a short time-lag it leads to an accelerating inflation that proceeds until unemployment is brought back to its 'natural' rate, and output is where it would have been in the absence of reflation.

If this were the right picture of the effects of reflationary action on the UK economy, we should presumably observe successive episodes in which unemployment drops below some 'natural' norm, followed by accelerating price rises, a drop back in the rate of increase in output and a return to the previous level of unemployment. The trouble is that the UK experience just does not look like this at all. There was a long period, up to 1966, with very low figures of unemployment, well under $2\frac{1}{2}$ per cent, and with no significant tendency for the rate of inflation to accelerate. Since 1966, unemployment has never fallen below $2\frac{1}{2}$ per cent, trending strongly upwards, accompanied by accelerating inflation. It is very difficult, even with elaborate econometric prestidigitation to fit actual UK experience to this hypothesis; it is difficult to get an equation in which any series representing the pressure of demand for labour is significant, and of the right sign, in explaining the movement of money earnings if the last seven years are included.

Those who put forward this counter-hypothesis differ about whether or not reflation is permissible when unemployment is above the 'natural' rate. Some consider it might perhaps be used, in moderation, to accelerate a little the return to natural unemployment – a return that certainly they consider will occur in any case. This concession, however, is not very helpful, since nobody is prepared to say where the natural rate is.

The second counter-hypothesis is that any stimulus from the public sector simply crowds out the private sector. The sequence tends to be described as follows. Any public sector stimulus implies an increase in the borrowing requirement; the increased borrowing will force the government to raise the rate of interest. This will reduce not only investment spending but consumer spending as well through a wealth effect; and the reduction in private spending will neatly offset the public sector's increase. This concatenation of economic events is, of course, conceivable – as are many other such concatenations. But it is not enough to describe a possible sequence of effects. The important question is the size of the effects, and whether or not they are more powerful than other sets of possible effects working in the contrary direction – such as the effect on investment of the higher expectations of demand, or the direct effect on consumer spending of tax reductions.

What are the supposed numerical relationships between an increase in the PSBR and the rate of interest, and what in turn are the numerical relationships between changes in the rate of interest and consumer or investment expenditure?

If private investment is crowded out as a consequence of public reflationary methods, then this should, of course, be observable. So it is perhaps helpful, in assesing this counter-hypothesis, to look at two of the major reflations of recent years – 1963 and 1972 – and to observe whether, as a consequence, private sector investment rose or fell. Between 1963 and 1965, investment in manufacturing industry, at constant prices, rose 25 per cent; between 1972 and 1974, it rose 17 per cent. The postwar experience appears to be much more consonant with the view that reflation leads to upswings in demand and output, and private investment responds as output moves up more closely to capacity. The postwar pattern does not fit crowding out.

The third counter-hypothesis is of a rather different nature. It is not that reflation, considered globally, is ineffective, but rather that the industrial world has developed in such a way that it is more difficult than it used to be for individual countries to reflate on their own. The proportion of total expenditure that goes on imports has risen substantially, and exchange rates are now floating. As a consequence, a good deal of the effect of any national reflation leaks abroad; the balance of payments worsens, the exchange rate falls, the internal rate of inflation is thereby worsened, thus neutralising some of the internal reflationary effect. One might add that hot money will move away from the reflating country, intensifying the exchange rate movements.

This is an objection to reflation of a rather different nature; the implication is not that all reflations are ineffective, but that national reflations are more difficult than they were.

There is, as usual, the problem of fitting numbers to this series of effects. All forecasters at the moment have a significant 'import leakage' in the current rise in UK demand – though the forecasts differ about its size. For example, between the second half of 1977 and 1978, the Financial Statement forecast assumes that over 40 per cent of the rise in total final expenditure (at constant prices) goes on imports of goods and services; the NIESR forecast over the same period has a figure of 30 per cent for the important leakage – though it should be noted that these forecasts probably have different exchange rate assumptions. However, for the other steps in the sequence of effects, quantification is much less certain. The experience of floating exchange rates is short, and there is no certainty at all about the effect on the exchange rate of any particular size of change in the current surplus or deficit of the balance of payments. Nor is there certainty about the further effect of any consequent rise in import prices on the internal price level. For there are at the moment no good wage equations from which this effect can confidently be predicted. It is true that most wage equations around at the moment have strong price terms in them; some – the 'wage bargaining' type – include a direct effect for the movement of past prices, on the grounds that trade unionists begin, as a minimum, to try to recover the loss in real wages since the last award; other equations include the movement of past prices as a proxy for price expectations. It is clear why price terms have been introduced into wage equations – obviously they help the explanation a great deal at a time when both prices and wages are moving up sharply. However, all these equations are very bad at explaining what has happened from mid-1975 on. They cannot really be used to forecast with any certainty the effect of an increase in import prices on the subsequent movement of money earnings. There is a further complication that one of the front runners in wage equations gives significant weight to the movement of real post-tax earnings. There is a potential counter-force here, insofar as reflation serves to improve the movement of post-tax earnings.

We are left with the conclusion that certainly there is a sizeable import leakage; this is hardly news. It is much harder to make any precise statements about the other alleged chain of effects – the worsening of the balance of payments leading to a fall in the exchange rate, leading to a rise in import prices, leading to a further increase in money earnings, and so on. It is much more open to question how strong the links are in this particular chain.

I think the sensible conclusion to all this is that the Chancellor's statement in the 1978 budget, implying that as a consequence of tax reductions output would be higher than it would otherwise be, was right.

'RULES FOR DEMAND MANAGEMENT'

So far, I have argued that it was quite wrong to draw from the UK's postwar experience the lesson that the concept of demand management is wholly misconceived. I want to turn to another question: can one deduce from postwar experience 'rules' for its conduct? My answer is that there are no simple rules.

Early in 1975 the General Sub-committee of the House of Commons Expenditure Committee put this same question to a number of individuals and institutions: 'By what rule should the size of the financial deficit or surplus of the public sector be settled?' The National Institute submitted a memorandum, giving the answer that I have just given; this was not what the Sub-committee wanted to hear, and the National Institute was not invited to give oral evidence.

The National Institute argued that the decision on whether to increase or decrease effective demand, and how much, should be based on a forecast of the course of the economy in which the public sector is not put in as a single item. The various component parts of public revenue and expenditure should be incorporated, according to an economic classification, in the pigeonholes to which they appear most appropriately to belong. This is on the grounds that increases in different types of public expenditure have very different effects on the rest of the economy. Increases in pensions, for example, will by and large be spent, and will add to demand; the 'savings ratio' applicable to them is very different from the 'savings ratio' applicable to an increase in the amount of interest on the national debt that is paid to the personal sector. To take another form of government expenditure, investment grants may or may not increase total demand for investment goods; in some circumstances the volume of investment expenditure may change little, and companies may simply use investment grants to finance investment that they would in any case have undertaken. On the tax side, the same applies: increases in capital taxes have a very different effect on demand from increases in National Insurance contributions deducted from pay packets. To take a third example, the investment expenditure of a nationalised industry such as steel is much more clearly akin to the investment expenditure of private manufacturing industry in general than it is to, say, public expenditure on additional social workers in the London Borough of Sutton.

The procedure that is in fact followed is therefore a rational procedure. Public expenditure and taxation items are entered where they belong in the forecasting structure. For example, current grants to persons are added to the forecast of personal income, and income taxes are part of the same process by which an estimate of consumers' expenditure is derived from an estimate of personal incomes. The whole course of the economy is then considered, both public and private. If, as a result of the whole forecast, it appears likely that output will be rising either slower or faster than productive potential, then – other things being equal, and depending on the unemployment target that the government has chosen, and depending also on the price and balance of payments forecasts – it would be appropriate to adjust expenditure or, more normally, revenue.

It follows that there is no rule. The same size of aggregate public sector deficit in two successive years can have different economic consequences if the patterns of expenditure leading to that deficit are different. The decision about adjustments to public sector revenue or expenditure will depend, at any particular time, on the expectations about the movements of private expenditure.

In this process of trying to fix the appropriate size of the stimulus or the deflation, what should be the role of the calculations of the public sector's acquisition of financial assets, or the public sector borrowing requirement, either on a weighted or an unweighted basis, or the various 'full employment' calculations?[1] In my view, these calculations help very little in deciding what the number should be. Here are five reasons.

First of all, 'unweighted' figures are not very useful for estimating the effect of revenue and expenditure decisions. To quote Professor Artis:

> The actual unweighted public sector deficit ... is open in principle to two crucial objections. In the first place it implicitly treats every £1 of expenditure (of whatever kind) as equal in impact to every £1 of taxation (of whatever kind), whereas in fact the output generating (or, in the case of taxes, output-destroying) content differs from item to item ... Similarly the output generated by public expenditure as a whole may be judged greater than the reduction in competing demands on output implicit in a matching amount of tax revenues raised by the public sector. [1972, p. 294]

Various people who write City columns are coming to this point for the first time. They have discovered that the figure for the PSBR for the financial year 1977/78 is 'unreal' (in their phrasing), because it includes sales of BP shares and because the government cajoled the banks into undertaking a significant part of the provision of export credit. Unwittingly, these commentators are conceding the necessity for demand-weighted calculations, if one is to have such calculations at all.

Second, 'demanded-weighted' calculations of public sector revenue and expenditure are simply winkling out of the forecasting process the various public sector bits incorporated in it. This procedure really does not help much, since the decision on what the public sector sum should be depends on the sum of the private sector items that have been left behind.

Third, the prominence that has been given to forecasts of public sector deficits or borrowing requirements puts a load on these figures that they are wholly unable to bear. The forecast of the public sector borrowing requirement demands not only forecasts of central government revenue and expenditure, including debt interest, but also forecasts of the transactions of public corporations and the current expenditure and the borrowing of local authorities. By no means all of these separate components are in fact forecast in the main demand-forecasting model. The official forecasts tend regularly to be wrong by enormous margins. Thus in March 1974, in the budget speech, the Chancellor forecast a public sector financial deficit of £1.2 billion. Already by November 1974, *before* the changes in taxation made in the second budget of that year, the forecast was revised upwards to £4.1 billion. The record of 1977/78 provides an example of an error in the other direction. The budget forecast of the PSBR was £8½ billion; in the absence of the further tax reliefs announed in October 1977, the out-turn (on present figures) would have been £5½ billion. There is no point in basing policy on figures of this kind.

Fourth, partly but not wholly because of the unforecastable nature of these figures, it is not possible to make sensible deductions about the future movement of monetary aggregates from the PSBR forecasts. In the period from 1963 to 1967, if one subtracted external financing from the borrowing requirement, one could make a reasonable guess at the movement of the money supply (M3). Since 1969, that has not been the case. If the PSBR could be forecast with any degree of accuracy; if one could deduce from that forecast the likely movements either of the rate of interest or of the money supply; then there would be some point in that operation. Neither of these conditions is fulfilled.

Finally, there are the calculations of revenue and expenditure adjusted for full employment. I can see that these calculations may have a certain propaganda value in reminding people that the size of the deficit is the consequence of the depression, since proponents of balanced budgets appear to be getting an audience of some kind in this country. But I do not see how the calculation of a full employment budget surplus or deficit assists in the judgement of the size of an appropriate stimulus or an appropriate measure of deflation.

In my view, therefore, the basic framework of the Treasury model is unlikely to be substantially changed. It will still be centrally concerned with assessing the movement of demand in real terms for the economy as a whole; and it is on the basis of that assessment that various fiscal policy adjustments will periodically be stimulated, to see whether the outcome could be improved. None of this should be taken to imply, however, that demand management in any way holds a solution to Britain's general economic weakness; demand management could be described as the process of making the best of a bad job. We have a relatively inefficient manufacturing sector and an unreformed pay bargaining system; demand management does not help us with either of those problems.

THE POLITICS OF DEMAND MANAGEMENT

Politicians are genuinely concerned to improve the performance of the economy – as measured by the standard criteria of full employment, stable prices and rapid economic growth – because these objectives indicate reasonably well what the electorate want themselves. There is no great conflict here between the criteria that economists tend to use in judging economic performance, and the changes that politicians try to bring about. Good economic performance is electorally rewarding.

However, this general statement needs some qualification. First of all, governments can try to window-dress the economy in such a way that they can go to the country when things appear to be going well, just before they begin to go badly again. The standard way of doing this is to take advantage of the lag before increases in earnings work through to prices: there is a temporary rise in the standard of living until the movement of prices catches up. There are other devices, too, for postponing days of reckoning until after some chosen date: by using reserves to hold the exchange rate for example, or by buying off present wage claims by large future promises. So there is certainly a 'political trade cycle' (see chapter 6 and the Prologue in this volume).

Should one consider this a major blemish in the democratic process? Certainly in the UK, it does not in fact seem to have tilted the balance so fiercely towards the party in power that we have had no changes in government; and in any case it is rather difficult to see what could be done about it. The only sensible weapon is sophisticated public understanding of the economic situation; and that is asking a great deal.

However, distrust of politicians' manipulation of the economy has led recently to a number of suggestions that the government's freedom to manage demand should be in some way limited. There are the suggestions that the Bank of England should be made independent of the government and instructed to pursue a money supply rule: this is a suggestion much favoured by the editor of *The Times*. There have also been some more extreme suggestions that the government should be required to balance the budget each year; thus it should be specifically prohibited from undertaking *any* fiscal demand management.[2]

Three comments on these suggestions. First, they are politically rather fanciful. It is not easy to see why any government should introduce measures into the House of Commons that limit its powers. Once power has been taken by a government, it is not easily surrendered; just as individuals do not willingly put themselves into straight-jackets, in much the same way governments do not introduce self-imposed limits on what they are allowed to do.

Second, I think both these proposals embody a misunderstanding of the nature of UK inflation. The implication of the second proposal – that the budget should always be balanced – is presumably that deficit finance is at the root of the UK's inflationary problem. The argument is presumably that our inflationary troubles are caused by politicians who raise public expenditure in an irresponsible way because they have no need to increase revenue *pari passu*. The argument must be, presumably, that this has led to excess demand in the economy, and that it is excess demand that is driving up prices and wages. This proposition is, of course, very difficult to reconcile with the current high level of unemployment in Britain.

Indeed, it seems very possible that if we are to avoid continuing substantial depression in the UK economy, we may have to accept the idea that the public sector should normally be a substantial net borrower. This is simply because we have moved into a world in which the personal sector wishes each year to add substantially to its financial assets; and it seems most unlikely that the company sector will be willing to create sufficient financial liabilities to meet this demand. The argument here is that the rise in personal savings is not simply a consequence of the acceleration of the rate of inflation; it is that the personal sector (which, it must be remembered, includes pension funds) collectively wishes each year to put aside a larger portion of its income than it used to do in provision for the future.[3] The personal sector's own expenditure on capital goods – mainly on housing – takes up only a small part of this flow of savings; thus in 1977 the personal sector's net acquisition of financial assets was nearly £9 billion. There was no likelihood that the company sector would create financial liabilities of anything like this figure: their financial deficit was only of the order of £3 billion. So what would have happened to the economy if the public sector had refused to borrow? This is a question not only for 1977, but for future years as well: it seems most improbable that the personal sector's desire for additional financial assets will be matched by the company sector's desire to borrow. We had better reconcile ourselves to a public sector borrowing requirement for ever.

The third comment on this proposal for a constitutional requirement to balance the budget is to suggest a very different line of criticism of the possible political bias in politicians' weighting of economic objectives. The implication of the 'balanced budget' recommendation is that politicians are zealous in providing employment in the public sector and are careless of the inflation that results. Leaving aside the question of whether inflation has in fact resulted in recent years from excessive government borrowing, this misrepresents politicians' priorities. By now they know very well that there are more votes to be had by bringing down the rate of inflation than by bringing down unemployment. They have discovered that high unemployment is not much of a political liability. Large numbers of the unemployed – who indeed include those who for various reasons are on the margin of the labour force – do not vote. The employed are not much concerned with the plight of the unemployed – and indeed the unemployed are widely regarded as scroungers. The danger, therefore, is not that politicians are giving too big a weight in their judgements about economic policies to the reduction of unemployment, but rather that they are giving too small a weight. The unemployed have little voting strength, no organisation and consequently no power to disrupt society; and as a result the government is not effectively deterred from undertaking policies that impose a relatively miserable life on this small and unprotected group. There is a growing danger, not only in Britain but in the Western industrial world in general, that a high figure of unemployment will increasingly be accepted as a norm, because there is no sufficient effective democratic pressure on politicians to find non-inflationary ways of raising the effective demand for labour.

It is not sensible at all to suggest imposing constitutional constraints on the economic policies that governments adopt; but if it were sensible, then there might be some point in attempting to impose on governments the obligation to see that jobs are available for those who want them. There would be very little point in attempting to impose constraints on the way particular instruments of policy are used.

NOTES AND REFERENCES

1. See the discussion of alternative measures of fiscal influence by Keith Shaw in chapter 2 of this volume.
2. Buchanan, Burton and Wagner (1978). The authors want a written constitutional rule 'that total Government expenditure does not exceed total Government revenue from taxation and charges'. 'Government' is not defined, so it is not clear whether they are referring to the central government financial deficit or to the public sector financial deficit, or to the borrowing requirement of either of these groups.
3. Discussion of the recent increase in the personal sector savings ratio is to be found in Coghlan and Jackson (1978).

CHAPTER 10

The Future of Demand Management: Reviewing the Choices

A. Budd

INTRODUCTION

The natural reaction of economists, when asked to talk about the future, is to talk at considerable length about the past. I shall not completely resist the temptation since it is reasonable for a forecaster to see whether there has been any systematic behaviour in the past that will help him make predictions; but I shall practise restraint, partly because the past has been considered in Chapter 9 and partly because I take the phrase 'Reviewing the choices' as allowing me to say what I would *like* the future to be as well as what I expect the future to be.

I shall assume that 'demand management' is not confined to the conventional instruments of fiscal and monetary policy but also includes measures such as incomes policies and import controls. I shall also assume that the objectives of demand management include price stability as well as the stabilisation of output.

It would be foolish to attempt to make straightforward predictions about the future of demand management. Demand management will change as knowledge about the economy and technical skills change, and such developments are, by their nature, unpredictable. How could one answer the question: what shall we know about the economy in ten years' time? However, the whole question of demand management is so open at the moment that it seems worthwhile to consider the debate at some length since its outcome will be a major factor in the future of demand management. There is also a debate about the techniques, in the narrow sense of demand management, which has been concerned with the possible usefulness of the techniques of optimal control. I shall not deal with that particular debate. A complete account of it is to be found in the *Report of the Committee on Policy Optimisation* (HMSO, 1978).

198

QUESTIONS ABOUT DEMAND MANAGEMENT: OLD OR NEW?

Questions about demand management were raised most prominently in the mid-1970s when there were reasonable fears that the UK economy would collapse. The reaction mirrors the response to the economic crisis of the 1930s; as Strachey (1934) wrote:

> Both [schools] admit that the present situation is impossible. But each proposes a remedy which appears to be antithetical to the other. One school proposes to attempt to restore the free market in all its pristine purity: the other proposes to hasten forward the process by which the freedom ,of the market is being curtailed.

On the one hand we had the call for the revival of the market economy by Sam Brittan and Sir Keith Joseph, among others; on the other, we had the call for import controls and the reintroduction of economic planning by those on the Left of the Labour Party. So far the power of British compromise seems, as usual, to have triumphed, and economic policy is continuing much as before though with a greater leaning towards monetary measures and, possibly, with humbler aspirations.

The events of recent years, which are not solely confined to the UK have brought a variety of criticisms to bear on conventional demand management. The grounds for criticism can be listed as follows:
(a) stabilisation of output is impossible;
(b) stabilisation is possible but unnecessary, (i) because the economy is self-correcting, or (ii) because fluctuations in output are desirable;
(c) stabilisation is possible but requires different instruments from those currently used.
'Stabilisation' can be extended to cover any attempt to make the level of output and employment different from what it is otherwise expected to be. It thus includes attempts to raise the level of employment permanently.

Each ground for criticism is not necessarily linked with a single point of view. The Cambridge Economic Policy Group, for example, rub shoulders with their enemies, the monetarists, in more than one place. But the list provides a useful framework within which to discuss the debate. As a preliminary, we can consider the developments that have caused these criticisms of economic policy to emerge.

Common to all schools of thought, there has been a recognition that the constraints on the economy and hence on the achievements of economic objectives are far more severe than was previously thought. One could modify the above list to suggest that the limitations apply not to stabilisation on its own, but to the combination of stabilisation with a satisfactory outcome for inflation and/or the balance of payments. A remarkable statement of this view was made by Mr Callaghan in his speech to the Labour

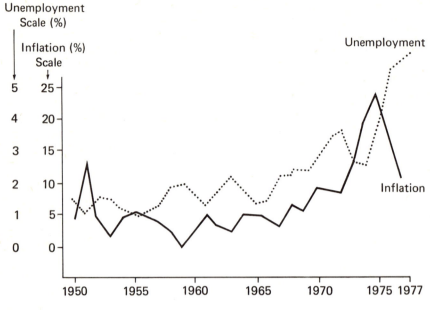

FIGURE 10.1   *Inflation and unemployment*

Party conference in 1976 (quoted in Chapter 9, p. 187). This statement represents an apparent rejection of both the methods and achievements of postwar economic policy. Mr Callaghan leaves it slightly unclear whether it is the world that has changed or merely our understanding of it. However, it does seem clear that it has become increasingly difficult to manage economic policy successfully. Figures 10.1 and 10.2 compare unemployment with inflation and the balance of payments for the UK (expressed as a ratio of GNP). Figure 10.1 would appear to show that unemployment and the rate of inflation were inversely related until the mid-1960s. Even after that period there is a general tendency for the rate of inflation to fall when unemployment rises, but the most striking feature has been the tendency for both inflation and unemployment to rise far above earlier levels. By the end of 1977, although unemployment was twice as high as in past peaks, inflation was well above its postwar average. A crude unemployment–inflation trade-off would suggest that persistently high levels of unemployment would be necessary to keep inflation below 10 per cent.

The balance of payments figures provide an equally depressing picture. Most economists would accept that improvement on the current account can be 'bought' by high enough unemployment; but the price has increased dramatically. In 1960, balance on the current account could be 'bought' for about 360,000 unemployed, in 1972 it cost 800,000, and by the end of 1977 it

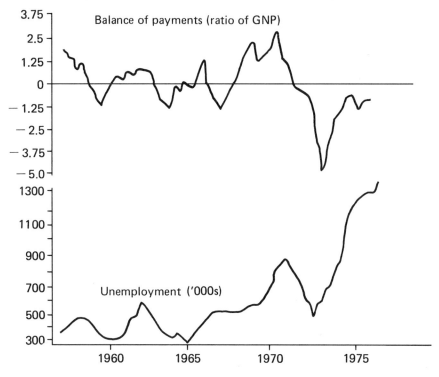

FIGURE 10.2   *Balance of payments and unemployment*

was costing about 1.3 million unemployed – even with the help of North Sea oil.

Alongside this apparent tendency for economic policy to become increasingly difficult, there has been disillusionment with an instrument that at one stage it was hoped would cure everything – a flexible exchange rate. One can say that the consensus during the 1950s and 1960s was that any combination of output and the balance of payments was feasible (subject to the physical limits of capacity) provided that the government gave itself the instruments of fiscal–monetary policy *and* the exchange rate. It was the failure to allow the exchange rate to change that forced the government to choose between output and the balance of payments. It oscillated between the two and the result was the familiar cycle of stop–go. Failure to change the exchange rate, it was argued, also caused the failure of the planning experiment of the 1960s. The persistence of balance of payments problems (even if their precise nature has changed), in spite of devaluation in 1967 and the adoption of flexible exchange rates in 1972, seems to be one of the most important events of recent years. It calls into question the whole analysis applied to the 1950s and 1960s. It has become necessary not only to consider why the adoption of flexible exchange rates has been so unsuccessful but also to find a new explanation for the policy difficulties of the 1950s and 1960s (although by recent standards they were years of outstanding economic success).

AN ANALYSIS OF THE ECONOMIC POLICY OF THE 1950s AND 1960s

I start by presenting what seems to me to be the most convincing explanation of these events. The account is provided in an article by Ball and Burns (1976) and has the desirable quality that it covers the periods of fixed and flexible exchange rates. The two key ideas in that article are that the prices of traded goods tend to be the same in all countries in terms of a common currency (the 'law of one price') and that real wages are, in the long run, unaffected by changes in the nominal exchange rate. From these two ideas it will follow that any change in the exchange rate will cause only a temporary improvement in the trade balance, since wages will adjust to remove the terms of trade effect of the devaluation. (In their valuable guide to the discussion, Odling-Smee and Hartley, 1978, seem to argue that the 'law of one price' on its own is sufficient for the Ball–Burns result. That would seem to be wrong unless the law also covers wages. Devaluation would be effective if it permanently improved the profitability of exports and it could do this, even if exports sell at world prices, provided it could alter real wages.)

In addition to an explanation of why devaluation will not work except in the short run, Ball and Burns are able to explain the major features of postwar economic history. A further theoretical implication of their approach is that, under fixed exchange rates, the United Kingdom's overall rate of inflation will depend on what is happening in the rest of the world. It will not equal inflation in the rest of the world since there can be a divergence between the rates of inflation of traded and non-traded goods. A full account of this is given in Burns, Lobban and Warburton (1977).

In terms of postwar history, the low rate of inflation under fixed exchange rates can be explained by the low rate of inflation in the rest of the world. Under fixed exchange rates, no other means of adjustment was possible. The shift in real wages raised the level of unemployment consistent with a given balance of payments target.

There were also other factors that were favourable to the United Kingdom in the early postwar years but where the benefits were fading. The UK became more vulnerable to foreign competition as trade was progressively freed and the tendency for the terms of trade between manufactured goods and raw materials to move in favour of manufactured goods was coming to an end. The government continued to try to repeat the successes of the early 1950s but failed. Critics of the government argued that the problem was an over-valued currency. But that diagnosis was mistaken. The problem was that, once real wages had reached their equilibrium level, attempts to raise output further would lead to an unacceptable loss of reserves. The pressure on the exchange rate was the point at which the inconsistency of policy objectives became evident; but the exchange rate was not a cause of the difficulties.

When sterling was eventually devaluated in 1967, the adjustment of real wages was much more rapid than it had been in 1949. From 1968 to 1970, however, fiscal and monetary restraint kept pressure off the exchange rate and in 1971 some revaluation against the dollar was possible in the light of the rapid growth of the US money supply. But after 1971 the rapid growth of the UK money supply generated pressures that were released by the abandonment of the fixed exchange rate and that eventually swept inflation to nearly 30 per cent a year.

That account raises two important questions. The first is how rapidly do real wages adjust after a change in the exchange rate? Even those who accept the general analysis may argue that it is possible to gain a succession of short-run benefits from a series of exchange rate changes and that these benefits are worth having. Alternatively, it may be argued that what is needed is a combination of exchange rate changes and incomes policy. The second question is more fundamental. Does the analysis provide an adequate or even relevant account of postwar developments? The key issue is the nature of the balance of payments constraint. The Ball–Burns approach sees balance of payments problems essentially as a reflection of domestic problems. Under fixed exchange rates, excess demand (whether caused by fiscal or monetary policy) causes losses of reserves that lead either to devaluation or to a reversal of domestic policy. Under flexible exchange rates, excess demand – especially excessive growth of the money supply – leads directly to exchange rate depreciation and an increase in the rate of inflation. The performance of the world economy is important but only insofar as it sets the level of demand for the United Kingdom's economy. The attempt to regulate UK output independently will fail because such regulation would require changes in real wages that are unattainable, except in the short run. One implication of this approach (although Ball and Burns do not advance it) is that the problem can be described as one of the level of real wages. The equilibrium rate of unemployment is the one at which there are neither inflationary nor balance of payments problems. Labour supply conditions are such that this equilibrium level is now much higher than it used to be (and it is certainly much higher than the level achievable under the conditions of artifically low real wages after the 1949 devaluation). This approach is rejected as wrong or, at best, irrelevant by the Cambridge Economic Policy Group (CEPG) (1978). They emphasise trade performance as the key to the problem:

> Discussion of the problems of stagnation and unemployment has been confounded by a failure to recognise the central importance of the balance of payments as a constraint on the growth of output and loss of industrial markets as the main cause of this constraint.
>
> Thus the monetarist school of analysis has fostered the false belief that much of the increase in unemployment has been voluntary, or has been caused by real wages being too high. These views are more pernicious than the misguided emphasis on the role of monetary policy as such, because they imply that the onus for curing unemployment and stagnation lies with workers and that there is little the government can do.

It can be objected that the CEPG do not explain the loss of industrial markets. In the Cambridge tradition, the loss is a 'stylised fact' that must dominate any search for the correct economic policies. But it is equally true that monetarist models do not explain it either. Estimated models in any tradition tend to show that the United Kingdom suffers a steady deterioration in its trade balance even if competitiveness is held constant. Monetarist models may show that a sufficient reduction in real wages, if it could be achieved, would solve the balance of payments problem; but it would be wrong to confuse the cure with the cause. To put it slightly differently, the Ball–Burns account provides an adequate demonstration that balance of payments problems and exchange rate problems are in practice excess demand problems, but it does not fully explain why the excess demand problems emerge at ever higher levels of unemployment. The CEPG make this development the central part of their policy analysis.

To be somewhat eclectic one can say that postwar history shows that it has become increasingly difficult to use the exchange rate as an effective instrument for changing real wages. Whereas it was once believed that a combination of fiscal and monetary policy with flexible exchange rates would allow the government to choose its desired level of output and balance of payments, experience of using flexible exchange rates shows that the belief was mistaken. The successes of the 1950s were due to temporary success in reducing real wages below their equilibrium level, but such successes cannot be repeated without effective incomes policies. At the same time there has been a steady loss of home and foreign markets to foreign competition that goes beyond any explanation in terms of movements of real wages. With conventional policies, including flexible exchange rates, the prospects are for static or rising levels of unemployment.

Against that background one can now consider the list of objections to conventional demand management.

SOME OBJECTIONS TO CURRENT METHODS OF DEMAND MANAGEMENT

Stabilisation of Output is Impossible

I consider the assertion that the stabilisation of output is impossible, first in the narrow sense of the attempt to smooth out economic fluctuations. The strongest statement would be that stabilisation is absolutely impossible whatever instruments one was prepared to use and whatever political and economic consequences one was prepared to tolerate.

That statement is surely not sustainable and, indeed, it would be difficult to find anyone to propose it. The more reasonable view is that stabilisation is in practice impossible within the limits of a liberal democracy. Since a large part of economic activity within a liberal democracy is left to the operation of markets in which there are bound to be occasional unpredictable shocks to supply or demand, it will not be possible to stabilise output completely. But that would seem to attack a claim for demand management that is rarely made. Few would argue that stabilisation policy claims to avoid fluctuations completely; the more normal claim is that it reduces their severity. It is, however, occasionally argued that even this modest ambition is unattainable because we do not know enough either about the structure of the economy or about shocks to it. This can be described as the 'early-Friedman' view, which was presented in *Essays in Positive Economics* (1953). His argument was, briefly, that attempts to stabilise output are as likely to be wrong as right. With a quadratic loss function, the costs of the errors will be larger than the benefits of the well-timed interventions; therefore it will be better not to intervene at all.

That view may still have its adherents. The record of intervention in the United Kingdom shows some tendency for reflationary measures to be introduced just as the economy is about to turn up of its own accord and the reverse at the beginning of the down-turn. Such errors can be explained in terms of the delay between changes in output and changes in politically sensitive indicators such as unemployment and inflation; but it would be a poor outlook if experience had not removed systematic errors of that type. Forecasters have not been notably good at forecasting turning-points in the UK economy, and users of forecasts are, or should be, aware of this; but apart from major forecasting errors in such years as 1975, forecasters should generally be able to distinguish between years of above and below trend growth and that should be sufficient for moderate success in stabilisation, provided that the policy-makers have adequate instruments to regulate demand.

The more serious question about the feasibility of demand management is derived from Friedman's (1968) later argument about the natural rate of unemployment. That argument is directed not so much towards stabilisation as towards attempts to reduce unemployment permanently below its 'natural' level. With conventional instruments of demand management, the result of attempting to do so would be ever-accelerating inflation or loss of reserves. Stabilisation in the narrow sense is not ruled out: if for some reason unemployment is above its natural level, the government can in theory hasten its return to equilibrium. (There are objections to this view, as will be discussed later.) A further implication of the model that generates the concept of the natural rate of unemployment is that attempts to reduce the rate of inflation will require unemployment to rise temporarily above its natural rate. It could be argued that the current policy stance towards inflation and unemployment, including Mr Callaghan's statement quoted earlier (p. 187), is close to this general approach. It is not clear whether the government believes that unemployment is currently at its natural level or whether it is deliberately leaving it above it as part of its attempt to reduce inflation; but its rather fatalistic attitude towards unemployment is consistent with the Friedmanite approach, even if it does not think in those terms.

To summarise, one could perhaps say that, rather than being 'impossible', recent experience may suggest that stabilisation is extremely difficult, certainly if one is limited to conventional instruments of demand management, if one wishes to avoid inflationary and/or balance of payments problems and if one is concerned with long-run as well as short-run effects.

Stabilisation is Unnecessary

The assertion that stabilisation is unnecessary is usually based on a mixture of positive and normative views. The positive views assert either that the economy is self-stabilising or that there is a revealed preference for instability. The normative views assert either that the costs involved in a slow adjustment to full employment should be ignored or that the revealed preference for stability should be respected.

The main sources for the view that the economy is self-stabilising have been the neo-classical/monetarist school and the early version of the CEPG model. The former relied on market behaviour in the markets for labour, goods and financial assets; the latter relied on stable propensities to spend by the private sector. The CEPG view has been very much modified by the recognition that private expenditure depends, *inter alia*, on the rate of inflation. The neo-classical/monetarist view varies from a rather weak version as propounded by Friedman, for example, to the much stronger view expressed by the supporters of rational expectations (see Sargent, 1973, for example).

A major difference between the CEPG and the neo-classical/monetarist approach concerns the nature of the equilibrium at which the economy settles. For the neo-classicals the equilibrium is one of full employment; for the CEPG it is not. Thus the CEPG case is not so much that stabilisation is unnecessary as that it is irrelevant. If it is conducted according to conventional means it is actually harmful since the government's attempts to reduce unemployment will simply lead to severe balance of payments problems and to increased instability.

The rational expectations case is, briefly, that all actors in the economy understand its structure as well as does the government and are as capable of forecasting exogenous shocks to it. The only inside knowledge that the government has concerns its own policy intentions; but it would be much more sensible to share this knowledge. The conclusion of the argument is that the government has no role to play in economic stabilisation. If the economy displays cycles, this may be due either to the erratic behaviour of governments or to a rational response to shocks. If companies reduce output rather than prices and do not switch to domestic production during a world depression, this represents their rational choice. If workers become unemployed rather than cut their wages or switch jobs, this too represents their rational choice. Attempts by the government to interfere merely makes it more difficult to shift back to export production, for example, when world demand recovers.

It can also be argued that excessive stabilisation makes it more difficult to generate structural change in the economy. Successful short-term stabilisation may have involved costs in terms of the long-run growth of productivity.

The arguments about the need for stabilisation should at least have raised serious questions in policy-makers' minds about whether they believe the economy is stable in the longer term. The rational expectations argument should have reminded them that the naive model of percipient policy-makers and short-sighted workers and employers that seemed to provide the basis of much intervention should be questioned, if not abandoned.

Stabilisation Requires New Instruments

The previous arguments have questioned the ability of fiscal and monetary policy to reduce fluctuations in output or to raise the level of employment permanently without harmful consequences for inflation and/or the balance of payments. The question is therefore raised whether new instruments should be adopted. The two most seriously canvassed are incomes policies and import controls. The debate has centred on the issue of whether the policies can work and whether if they did work the costs would be acceptable. The arguments again involve positive and normative views. There has been no convincing evidence on the former and the latter are, by definition, not resolvable by fact or logic.

The debate on import controls is the least satisfactory. Within a simple

Keynesian model it is easy to see that a reduction in the propensity to import will raise the equilibrium level of output. As the CEPG have argued, the potential welfare losses through the limitation on trade are minor compared with the increase in total output. But it is the question of the change of output that is most at issue and there is almost no common ground between the Keynesians and the monetarists. If unemployment is currently above its equilibrium level, import controls are one device among others (including devaluation for lowering real wages and increasing employment). But, for the monetarists, if unemployment is at its natural level, output will only rise without accelerating inflation if import controls shift the demand curve for labour (there is no reason to suppose they will shift the supply curve).

One point that can be made about import controls is that, even if they do not allow unemployment to be reduced permanently, they may increase the government's control over output. It has been pointed out by Burns that the ratio of imports to GDP has now reached a level last observed just before the outbreak of war in 1914. It may well be that political pressures will not allow governments to abandon control over the economy to the extent implied by the increasing share of foreign trade in output. Thus import controls may be adopted even if they are not expected to reduce unemployment permanently.

It is natural when considering demand management to limit attention to methods currently in use or to methods used in the past. Economic models are designed to investigate a narrow range of problems using a narrow range of policies. The odds are weighted against a completely new approach and it is not easy to identify any serious contenders, though it would be foolish to think that there are no advances to be made in devising new instruments.

REVIEWING THE CHOICES

It seems sensible to consider the future under the separate headings of objectives and techniques. That would at least correspond to the simple textbook view that there are problems about objectives, which are the responsibility of politicians, and technical problems, which are the responsibility of economists (among others). It is fairly clear, however, that the distinction is inadequate. At any time, economic policy is concerned with a restricted set of economic variables. Variables are included only if it is believed that they are capable of being affected by economic policy. That may sound obvious, but the process by which the policy-makers – and the general public – decide what is feasible is a mixture of the technical and the political. Full employment became an objective of policy when Keynes showed how to achieve it. Economic growth, however, became an objective of economic policy in the early 1960s before the techniques were available to generate it. The Labour Party could have said so, but instead successfully outbid the Conservative Party in its claim to mastery of the necessary techniques. The complete failure of the attempt to accelerate economic growth removed it from the objectives of economic policy. It would be extremely difficult to say how far the current downgrading of unemployment as an objective of policy is a political choice and how far it is a recognition of economic constraints.

The safest forecast always is that the future will be much like the past. It would be surprising if there were any major changes in either objectives or techniques in the near future. The policy failures of recent years accompanied extreme external problems in terms of world output and inflation. Now that the smoke has cleared, the feeling that drastic changes in policy will be required has faded. The exceptional experiences have, however, emphasised the limitations of demand management. One way of describing the lessons is to say that there is greater recognition of the role of markets. This has been particularly true in the case of financial assets, currencies and traded goods, but it has also been true in the case of labour markets (however imperfect they may be). The CEPG remain something of an exception to this development; but their policy recommendations have not so far been accepted.

Recognition of the role of markets suggests that certain experiments will not be repeated. There will not be monetary explosions of the style of 1972–73, nor will there be attempts to expand demand rapidly while attempting to hold down money earnings by incomes policies. (The CEPG would, however, propose such a combination.) One can also suggest that the experiences of 1977 show that it is not possible simultaneously to control the money supply and the exchange rate.

The broad choices are between intervening rather less, intervening rather more and carrying on as at present. As far as present policies are concerned, it would seem that monetary policy has moved back towards the centre of attention and that monetary and fiscal policy will, in future, be considered jointly. Ambitions towards the control of unemployment have apparently been much reduced; but the hope must be that conventional policies are consistent both with single figure inflation and with unemployment at somewhat below its current levels. The key issue, then, is whether the trend towards higher import propensities will steadily raise unemployment or whether market forces will cause an adequate change in relative prices that will keep unemployment at about its present level. The CEPG view is that on current policies unemployment will rise to $4\frac{1}{2}$ million by 1990. If such a prospect were to seem likely, the government would have to choose between either accepting it as inevitable or adopting a different set of policies.

If current policies do not at least hold unemployment at about its present level, the debate will have to shift to the political choice between free behaviour and increased intervention in labour and foreign trade markets. The government is trying to avoid this choice by its attempts to persuade other countries to expand demand. There is a possible inconsistency between the government's announcement that it cannot spend its way out of unemployment on its own but that the world can do so if certain countries coordinate their expansion. But it is possible that all countries are stuck at a local equilibrium through fears of balance of payments consequences of expansion, whereas a higher level of output is in fact feasible for all. Import controls, it has been suggested, may even be one way of moving to the new equilibrium. Such questions remain completely open.

If civil engineering were like economics, engineers would have to decide how the universe began before they could build a bridge. It is therefore largely an act of faith for me to assert that the future of demand management lies with less short-term intervention rather than with more. The result is likely to be greater fluctuations in output but possibly smaller fluctuations in inflation. I would at any rate expect a steady return to fixed exchange rates that will itself bring steadier and, almost certainly, lower inflation. I accept the arguments in Modigliani's (1977) presidential address that it would be quite wrong to maintain an unchanged monetary policy in the face of shocks such as the increase in oil prices; but such changes in policy would be the exception rather than the rule.

If there is to be less short-term intervention, the major question is whether the long term can be left to look after itself. The experiences of the mid-1960s and of 1972–1974 suggest that conventional demand management cannot be used successfully to raise the underlying growth of the economy. There is no virtuous circle of demand management. The CEPG strategy is for protection accompanied by investment incentives. My fear is that such a strategy would slow down rather than encourage structural change. The defender of market forces always appears to be on weak ground simply because he refuses to say what should or will happen to the structure of the economy; but it is precisely because such questions cannot be answered that it is wise to use a system that disseminates information efficiently and that provides incentives to use it correctly.

Comment and Discussion

For the final morning of the seminar Alan Budd and Frank Blackaby were invited to review the past and likely future development of demand management policy in the UK.

Michael Posner took the chair and John Odling-Smee joined Frank Blackaby and Alan Budd for the discussion of their papers.

Following the two introductory papers is a brief summary of the debate they provoked.

THE UK ECONOMY IN THE 1970s

Michael Posner opened the discussion by asking what had caused the sharp deterioration in the United Kingdom's economic health in the early 1970s. Could the widening deficit on current account, accelerated domestic inflation and the depreciation of the sterling exchange rate be attributed solely to our excessive monetary expansion brought about by a succession of allegedly misjudged budgetary stimuli; or were there other circumstances independent of the budget deficit that had stimulated inflationary pressures, or weakened monetary controls?

Frank Blackaby argued that inflation in the United Kingdom was wage driven; that the movements of wages could not be satisfactorily explained by economic determinants; and that it was a mistake to look for explanations of the acceleration of inflation in recent years to budgetary deficits or to the money supply. Thus if one wanted to understand why the rate of price increase moved up from the end of 1973 to a peak figure of around 25 per cent in the year ending in the middle of 1975, the proper thing to study was the course of wage bargaining. Stage III of the Conservative government's incomes policy embodied a 'threshold clause' by which negotiating groups could obtain full compensation for any increase in the retail price index over and above 7 per cent. This indexation provision coincided with the quadrupling of oil prices and a very sharp increase in world commodity prices in general; and it was the one part of the Conservative government's incomes policy that was kept in being after the return of the Labour government in the spring of 1974. The threshold provision was triggered eleven times during 1974.

This was not the only force producing a wage explosion. The miners had broken the government's incomes policy for the second time; however, on this occasion other unions were not willing to allow the NUM to push themselves so far ahead – so that throughout the 1974/75 wage round claims were pressed that effectively gave earnings increases of the order of 30 per cent. It is here that explanations of the great inflation of 1974/75 are to be found. The fact that the move to allow greater competitive freedom to the clearing banks led to a property boom was essentially a peripheral matter. The wage bargaining process was central.

Alan Budd challenged Frank Blackaby's interpretation of the UK's experience in the early 1970s. He argued that the authorities could have resisted the pressure generated by the UK's internal and external problems for monetary and fiscal expansion. Had they done so then the sterling exchange rate would now be higher and the UK would have experienced a slower rate of price inflation. The probable cost of a more determined resistance would have been an earlier rise in unemployment; but since most other industrial countries had responded to the oil price rise with restrictive domestic measures, the UK government acting alone could do no more than slightly delay the inevitable.

THE ROLE OF EXCHANGE RATE POLICY

Alan Budd emphasised that his interpretation of the experience of the UK in the early 1970s rested on a view of the role of exchange rates in linking domestic and world inflation rates articulated forcefully by Ball and Burns (1976). The essence of their thesis is that prices of domestically produced tradeable (primarily manufactured) goods are competitively determined in world markets. Changes in domestic manufacturing wages are determined in turn by changes in the world price of manufactures measured in domestic currency and changes in the level of output per man in domestic manufacturing. An increase or decrease in the world price of manufactures thus increases, or decreases, the marginal product of labour in manufacturing.

The resulting upward, or downward, pressure on wage rates in that sector is transmitted to the non-tradeable (primarily non-manufactured) sector by changes in the pressure of demand and trades union enforcement of the principle of comparability in collective bargaining. If prices in the non-manufacturing sector are determined by a mark-up on unit costs of production and if productivity increases less rapidly than in manufacturing, it follows that domestic prices rise more rapidly than the price of manu-factured exports, by an amount equal to the product of the share of non-manufacturing in total output and the difference between the rate of increase of output per man in manufacturing and non-manufacturing. If the differ-ence between fast- and slow-growing economies is explained by differences in the rate of growth of labour productivity in their manufacturing indus-tries, while productivity in the service sector grows at more or less the same (slow) rate in all countries, then fast-growing economies will tend to man-ifest a faster rate of domestic inflation and a bigger gap between this rate and the rate of increase of their manufactured export prices.

With fixed exchange rates and stable demand for money functions the domestic rate of inflation in an open economy is thus determined by the world rate of inflation (which sets the price of tradeable manufactures) and the growth of labour productivity in domestic manufacturing (which sets the cost and, therefore, the price, of non-tradeable non-manufactures). The dom-estic authorities have no control over the domestic rate of inflation in the long run. To maintain a system of fixed exchange rates the authorities must not allow the rate of domestic credit expansion to exceed, or fall short of, the growth of nominal national output by more than the rest of the world. If, for example, they permit the rate of domestic credit expansion to exceed the rate warranted by the rest of the world, there will be an outflow of reserves that must be countered either by monetary restriction or by a depreciation of the exchange rate. In the latter case the exchange depreciation brings in its wake an equal increase in the domestic price level disseminated through the economy by demand pressure and collective wage bargaining. In the limit, the acceptance of a floating exchange rate characterised by continuous appreciation or depreciation returns to the national authorities some con-trol over the rate of inflation, but not over the level of output.

Clearly, in this sort of world the authorities cannot lean against the ex-change rate in pursuit of either external balance or a higher rate of domestic output in the long run. Devaluation can, at best, only buy a temporary increase in output and employment at the cost of higher inflation during the period in which the domestic price level is moving back to its equilibrium level. The 'temporary' advantage conferred on the UK by the 1949 devalua-tion appeared to have persisted for almost a decade and a half; but that conferred by the 1967 devaluation had lasted only five years. The almost continuous depreciation of sterling since mid-1972 seems to have conferred little advantage, or none at all. Why the lag between exchange depreciation and adjustment of the domestic to the world price level should be shortening was unclear. It was thought by some to reflect learning: trades unions, for example, might now expect monetary expansion to lead to faster inflation via devaluation and might therefore be quicker to resist the implied transfer from wages to profits.

Whatever the reason, price elasticities of demand and supply for exports and imports now seemed irrelevant to the task of securing external balance, because the one instrument that had offered some control over relative prices no longer worked in the way it had once been thought to. Attaining external balance depended now upon income elasticities and relative growth rates. Balance of payments deficits implied a slower rate of domestic expansion and some combination of lower than otherwise real wages or higher than otherwise unemployment.

Frank Blackaby said that he was as unconvinced by Ball and Burns as he was by all varieties of international monetarism. Even if there was a long-run relationship between the growth of the domestic money stock and nominal national expenditures, that only made monetary growth an indicator of future changes in nominal expenditure. It did not justify the use of a monetary aggregate as an instrument for controlling the short-run behaviour of the economy. Apart from the problems of defining an appropriate monetary aggregate and a demand for money function that was stable in both the short and long runs, a change in nominal expenditures could not be decomposed into its volume change and price change components, even in the long run. Clearly the use of monetary targets to achieve some desired configuration of output and price levels was a haphazard business. Monetary restriction might bring substantially lower output and employment but have only a minor effect on the inflation rate: that was what appeared to happen when such policies were simulated on the current vintage of forecasting models.

Admittedly, wages were determined exogenously in all the major models, but that seemed to reflect the importance of non-economic factors in wage determination; hence the persistent failure to identify satisfactory wage forecasting equations. Since wage inflation did not appear to abate in the face of restrictive policies there were strong reasons for expecting the impact of such policies to fall almost entirely upon output.

Other seminar members took up a number of different questions concerning exchange rate policy. One argued that since both the NIESR and the Treasury assumed that workers bargained for a target *net* wage (so that reductions in income tax reduced the rate of wage increase), tax policy could fill the place vacated by exchange rate policy. Current marginal rates of direct tax amounted to roughly 50 per cent and of indirect tax to less than 5 per cent, so there was substantial scope for switching the burden of taxation from domestic costs of production to import prices. Another member wondered whether attempts to increase the price competitiveness of existing UK exports were misguided because they delayed a necessary shift of resources out of the production of standardised low technology commodities into innovative high technology products. Similarly it was argued that the use of import controls to protect the balance of payments and support the exchange rate might provide the right environment for an attempt to raise productivity through faster growth. None of these suggestions found much support among seminar members. It seemed unlikely that a switch from direct to indirect taxes would do much to reduce domestic costs of production if wage negotiators had in mind a target net *real* wage. Supporting the exchange rate was thought likely to stifle demand for traditional UK exports but unlikely to stimulate a shift of resources into new forms of production for export; and the effect would be intensified by reflation and trade protection as existing export capacity was drawn into import-replacing forms of production.

Furthermore, it was unrealistic to suppose that the rate of increase of output per man would ever approach the rate of wage increase experienced in the UK since the late 1960s; and if productivity in manufacturing did increase, then, if Ball and Burns were correct, so would the domestic rate of inflation.

In short, demand management policies are not the right instrument with which to bring about structural reform, particularly when so little is known about the response of aggregate supply to changes in aggregate demand.

DEMAND MANAGEMENT AND THE WORLD RECESSION

Michael Posner then asked what part domestic demand management could play in combating the current world-wide deficiency of aggregate demand. The oil price rise had precipitated the world recession; but it was the un-coordinated lapse into restrictive policies by many industrial countries in 1973 and 1974 that had both deepened and prolonged the period of high unemployment. Some commentators (particularly at the London Business School) had argued that a solution could be found if the so-called locomotive countries, particularly Germany and Japan, could be persuaded to accept an appropriate share of the growth in world money supply. This appeared to be in deliberate contrast with the more conventional recommendation that the locomotive economies should pursue expansionary fiscal policies.

But what was the difference? Monetary expansion would follow automatically from an increase in the budget deficit; and monetary expansion could only be achieved through the medium of an increased deficit. The Germans, in particular, had resisted the blandishments of other countries to relax their fiscal stance because they feared the monetary expansion that would inevitably follow.

In support of the LBS Alan Budd argued that putting the case in terms of monetary rather than fiscal expansion emphasised the political and social difficulties facing the industrial countries. A return to stable exchange rates required national monetary authorities to ensure that domestic stocks of money grew at the right rate in relation to the world average. In present conditions that meant countries like Italy and the UK adopting extremely restrictive policies, or other countries allowing a faster expansion of their money supply, or the world accepting a very long period of adjustment while exchange rate changes brought about the required monetary adjustment. For the strong economies to (temporarily) share the weaknesses of the weaker economies offered the quickest solution for high unemployment. If the weaker economies attempted to mimic the strengths of their neighbours, the result would probably be a further sharp drop in the level of world demand and an increase in world unemployment. Sitting out the period of exchange rate adjustment seemed the most probable outcome; but it might involve a long and politically damaging wait for the return of stability. The political problem was to persuade the locomotive countries to make an adjustment that would be forced on them anyway and thus minimise the cost of returning the world to full employment.

THE LIMITS OF DEMAND MANAGEMENT

The preceding discussion led Michael Posner to question whether demand management had a substantial role to play in an economy like that of the UK, small, open and possessing a weak manufacturing industry. Could it be that Britain's difficulties reflected not technical failures in the implementation of fiscal and monetary policy but a failure to develop other sorts of policy?

Alan Budd thought that even without adopting the perspective of those who believed in full rational expectations it seemed obvious that short-run demand management had only a limited role to play. There were some big and unpredictable shocks that had to be absorbed by changes in government expenditures and revenues, the effects of the oil price rise being an obvious example; but, generally, the economy would return automatically to its long-run equilibrium growth path if markets operated in anything like the manner that most economists believed. For example, the high imports propensities that led the Cambridge Economic Policy Group to forecast 4 million unemployed by 1982 probably reflected a too high real wage. If this was so, then it is reasonable to suppose that expectation of rising unemployment will reduce real wages and, therefore, imports to a level lower than that anticipated by CEPG. Lower than anticipated domestic costs of production combined with an internationally determined price level would mean higher profits that should, in turn, bring higher levels of output and exports than CEPG were currently forecasting.

If expectations of rising unemployment failed to stem the rise in real wages, through either the process of collective bargaining or the acceptance of wage restraining incomes policy, the unemployment would be voluntary rather than involuntary, and it was not clear what, if anything, the government should do to reduce it. Attempting to increase employment by depreciating sterling and riding the adjustment lag would only increase the rate of inflation. It would be more reasonable for the government to pursue a money supply growth target consistent with the state of the cycle and then set fiscal policy to be consistent with the monetary target. In this context the role of fiscal policy would be limited; if, for example, it was proving difficult to dispose of gilt-edged stocks, or if companies were attempting to increase their borrowing, then fiscal policy would have to be tightened in relation to current monetary policy.

There was a widely held belief that the biggest obstacles to effective demand management were the complexity of the short-run behaviour of the economy (particularly of the structure of the lags in its responses to extraneous shocks and policy interventions) and the difficulty of obtaining timely and accurate information on the current state of the economy. Alan Budd thought this belief misguided. A far bigger obstacle was the failure of current forecasting models to capture the effects of longer-run market-driven adjustment processes.

It was this omission that tempted policy-makers to engage in futile attempts at short-term management and unnecessary attempts at medium- and long-run management. It was the number of interventions rather than defects in their scale or timing that stood in the way of good policy making.

Frank Blackaby attacked Alan Budd's apparent belief in the existence of long-run equilibrium. He argued that the concept of the steady state that economists had borrowed from the physical sciences had no counterpart in the social sciences. Thus it is naive to call unemployment 'voluntary' just because it results from a failure of real wages to adjust in the face of changing market conditions. If the institutional arrangements for collective bargaining preclude collectively rational decision-taking by trades union leaders, real wages might fail to find their 'equilibrium' level and leave large numbers of workers unemployed, not as a result of their voluntary actions, but as a result of 'the million private dreams that make a public nightmare'.

Other members of the seminar, particularly John Odling-Smee argued that because so little was known about the long-run behaviour of the economy, except that major adjustments took a long time to work through the system, the desire to manage was rational. There clearly was some scope for judiciously playing on the lags in the adjustment process, although the authorities' response in any particular case would depend on the size and nature of the shocks and the range of policies available. If it was possible to smooth the cycle even slightly then, over a number of years, it was not unreasonable to expect some cumulative increase in productivity and output growth. Similarly, even a short-lived boost to demand generated by higher export volume could be sufficient to spark off quite rapid increases in productivity and changes in the pattern of output if investment increased rapidly enough in response to the increase in demand. But governments' ability to manage in this way was severely hampered by ignorance of the economy's responses to shocks of various kinds and the absence of data on the current state of the economy.

In the current vintage of forecasting models, the short-run behaviour of the economy was almost as uncertain as its long-run behaviour. For example, there was little agreement on either the strength of wealth effects on personal consumption or their speed of operation. Thus it was difficult to predict the effects of a falling inflation rate on the personal savings ratio. Sometimes the direction of change was as much in dispute as its size and speed. The LBS model showed output rising with the exchange rate because their model embodied powerful wealth effects that outweighed the trade balance effects of revaluation; but this did not occur in either the Treasury or NIESR models. It was this kind of uncertainty that most threatened to upset both the size and timing of interventions by the authorities.

Returning to the theme of long-term adjustment, it was observed that the corporate sector of the economy had been in financial surplus continually until the end of the 1960s and was so again in the late 1970s. In between, it had been heavily in deficit. The problem was whether the corporate sector would sustain financial deficits for long periods of time. If it could not then that implied that the government should have a larger financial balance in mind for the corporate sector and thus, implicity, for itself. Did this amount in effect to the adoption of a fiscal rule?

There was general agreement that the UK corporate sector's peculiar (by international standards) preference for internal funding and reluctance to borrow accounted for the persistent accumulation of financial assets up until the late 1960s. However, the personal sector's savings ratio had been rising since probably the 1930s (although the trend was distorted by the war and its aftermath), implying that the demand for financial assets was likely to rise in the long term. Presumably some of the demand would be met if the corporate sector were willing to borrow, but it was unlikely to borrow enough, despite the evidence of a recent change in corporate behaviour. The choice therefore was between meeting the personal sector's demand by continuing to run a public sector deficit or by attempting to run a balance of payments surplus and accumulating titles to overseas assets.

Whether the whole private sector's financial balance limited the scope for demand management was not clear. The relevant numbers for who wished to acquire what volume of financial assets were implicit in the forecasts of personal saving and of investment in housing, plant and equipment. There seemed no particular reason for the government to worry unless its own plans seemed inconsistent with its hopes for the balance of payments and the plans of the private sector; or unless the corporate sector itself seemed worried, for in that case industrial confidence might be at stake.

CONCLUSION

It seemed to Michael Posner that there was no real dispute about the nature of unemployment in the UK. In a small open economy the only long-run solution to high unemployment lay in reducing the relative real wage. The real debate revolved around the problem of how to attain a lower relative real wage. Reflation by the locomotive countries seemed to be a remote possibility, so that only domestic solutions could be implemented. Here the problem seemed to be whether the labour market would adjust automatically without some reform of the structure of collective bargaining; or whether we should continue to rely on wage restraining incomes policy. The most disturbing conclusion was the diminution of the role of exchange rate policy. Since the 1930s devaluation had been regarded as the key that would unlock the balance of payments constraint on the growth of small open economies. If we accepted the view that devaluation did not work at all, or, at least, that it did not work as well as we used to think it did, then governments had substantially less room for manoeuvre than we had thought.

Bibliography

ALT, J. and CHRYSTAL, K. A. (1977) 'Endogenous government behaviour: overture to a study of government expenditure', University of Essex, Department of Economics, Discussion Paper No. 108.

ANDERSON, L. C. and JORDAN, J. L. (1968) 'Monetary and fiscal actions: A test of their relative importance in economic stabilisation' *Federal Reserve Bank of St Louis Review* November.

ARGY, V. and PORTER, M. G. (1972) 'The forward exchange market and the effects of domestic and external disturbances under alternative exchange rate regimes', International Monetary Fund *Staff Papers* November

ARTIS, M. J. (1972) 'Fiscal policy for stabilisation' in W. Beckerman (ed.) *The Labour Government's Economic Record, 1964–70*, London, Duckworth.

ARTIS, M. J. and NOBAY, A. R. (1969) 'Two aspects of the monetary debate' *National Institute Economic Review* No. 49, August.

AULD, D. A. L. (1967) 'A measure of Australian fiscal policy performance, 1948–49 to 1963–64' *Economic Record* September.

AULD, D. A. L. (1969) 'Fiscal policy performance in Canada 1957–1967' *Public Finance* No. 3.

BACON, R. W. and ELTIS, W. A. (1976) *Britain's Economic Problem: Too Few Producers* London, Macmillan.

BAILEY, M. J. (1962) *National Income and Price Level* New York, McGraw-Hill.

BALL, R. J. and BURNS, T. (1976) 'The inflationary mechanism in the United Kingdom economy' *American Economic Review* Vol. 66, September.

BARRO, R. J. (1974) 'Are Government bonds net wealth?' *Journal of Political Economy*, Vol. 82, No. 5.

BARRO, R. J. (1976) 'Reply to Feldstein and Buchanan' *Journal of Political Economy*, Vol. 84, No. 2.

BARRO, R. J. and GROSSMAN, H. (1976) *Money, Employment and Inflation* Cambridge University Press.

BATCHELOR, R. A. (1977) 'Sterling exchange rates: A Casselian analysis', *National Institute Economic Review*, No. 81, August.

BAUMOL, W. J. and PESTON, M. H. (1955) 'More on the multiplier effects of a balanced budget' *American Economic Review* Vol. 45.

BLACKABY, F. T. (1978) *British Economic Policy 1960–74* Cambridge University Press.

BLINDER, A. S. and GOLDFELD, S. M. (1976) 'New measures of fiscal and monetary policy 1958–73' *American Economic Review* Vol. 66, December.

BLINDER, A. S. and SOLOW, R. M. (1973) 'Does fiscal policy matter?' *Journal of Public Finance*, Vol. 2, November.

BLINDER, A. S. and SOLOW, R. M. (1974) 'Analytical Foundations of Fiscal Policy' in A. S. Blinder, R. M. Solow *et al. The Economics of Public Finance* Washington, The Brookings Institution.

BORPUJARI, J. G. and TER-MINASSIAN, T. (1973) 'The weighted budget balance approach to fiscal analysis: A methodology and some case studies' International Monetary Fund *Staff Papers* November.

BRANSON, W. H. (1972) *Macroeconomic Theory and Policy* New York, Harper and Row.

BROWN, C. V. and JACKSON, P. M. (1978) *Public Sector Economics* Oxford, Martin Robertson.

BROWN, E. C. (1950) 'Analysis of consumption taxes in terms of the theory of income determination' *American Economic Review* Vol. 40, March.

BROWN, E. C. (1956) 'Fiscal policy in the thirties: A reappraisal' *American Economic Review* Vol. 46, December.

BRUCE, N. (1977) 'The *IS-LM* model of macroeconomic equilibrium and the monetarist controversy' *Journal of Political Economy*, Vol. 85, No. 5.

BRUNNER, K. and MELTZER, A. H. (1972) 'Friedman's monetary theory' *Journal of Political Economy* Vol. 80.

BUCHANAN, J. M. (1976) 'Barro on the Ricardian equivalence theorem' *Journal of Political Economy*, Vol. 84, No. 2.

BUCHANAN, J. M., BURTON, J. and WAGNER, R. G. (1978) *The Consequences of Mr Keynes* Hobart Paper 78, London, Institute of Economic Affairs.

BUITER, W. E. (1977a) 'Crowding out and the effectiveness of fiscal policy *Journal of Political Economy* Vol. 85, No. 3.

BUITER, W. E. (1977b) 'Capacity constraints, government financing and the short and long run effects of macroeconomic policy', discussion paper presented to SSRC Money Study Group meeting, London School of Economics.

BURNS, T., LOBBAN, P. W. M. and WARBURTON, P. (1977) 'Forecasting the Real Exchange Rate', London Business School Centre for Economic Forecasting, *Economic Outlook* Vol. 2, No. 1, October.

BURROWS, P. and HITIRIS, T. (1974) *Macroeconomic Theory, A Mathematical Introduction* New York, Wiley.

CALLAGHAN, J. MP (1976) Labour Party conference address, *Report of the 75th Annual Conference of the Labour Party* Blackpool, 28 September 1976. Published by the Labour Party.

CAMBRIDGE ECONOMIC POLICY GROUP (1975–78) *Economic Policy Review* various issues.

CARLSON, K. M. and SPENCER, R. W. (1975) 'Crowding out and its critics' *Federal Reserve Bank of St Louis Review*, December.

CHAND, S. K. (1977) 'Summary measures of fiscal influence' International Monetary Fund, *Staff Papers* November.

CHICK, V. (1973) *The Theory of Monetary Policy* London, Gray-Mills.

CHRIST, C. F. (1968) 'A simple macroeconomic model with a government budget restraint' *Journal of Political Economy*, Vol. 76.

CHRIST, C. F. (1969) 'A model of monetary and fiscal policy effects on the money stock, price level, and real output' *Journal of Money, Credit and Banking*, Vol. 1.

COGHLAN, R. T. and JACKSON, P. M. (1978) 'The UK personal savings ratio; past, present and future', PSERC Discussion Paper, University of Leicester.

COUNCIL OF ECONOMIC ADVISERS (1962) *The Economic Report of the President* Washington, DC. US Govt. Printing Office.

CRIPPS, F. and GODLEY, W. (1976) 'A formal analysis of the Cambridge Economic Policy Group model' *Economica* Vol. 43, May.

CRIPPS, F., GODLEY, W. and FETHERSTONE, M. (1974) *Public Expenditure and the Management of the Economy*, Minutes of Evidence Taken Before the Expenditure Committee (General Sub-Committee), Sessions 1974, 30th July 1974, HC 328, HMSO.

CURRIE, D. A. (1976) 'Optimal stabilisation policies and the government budget constraint' *Economica* Vol. 43, May.

CURRIE, D. A. (1978a) 'Macroeconomic policy and government financing: a survey of recent developments' in M. J. Artis and A. R. Nobay, *Studies in Contemporary Economic Analysis* Vol. 1, London, Croom-Helm.

CURRIE, D. A. (1978b) 'Monetary and fiscal policy and the crowding-out issue', Queen Mary College (London) Discussion Paper in Economics.

DAVID, P. A. and SCADDING, J. L. (1974) 'Private savings: ultrarationality, aggregation and "Denison's Law"' *Journal of Political Economy* Vol. 82, no. 2.

DIXIT, A. (1978) 'Public finance in a Keynesian temporary equilibrium' *Journal of Economic Theory* Vol. 12, No. 2.

DIXON, D. A. (1973) 'The full employment budget surplus concept as a tool of fiscal analysis in the United States' International Monetary Fund *Staff Papers*, March.

DORNBUSCH, R. (1976) 'Exchange rate expectations and monetary policy' *Journal of International Economics*, Vol. 5.

DOW, J. C. R. (1965) *Management of the British Economy 1945–60* NIESR, Cambridge University Press.

DUGGAL, V. J. (1975) 'Fiscal policy and economic stabilisation' in G. Fromm and L. R. Klein (eds.) *The Brookings Model: perspectives and recent developments*. Amsterdam, North Holland.

FANE, C. G. (1977) 'National Institute Model II: an illustrative model and the model in detail', National Institute of Economic and Social Research (London), Discussion Paper No. 10a.

FELDSTEIN, M. (1976) 'Perceived wealth in bonds and social security: A comment' *Journal of Political Economy* Vol. 84, No. 2.

FISCHER, S. (1977) 'Long term contracts, national expectations and the optimal money supply rule' *Journal of Political Economy*, Vol. 85, No. 2.

FLEMING, J. M. (1962) 'Domestic financial policies under fixed and under floating rates' International Monetary Fund, *Staff Papers 9*.

FORTE, F. and HOCHMAN, H. (1969) 'Monetary and fiscal policy: Ambiguities and definitions' in Haller and Recktenwald (eds.) *Finanz und Geld Politik in Umbruch* Mainz, Von Hase & Kochler.

FREY, B. (1978) *Modern Political Economy* Oxford, Martin Robertson.

FREY, B. and SCHNEIDER, F. (1978) 'A politico-economic model of the UK' *Economic Journal* Vol. 88, No. 350, June.

FRIEDMAN, B. M. (1977) 'Even the St Louis model now believes in fiscal policy' *Journal of Money, Credit and Banking* Vol. 9, May.

FRIEDMAN, M. (1953) 'The effects of full-employment policy on economic stability: A formal analysis' in *Essays in Positive Economics* University of Chicago Press.

FRIEDMAN, M. (1957) *A Theory of the Consumption Function* Princeton, National Bureau of Economic Research.

FRIEDMAN, M. (1962) *Capitalism and Freedom* University of Chicago Press.

FRIEDMAN, M. (1963) 'The role of monetary policy' *American Economic Review* Vol. 58, March.

FRIEDMAN, M. (1970) 'A theoretical framework for monetary analysis' *Journal of Political Economy* Vol. 78.

FRIEDMAN, M. (1971) 'A monetary theory of nominal income' *Journal of Political Economy* Vol. 79.

FRIEDMAN, M. (1972) 'Comments on the critics' *Journal of Political Economy* Vol. 80.

FRIEDMAN, M. and HELLER, W. W. (1969) *Monetary versus Fiscal Policy: A Dialogue* New York, Norton & Co.

FROMM, G. and KLEIN, L. R. (1976) 'The NBER/NSF model comparison seminar: an analysis of the results', *Annals of Economic and Social Measurement*.

GOLDFELD, S. and BLINDER, A. (1972) 'Some implications of endogenous stabilisation policy' *Brookings Papers on Economic Activity*, Washington D.C., Brookings Institution.

GOODHART, C. A. E. (1975) *Money, Information and Uncertainty* London, Macmillan.

GORDON, R. J. (1976) 'Can econometric policy evaluation be salvaged – a comment' in K. Brunner and A. G. Meltzer *The Phillips Curve and Labour Markets*. Amsterdam, North Holland.

GORDON, R. J. (1977) 'Interrelations between domestic and international theories of inflation', in R. Z. Aliber (ed.) *The Political Economy of Monetary Reform* London, Macmillan.

GUPTA, S. (1967) 'Public expenditure and economic growth: A time-series analysis', *Public Finance* Vol. 22, 1967.

GURLEY, J. and SHAW, E. (1960) *Money in a Theory of Finance*, Washington, DC., Brookings; London, Allen and Unwin.

HACCHE, G. (1974) 'The demand for money in the UK; experience since 1971' *Bank of England Quarterly Bulletin* September.

HALL, R. L. (1965) 'Introduction' to J. C. R. Dow (1965).

HANSEN, B. (1969) *Fiscal Policy in Seven Countries 1955–1965*' Paris, OECD.

HANSEN, B. (1973) 'On the effects of fiscal and monetary policy: A taxonomic discussion', *American Economic Review* Vol. 63, September.

HARTLEY, N. and BEAN, C. (1978) *The Standardised Budget Balance* Government Economic Service Working Paper No. 1, London, HM Treasury, February.

HEALEY, D., MP (1978) Budget Statement, Official Report, House of Commons *Parliamentary Debates* Vol. 947, No. 3, Tuesday 11 April, Vols. 1183–1208.

HIBBS, D. (1976) 'Economic interest and the politics of macroeconomic policy' MIT Center for International Studies, mimeo.

HIRSCH, F. and GOLDTHORPE, J. H. (1978) *The Political Economy of Inflation* London, Martin Robertson.

HMSO (1978) *Report of the Committee on Policy Optimisation*, Cmnd. 7148, London, HMSO.

HOLT, C. (1962) 'Linear decision rules for economic stabilisation' *Quarterly Journal of Economics* Vol. 76.

HOPKIN, W. A. B. and GODLEY, W. A. H. (1965) 'An analysis of tax changes' *National Institute Economic Review*, No. 32, May.

HUTTON, J. P. (1976) 'A model of short term capital movements, the foreign exchange market and official intervention in the UK, 1962–1970' *Review of Economic Studies* Vol. 43.

INFANTE, E. F. and STEIN, J. L. (1976) 'Does fiscal policy matter?' *Journal of Monetary Economics* Vol. 2, November.

JOHNSTON, J. (1973) *Econometric Methods* New York, McGraw-Hill.

KATZ, E. (1977). 'The efficacy of fiscal and monetary policies under floating exchange rates: the implications of capital mobility reconsidered', Queen Mary College (London) Discussion Paper in Economics.

KENEN, P. B. (1978) 'New views of exchange rates and old views of policy', *American Economic Review* Vol. 68.

KERAN, M. (1969) 'Monetary and fiscal influences on economic activity – the historical evidence' *Federal Reserve Bank of St Louis Review* November.

KEYNES, J. M. and HENDERSON H. D. (1929) 'Can Lloyd George Do It?' *The National and Athenaeum*, London.

KLEIN, L. R. (1947) 'The use of econometric models as a guide to fiscal policy' *Econometrica* Vol. 15.

KLEIN, L. R. (1978) 'The supply side' *American Economic Review* Vol. 68, No. 1.

LAIDLER, D. (1971) 'The influence of money on economic activity' in O. Clayton, J. C. Gilbert and R. Sedgwick (eds) *Monetary Theory and Monetary Policy in the 1970s* London, Oxford University Press.

LAIDLER, D. (1973) 'Simultaneous fluctuations in prices and output' *Economica*, Vol. 40, February.

LAURY, J. S. E., LEWIS, G. R. and ORMEROD, P. A. (1978) 'Properties of macroeconomic models of the UK economy: A comparative study' *National Institute Economic Review* No. 83, February.

LINDBECK, A. (1976) 'Stabilisation policy in small open economies with endogenous politicians' *American Economic Review: Papers and Proceedings*, May.

LUCAS, R. B. (1976) 'Econometric policy evaluation: a critique' in K. Brunner and A. N. Meltzer (eds) *The Phillips Curve and Labour Markets*, Amsterdam, North Holland.

McGRATH, B. (1977) 'Implications of the government budget constraint: A comparison of two models' *Journal of Money, Credit and Banking*, Vol. 9.

McKINNON, R. I. (1969) 'Portfolio and international payments adjustment' in R. A. Mundell and A. Swodba (eds) *Monetary Problems of the International Economy* University of Chicago Press.

McKINNON, R. I. (1976) 'The limited role of fiscal policy in an open economy' *Quarterly Review of the Banca Nazionale del Lavoro*, September.

McKINNON, R. I. and OATES, W. E. (1966) 'The implications of international economic integration for monetary, fiscal and exchange rate policy' Princeton Studies in International Finance, No. 16, March.

MACMILLAN, H. (1973) *At the End of the Day 1961–63* London, Macmillan.

MALINVAUD, E. (1977) *The Theory of Unemployment Reconsidered* Oxford, Basil Blackwell.

MATTHEWS, R. C. O. (1968) 'Why has Britain had full employment since the war?' *Economic Journal* Vol. 78, September.

MATTHEWS, R. C. O. (1971) 'Fiscal policy and stabilisation in Britain' Ch. 2 in Sir Alec Caincross (ed) *Britain's Economic Prospects Reordered* London, Allen and Unwin.

MEYER, L. H. (1974) 'Lagged adjustment in simple macro models' *Oxford Economic Papers* Vol. 26, No. 2, November.

MEYER, L. H. (1975) 'The balance sheet identity, the government financing constraint and the crowding-out effect' *Journal of Monetary Economics* Vol. 85, January.

MEYER, L. H. and HART, W. R. (1975) 'On the effects of fiscal and monetary policy: completing the taxonomy' *American Economic Review* Vol. 65, September.

MILLER, M. H. (1976) 'Comment on Sparks' in M. J. Artis and A. R. Nobay (eds) *Essays in Economic Analysis* Cambridge University Press.

MILLER, M. H. (1978) 'Intersectoral flows of funds and the rate of interest', mimeo, University of Manchester, Department of Economics, March.

MILLER, M. H. and TEMPLE, P. (1977) 'Estimates of inflation taxation in the UK', mimeo, University of Manchester, Department of Economics.

MODIGLIANI, F. (1977) 'The monetarist controversy, or, should we foresake stabilisation policies?' *American Economic Review* Vol. 67, March.

MORSS, E. T. and PEACOCK, A. T. (1969) 'The measurement of fiscal performance in developing countries' in A. T. Peacock (ed) *Quantitative Analysis in Public Finance* New York, Praeger.

MUNDELL, R. A. (1962) 'The appropriate use of monetary and fiscal policy for internal and external stability' International Monetary Fund *Staff Papers* 9, No. 1, March.

MUNDELL, R. A. (1963) 'Capital mobility and stabilisation policy under fixed and flexible exchange rates' *Canadian Journal of Economics and Political Science* Vol. 29, November.

MUNDELL, R. A. (1968) *International Economics* New York, Macmillan.

MUSGRAVE, R. A. (1964) 'On measuring fiscal performance' *Review of Economics and Statistics* Vol. 46, May.

MUSGRAVE, R. A. and PEACOCK, A. T. (1967) *Classics in the Theory of Public Finance* New York, Macmillan, St. Martins Press.

MUTH, J. S. (1961) 'Rational expectation and the theory of price movements' *Econometrica*, Vol. 29.

NEILD, R. and WARD, T. (1976) 'The budget deficit in perspective' *The Times* London, 12 July.

NIEHANS, J. (1975) 'Some doubts about the efficacy of monetary policy under flexible exchange rates' *Journal of International Economics*, Vol. 5.

NORDHAUS, W. D. (1975) 'The political business cycle' *Review of Economic Studies* Vol. 42, April.

OAKLAND, W. H. (1969) 'Budgetary measures of fiscal performance' *Southern Economic Journal* Vol. 35, April.

OATES, W. (1966) 'Budget balance and equilibrium income: A comment on the efficacy of fiscal and monetary policy in an open economy' *Journal of Finance* Vol. 21.

ODLING-SMEE, J. and HARTLEY, N. (1978) *Some Effects of Exchange Rate Changes* Government Economic Service Working Paper No. 2, London, HM Treasury, March.

OKUN, A. (1971) 'The personal tax surcharge and consumer demand' *Brookings Papers on Economic Activity* No. 1, Washington D.C., Brookings Institution.

OKUN, A. (1977) 'Comment' on Springer (1975), *American Economic Review* Vol. 67, March.

ORMEROD, P. A. (forthcoming) 'The National Institute model: some current problems' in P. A. Ormerod (ed.) *Economic Modelling* London, Heinemann.

OTT, D. J. and OTT, A. F. (1965) 'Budget balance and equilibrium income' *Journal of Finance*, Vol. 20.

PARKIN, M. (1978) 'A comparison of alternative techniques of monetary control under rational expectations', paper presented to the SSRC Money Study Group Conference, April.

PEACOCK, A. and WISEMAN, J. (1961) *The Growth of Public Expenditure in the UK* Princeton, Princeton University Press.

PEACOCK, A. T. and SHAW, G. K. (1978) 'Is fiscal policy dead?' *Banca Nazionale del Lavoro Quarterly Review* June.

PERRY, G. L. (1976) 'Stabilisation policy and inflation' in H. Owen and C. L. Schultze (eds) *Setting National Priorities: The Next Ten Years* Washington D.C., Brookings Institution.

PESEK, B. and SAVING, T. (1967) *Money Wealth and Economic Theory* New York, Collier Macmillan.

PESTON, M. H. (1971) 'The tax mix and effective demand' *Public Finance* Vol. 26.

PISSARIDES, C. (1972) 'A model of British macroeconomic policy, 1955–1969' *Manchester School* Vol. 40.

POOLE, W. (1970) 'Optimal choice of monetary policy instruments in a simple stochastic macro model', *Quarterly Journal of Economics* Vol. 84.

POOLE, W. (1976) 'Rational expectations in the macro model', *Brookings Papers on Economic Activity* No. 2, Washington D.C., Brookings Institution.

POSNER, M. (ed) (1978) *Demand Management* London, Heinemann.

PREST, A. R. (1968) 'Sense and nonsense in budgetary policy' *Economic Journal* Vol. 78, March.

RENTON, G. A. (ed.) (1975) *Modelling the Economy* London, Heinemann.

RICHARDSON, G. (1978) 'Reflections on the conduct of monetary policy', the first Mais Lecture at the City University, London, 9 February; reprinted in *Bank of England Quarterly Bulletin*, March.

ROWAN, D. C. (1974) 'Output inflation and growth' London, Macmillan, 2nd edition.

SARGENT, T. J. (1973) 'Rational expectations, the real rate of interest, and the natural rate of unemployment' *Brookings Papers on Economic Activity* No. 2, Washington D.C., Brookings Institution.

SAVAGE, D. (1978) 'The channels of monetary influence: A survey of the empirical evidence' *National Institute Economic Review* No. 83, February.

SCARTH, W. M. (1975) 'Fiscal policy and the government budget restraint under alternative exchange-rate systems' *Oxford Economic Papers* Vol. 27 March.

SCHILLER, R. J. (1978) 'Rational expectations and the dynamic structure of macroeconomic models: a critical review' *Journal of Monetary Economics* Vol. 4.

SHAW, G. K. (1977) *An Introduction to the Theory of Macro-Economic Policy* London, Martin Robertson, 3rd edition.

SHEEN, J. R. and SASSANPOUR, C. (1976) 'A comparison of money and economic activity in France and West Germany: 1959–1973', London School of Economics Monetary Research Programme, Discussion Paper.

SHEPHERD, J. R. and SURREY, M. J. C. (1968) 'The short-term effects of tax changes' *National Institute Economic Review* No. 46, November.

SIEGEL, J. (1976) 'Inflation-induced distortions in national income accounts', paper prepared for the North America Meetings of the Econometric Society, Atlantic City, N.J., 18 September.

SILBER, W. L. (1970) 'Fiscal policy in *IS–LM* analysis: A correction' *Journal of Money, Credit and Banking* Vol. 2, November.

SMITH, R. P. (1976) 'Demand management and the new school' *Applied Economics* Vol. 8.

SMITH, W. L. (1970) 'Current issues in monetary economics' *Journal of Economic Literature* Vol. 3.

SMYTH, D. J. (1968) 'The measurement of fiscal performance' *Economic Record* Vol. 44, December.

SNYDER, W. W. (1970) 'Measuring economic stabilisation 1955–1965' *American Economic Review* Vol. 60, December.

SPARKS, G. R. (1976) 'An analysis of monetary and fiscal policy in a quantity theory model of wealth adjustments' in M. J. Artis and A. R. Nobay (eds) *Essays in Economic Analysis* Cambridge University Press.

SPRINGER, W. L. (1975) 'Did the 1968 surcharge really work?' *American Economic Review* Vol.

65, September.

SPRINGER, W. L. (1977) 'Reply' to Okun (1977) *American Economic Review* Vol. 67, March.

STEINDL, F. G. (1970) 'A simple macroeconomic model with a government budget restraint: A comment' *Journal of Political Economy*, Vol. 79.

STEINDL, F. G. (1974) 'Money and income: The view from the government budget restraint' *Journal of Finance* Vol. 29, September.

STRACHEY, L. (1934) *Eminent Victorians* London, Chatto and Windus.

STRINGER, Y. (1977) 'A quantitative appraisal of Canadian federal fiscal policy, 1955–1970', University of York D.Phil. dissertation, July.

SURREY, M. J. C. (ed) (1976) *Macroeconomic Themes* London, Oxford University Press.

TEIGEN, R. L. (1974) 'The theory of income determination', ch. 1 in R. L. Teigen and W. L. Smith (eds) *Readings in Money, National Income and Stabilisation Policy* 3rd edition, Homewood, Illinois, R. D. Irwin Inc.

TOBIN, J. (1952) 'Asset holdings and spending decisions' *American Economic Review, Papers and Proceedings* Vol. 42, May.

TOBIN, J. (1972) 'Friedman's theoretical framework' *Journal of Political Economy* Vol. 80.

TOBIN, J. and BUITER, W. H. (1976) 'Long run effects of fiscal and monetary policy on aggregate demand' in J. L. Stein (ed) *Monetarism* Amsterdam, North Holland.

TOWNEND, J. C. (1970) 'The personal saving ratio' *Bank of England Quarterly Bulletin*, March.

TURNOVSKY, S. J. (1976) 'The dynamics of fiscal policy in an open economy' *Journal of International Economics* Vol. 6.

TURNOVSKY, S. J. (1977) *Macroeconomic Analysis and Stabilisation Policy* Cambridge University Press.

TURNOVSKY, S. J. (1978) 'Macroeconomic dynamics and growth in a monetary economy' *Journal of Money, Credit and Banking* Vol. 10, February.

WALLIS, K. F. (1973) *Topics in Applied Econometrics* London, Gray Mills.

WASS, SIR DOUGLAS (1978) 'The changing problems of economic management' *Economic Trends* March, HMSO.

WHITMAN, M. VON NEUMANN (1970) 'Policies for internal and external balance' Special Papers in International Economics, Princeton University.

WILLIAMSON, J. E. (1971) 'On the normative theory of balance of payments adjustments' in G. Clayton, J. C. Gilbert and R. Sedgwick (eds) *Monetary Theory and Monetary Policy in the 1970s* London, Oxford University Press.

Index